7

PRACTICAL DIGITAL AND DATA COMMUNICATIONS

... With LSI Applications

PAUL BATES, P. ENG

Sheridan College
Brampton, Ontario

A Reston Book

Prentice-Hall, Inc., Englewood Cliffs, New Jersey 07632

Library of Congress Cataloging-in-Publication Data

BATES, PAUL, P. ENG.
    Practical digital and data communications—with
LSI applications.

    ''A Reston book.''
    Includes index.
    1. Digital communications.   2. Data transmission
systems.   I. Title.
TK5103.7.B38 1987   621.38'0413   86-30492
ISBN   0-8359-5572-9

Editorial/production supervision
and interior design: *Theresa A. Soler*
Cover design: *Diane Saxe*
Manufacturing buyer: *Carol Bystrom*

Printed in the United States of America

10 9 8 7 6 5 4 3 2 1

ISBN 0-8359-5572-9 025

Prentice-Hall International (UK) Limited, *London*
Prentice-Hall of Australia Pty. Limited, *Sydney*
Prentice-Hall Canada Inc., *Toronto*
Prentice-Hall Hispanoamericana, S.A., *Mexico*
Prentice-Hall of India Private Limited, *New Delhi*
Prentice-Hall of Japan, Inc., *Tokyo*
Prentice-Hall of Southeast Asia Pte. Ltd., *Singapore*
Editora Prentice-Hall do Brasil, Ltda., *Rio de Janeiro*

To my wife,

Wilma

Contents

Preface

The text is intended for students of 2-year to 4-year electronic technology programs. The material presented is concerned primarily with the whys, whats, and hows of data-digital communication hardware.

It is assumed that the student is familiar with basic digital electronics and is concurrently studying (or has studied) some microprocessor assembly language programming and bus interfacing, although the latter need not be extensive. Where possible, I have given equal treatment to Intel family and Motorola family devices. The instructor may emphasize the MPU family, with which the class is most familiar. Some understanding of the fundamentals of electronic communication, such as amplitude modulation, frequency modulation, sidebands, and signal spectrum, is also required.

The material is broken into easily managed chapters. Based on my experience in the classroom, the sequence I have chosen is best, but the placement of the chapters ''The Telephone Network'' and ''Modems'' is debatable; the instructor may want to present these earlier. Each chapter begins with an outline of the topics contained in the chapter and finishes with a practical problem set.

The chapter on Videotex is included as an interesting case study. The videotex system serves as an excellent example of the application of data communication fundamentals to which most students can relate.

In the chapter dealing with LANs (local area networks), I present the fundamentals associated with the various types of LAN topologies and protocols, recognizing that this is a very fast-changing field. The Ethernet LAN is presented in some detail, since it is most common of the ''mature'' LANs. Currernt work on IEEE and ISO standards, MAP (manufacturing automation protocol), TOP (technical and office protocol), and the IBM token ring are also discussed briefly.

In preparing the manuscript, I made extensive use of publications of XEROX, Motorola, Intel, Intersil, National Semiconductor, Texas Instruments, CSA (The Canadian Standards Association, and ANSI (The American National Standards Institute). Specific credits are contained throughout the text, but I would like to express my appreciation for their permission to use this material.

Of those who reviewed the manuscript, I would especially like to thank D. Roddy and H. B. Killen for their helpful comments.

Paul Bates

1

Introduction

1.1 ANALOG COMMUNICATION SYSTEMS

Figure 1.1 shows the functional block diagrams for two communication systems. In each case, the objective is to transmit and receive analog information, such as sound or a visual image.

Figure 1.1(a) illustrates a *baseband* system—so named because the transmitted signal has the same frequency spectrum as the source or base signal from the transducer. Its spectrum has not been shifted by modulating a higher frequency carrier with the baseband signal, for example. Signal processing within the transmitter may include amplification, filtering, impedance matching, and so forth.

Figure 1.1(b) shows an *analog* system, which uses modulation and demodulation. *Modulation* is used to shift the signal frequency spectrum to match that of the transmission channel being used and possibly to prevent interference with other signals using the same channel. The latter is known as *frequency-division multiplexing* (FDM). The most familiar example of such a system is the commercial AM or FM radio broadcast service.

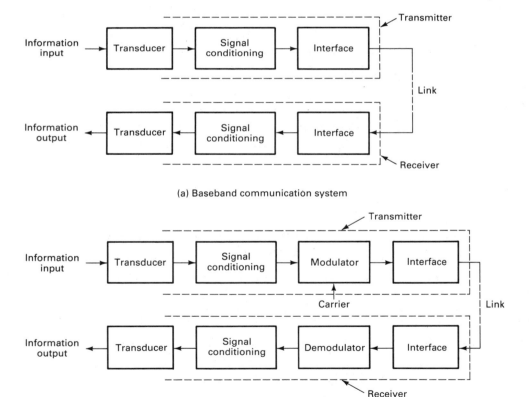

(a) Baseband communication system

(b) Modulated communication system

Figure 1.1   Analog communication systems

Communication systems are classified as simplex, half-duplex, or full duplex. *Simplex* describes a system that provides communication in one direction only. When communication can take place in both directions simultaneously, the system is said to provide *full-duplex* service. A system that provides for communication in either direction but not in both directions at the same time is called *half-duplex*.

1.2 CHANNEL AND SIGNAL CHARACTERISTICS

Level and attenuation.   Signal level, or strength, is usually expressed in terms of voltage and impedance, or power. For example, 100 mV at 75 Ω = 0.133 mW.

The ratio of two signal strengths, in the description of gain or attenuation factors, is most conveniently expressed by the logarithmic unit decibel (dB).

$$\text{Signal ratio} = 10 \log \left(\frac{P_2}{P_1} \right) \text{ dB}$$

The advantage of the logarithmic unit is that gains or attenuations of cascaded system components can easily be added algebraically to give the net system gain or loss.

Use of the decibel can be extended to express absolute signal power, provided that a fixed reference signal power is understood. A common reference signal level is 1 mW, denoted by the subscript m in dB_m.

$$\text{Signal strength} = 10 \log \left(\frac{P}{1 \text{ mW}} \right) dB_m$$

$$100 \text{ mV at } 75 \ \Omega = 0.133 \text{ mW} = -8.76 \ dB_m$$

The minus sign indicates that the level is 8.76 dB below 1 mW.

To relate decibels to a voltage ratio or dB_m to an absolute voltage requires knowledge of the circuit resistances (across which the signals appear). The relationship $P = V^2/R$ can then be used to solve for the rms voltage or voltage ratio. In audio and telephone systems, a 600-Ω reference resistance is often used.

$$100 \text{ mV at } 75 \ \Omega = 0.133 \text{ mW} = -8.76 \ dB_m = 0.282 \text{ V at } 600 \ \Omega$$

Bandwidth.   The *bandwidth* of a signal refers to the range of frequencies that contain most of its power. The bandwidth of a communication channel refers to the range of frequencies over which the attenuation or gain remains within a few decibels of the midband value. The half-powers, or 3 dB points, are often taken as the bandwidth boundaries. (See problem 1.4 for examples.)

The bandwidth of the communication channel should exceed that of the signal to avoid serious distortion and loss.

Signal delay introduced by a channel is relatively constant in its midband region but changes rapidly with frequency at the band edges.

Signal-to-noise ratio.   The *ratio S/N* is a measure of signal quality; it expresses the amount by which signal power exceeds noise power, in decibels. If a 2-dB_m signal is contaminated with noise power of -20 dB$_m$, the $S/N = 22$ dB. In other words, the signal level is 22 dB above the noise level.

1.3 MULTIPLEXING

Multiplexing is a process that allows the sharing of a communication link by two or more signals while retaining the ability to separate the signals at the receiving end.

There are two basic approaches to signal multiplexing: The signals can occupy unique frequency allocations within the bandwidth of the link, known as FDM, or they can occupy unique time slots, known as time-division multiplexing (TDM).

Frequency-division multiplexing.   The FDM of three analog channels, or signals, is illustrated in Figure 1.2. The carrier frequency for each modulator is chosen to locate uniquely each modulated signal within the available spectrum and provide some separation between channels. The signals can be separated, or demultiplexed, using high-Q-tuned circuits at the input of each receiver.

The bandwidth of the link must be wide enough to accommodate the modulated signal bandwidths (including sidebands) and allow for some frequency separation between them.

Besides commercial television and radio broadcasting, the telephone network makes extensive use of FDM. Twenty-four 3-kHz voice channels can be multiplexed onto a single twisted-pair line. Twenty-five of these 24-channel groups share a single coaxial cable, so thousands of voice channels are carried over one microwave or satellite link.

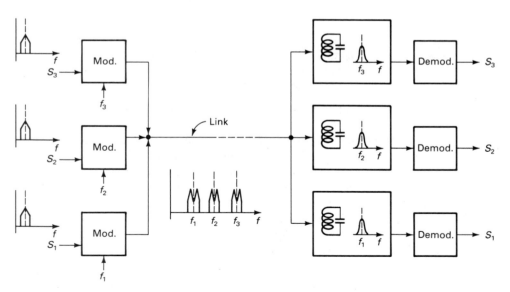

Figure 1.2   Frequency division multiplexing

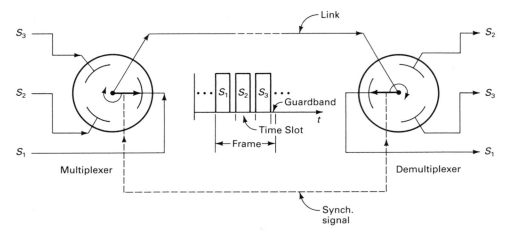

Figure 1.3   Time division multiplexing

Time-division multiplexing.   The concept of TDM is illustrated in Figure 1.3. Switching is used to connect each signal sequentially to the link for the duration of one time slot. Provided that switching of the demultiplexer is synchronized with that of the multiplexer, the signals will be separated properly.

Of course, portions of each signal are lost while the link is connected to other signals. If the rotation of the switch in Figure 1.3 is fast enough, these "gaps" in each signal will be relatively short and may be satisfactorily filled in by the receiver.

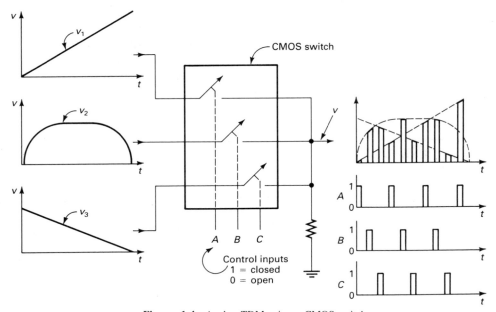

Figure 1.4   Analog TDM using a CMOS switch

For satisfactory reconstruction by the receivers, each signal must be sampled at a rate equal to at least twice the highest frequency contained in the baseband (input) signal. The formal statement of this relationship is known as the sampling theorem. The required link bandwidth for TDM can become quite large. This will be discussed more fully in a later chapter.

Use of TDM instead of FDM eliminates the need for critical tuned circuits—digitally controlled electronic switching performs the mux/demux functions. Figure 1.4 shows the application of an electronic switch to multiplex three analog signals. The multiplexer in this case is a CMOS bilateral analog switch, such as the MM74HC4016 (specified in the appendix).

1.4 DATA COMMUNICATION

In contrast to communication concerned with the transmission of signals representing analog quantities, such as audio or video, data communication is concerned with the transmission of sequences of binary codes. The codes are created, stored, and processed by computers and their peripherals. They comprise encoded messages, or files of text, graphics, numerical data, and the like.

The links used for data communication are *digital*—that is, the signal can take on only one of a limited number of discrete states—often one of two states, representing logic 1 or 0. (An analog signal can occupy any of a continuum of states over its range.)

The set of data elements, be it for text, graphics, or industrial control, uses *binary codes*. An *n*-bit code can uniquely represent 2^n elements.

Code sets to represent the alphabet letters and numerals are called *alphanumeric codes*. The most popular alphanumeric code set is 7-bit ASCII (American Standard Code for Information Interchange), shown in Table 1.1. The ASCII table has $2^7 = 128$ locations and contains codes for uppercase letters, lowercase letters, the numerals 0 through 9, several punctuation characters, and various special-purpose control codes, such as line feed and carriage return. Use of the control codes is described more fully in a later chapter.

EXAMPLE

From Table 1.1, the ASCII code for the character *A* is read as hexadecimal 41, or 41_{16}. In microprocessor literature hexadecimal numbers are often written as 41H or $41; the latter notation is used in this text.

Hexadecimal serves as a shorthand expression for the true binary ASCII code—in this case $41 represents $100\ 0001_2$.

Occasionally it is necessary to express the ASCII code for a character in decimal notation. For this example, the code for *A* may be written as $4 \times 16^1 + 1 \times 16^0 = 65_{10}$.

TABLE 1.1 7-BIT ASCII CODES

Hex Low	Hex High 0	1	2	3	4	5	6	7
0	NUL	DLE	SP	0	@	P		p
1	SOH	DC1	!	1	A	Q	a	q
2	STX	DC2	-	2	B	R	b	r
3	ETX	DC3	#	3	C	S	c	s
4	EOT	DC4	$	4	D	T	d	t
5	ENQ	NAK	%	5	E	U	e	u
6	ACK	SYN	&	6	F	V	f	v
7	BEL	ETB	'	7	G	W	g	w
8	BS	CAN	(	8	H	X	h	x
9	HT	EM	)	9	I	Y	i	y
A	LF	SS	*	:	J	Z	j	z
B	VT	ESC	+	;	K	Ä	k	å
C	FF	FS	,	<	L	Ö	l	ö
D	CR	GS	-	=	M	Å	m	ß
E	SO	RS	.	>	N	^	n	~
F	SI	US	/	?	O		o	DEL

Note: The code is the least significant 7 bits of the two-digit hexadecimal number.

Serial versus parallel transmission.   A character code can be sent in parallel, whereby all bits of the code are transmitted on separate lines simultaneously, or sent serially, whereby bits are transmitted one at a time, in sequence over one line. Figure 1.5 compares the two methods.

Parallel transmission is more costly than serial, since several parallel transmission lines are needed, but is inherently faster because several bits are sent at one time. Parallel transmission is most practical when the receiver is close to the transmitter—often in the same room.

Synchronous versus asynchronous transmission.   Besides being transmitted in serial or parallel, characters can also be sent synchronously or asynchronously. The two methods are illustrated for serial transmission in Figures 1.6 and 1.7.

Synchronous transmission, as the term suggests, means that the receiver shifts in the character bits in lock-step with the transmitter. Such transmission is accomplished by feeding the CLK inputs of both shift registers from a common clock source (located in the transmitter), as shown in Figure 1.6. Once synchronization of the receiver is established, long sequences of characters can be sent at high speed, limited only by the bandwidth of the link.

The disadvantage of synchronous transmission lies in the need to send the clock signal in parallel with the data, which requires a second transmission channel. Over long distances, where it is not possible to provide a separate channel for bit-timing information, synchronous receivers are equipped with special phase-locked loop (PLL) circuits,

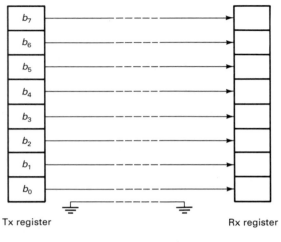

Tx register   Rx register

(a) Parallel

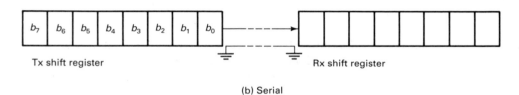

Tx shift register   Rx shift register

(b) Serial

Figure 1.5 Parallel and serial transmission

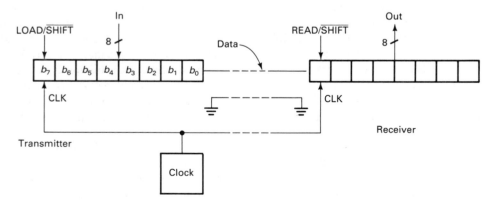

Figure 1.6 Synchronous serial transmission

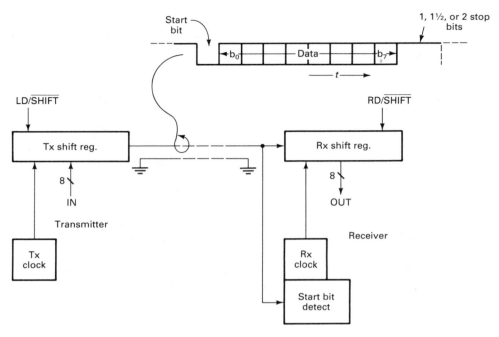

Figure 1.7 Asynchronous serial transmission

which can extract the timing information from the data stream itself and regenerate the bit clock locally. In either case, synchronous transmission is more costly than asynchronous transmission.

Although synchronous transmission implies that receiver bit timing is established directly, character bit boundaries must be established some other way. Usually a few special characters are sent before the data block for the receiver to achieve character synchronization; the ASCII SYN character is often used for this purpose (refer to Table 1.1).

Asynchronous transmission does not require a continuous synchronizing signal from the transmitter to the receiver. Characters are synchronized separately and can be sent with idle periods of random duration between them. In Figure 1.7, the data bits of each character are preceded by a start bit, which is detected by the receiver and triggers the start of the receiver shift clock. The nominal frequency of the receive and transmit clocks is the same and is determined by the bit rate being used. Because the frequencies of the two clocks are very close, the receiver remains sufficiently in phase with the data bits for the duration of the character, and resynchronization takes place at the beginning of each character. One or two stop bits are inserted after the data bits of each character to provide a minimum buffer period between characters.

Because start and stop bits must be added to each character for transmission, asynchronous transmission is generally slower than synchronous transmission, but it is less expensive. Standard data bit rates for asynchronous transmission are 75, 110, 300, and 1200 bits/s (bits per second). Rates for synchronous transmission are 2400, 4800, and 9600 bits/s.

Asynchronous transmission is particularly suitable when the input of data is not continuous, such as from a keyboard or other mechanical device. The sending of existing large files of data is best done synchronously.

Data communication hardware.   Figure 1.8 shows a typical arrangement of equipment for data communication. Two local links are included: between CPU A and the teletype (TTY), and between CPU A and the video data terminal (VDT). A long-distance telephone link between CPUs A and B is also shown, using modems. In this case, all links are asynchronous serial.

The UART, or asynchronous receiver transmitter, is often a CMOS or NMOS LSI chip. It performs parallel-serial and serial-parallel conversion between the parallel CPU data bus and the serial ports. The UART also includes logic to add and strip the start and stop bits for each character.

The *modems* convert the digital data to audio sine waves, or tones, which are more suited for transmission over the telephone network. The receiver portion of each modem demodulates the tones to recover the received data, and the transmitter section modulates the tones. Typically, two tones of equal amplitude but different frequency are used for each direction: one to send a logic 1 and the other to send a logic 0. This type of modulation is known as *frequency shift keying, or FSK*.

The local data links do not require use of modulation. Driver amplifiers are used on the output of each port to increase signal levels and reduce output impedance. This is necessary to overcome losses in the communication cables. Various industry standards exist for these communication interfaces. One such early standard was the 20-mA current loop, shown between CPU A and the TTY. It uses a loop current of approximately 20 mA to transmit logic 1 and 0 mA to transmit logic 0. The RS232 interface standard, shown between CPU A and the VDT and between each CPU/modem pair, is specified by the Electronic Industries Association (EIA). It uses approximately -12 V and $+12$ V to transmit logic 1 and logic 0 states. The RS232 standard also specifies a number of modem control and handshake lines (in addition to the receive and transmit data lines).

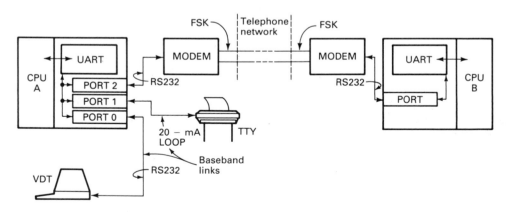

Figure 1.8 Data communication hardware

Data communication links that do not use modulation/demodulation are sometimes referred to as *baseband links*.

Asynchronous parallel interface.   Low-to-medium-speed data transfers over short distances may be made using a parallel asynchronous link. A common example is the connection between a microcomputer and a peripheral, such as a printer. One such link, referred to as the Centronics parallel interface, is shown in Figure 1.9. Character codes are transmitted in parallel, timed by the control, or handshake, lines: $\overline{\text{STROBE}}$, $\overline{\text{ACK}}$ (acknowledge), and BUSY. The sequence is as follows:

The CPU waits until BUSY is LOW, which indicates that the printer is ready to accept data (not busy).

The CPU outputs the code for the next character on the parallel port.

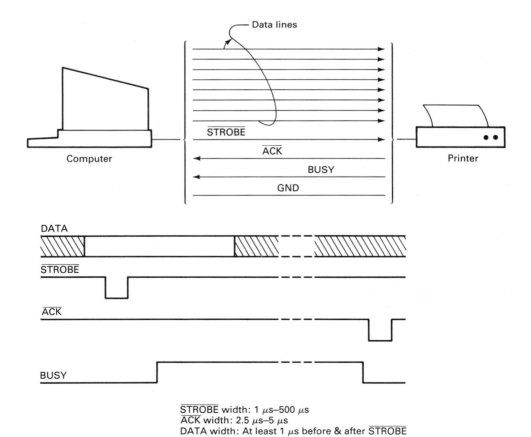

$\overline{\text{STROBE}}$ width: 1 μs–500 μs
$\overline{\text{ACK}}$ width: 2.5 μs–5 μs
DATA width: At least 1 μs before & after $\overline{\text{STROBE}}$

Figure 1.9   Parallel asynchronous (Centronics) interface

The CPU then pulses the $\overline{\text{STROBE}}$ line LOW. This signals the printer that new data has been put on the interface for it to print.

After the printer has completed the operation associated with the last character, it returns BUSY to LOW.

The printer pulses $\overline{\text{ACK}}$ LOW to inform the CPU that it is ready for another character.

1.5 DIGITAL COMMUNICATION

In digital communication of analog signals the analog information—such as an audio waveform—is sampled and digitized before transmission. The sample values are encoded using a binary code, and the sequence of codes is sent in a manner identical to that used for data communication. The codes can be sent serially, in parallel, asynchronously, or synchronously.

This process is known as *pulse code modulation,* or PCM. A/D and D/A conversion form the heart of the transmitter modulator and receiver demodulator, respectively. The components of such a system are shown in Figure 1.10. The system shown uses asynchronous serial transmission, with the necessary parallel-serial and serial-parallel conversion performed by two UARTs.

The sampling rate is determined by the frequency of the sampling clock, f_s, and it must be at least twice the highest input signal frequency. As shown, a low-pass filter is often included at the input to restrict the maximum input frequency (to f_a). If $f_s < 2f_a$, the

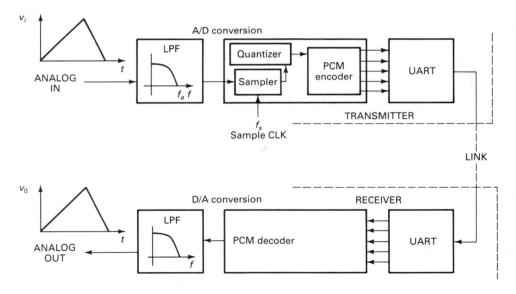

Figure 1.10   Digital communication system

signal is said to be *undersampled,* and it is impossible to reconstruct the analog signal in the receiver.

A digital communication system using n bits for each sample can encode only 2^n different sample values. Therefore, the analog samples must be quantized, or their values rounded, to match one of the codable levels before encoding can take place.

Figures 1.11 and 1.12 show example waveforms for the PCM transmitter and receiver, assuming 5-bit codes. Since transmission is asynchronous, each code is preceded by a LOW start bit and followed by two HIGH stop bits. The codes are transmitted LSB (least significant bit) first.

Notice that the output bit rate from the transmitter is very high compared with the input frequency, f_a. This necessitates a very wide link bandwidth and is the main disadvantage of PCM (versus analog communication).

For the example shown in Figure 1.11, the various frequencies and times are as follows:

$$\text{Maximum input frequency} = f_a \text{ Hz}$$
$$\text{Minimum sampling rate, } f_s = 2f_a \text{ samples/s}$$
$$\text{Sample interval, } T_s = \frac{1}{f_s} \text{ s}$$
$$\text{Output bit rate, } br = 8f_s \text{ bps}$$
$$\text{One bit time, } T_b = \frac{1}{br} \text{ s}$$

In this case the bit rate is $8f_s$, because 8 bits must be sent for each 5-bit code. In general, to transmit n-bit PCM serially will always require a bit rate of at least nf_s.

As will be explained more fully in the following chapters, when the data form a 1-0-1-0 square wave, there are effectively two bits per cycle, which means the minimum link bandwidth must be at least one-half the bit rate, or $nf_s/2$. For example, to transmit serially 4-kHz audio using 8-bit PCM requires a link bandwidth of at least 32 kHz and a bit rate of 64 kbps! This far exceeds the bandwidth of a telephone voice channel.

Figure 1.10 shows a baseband system: The digital signal is not modulated onto a sine-wave carrier for final transmission. With a high-frequency link, such as microwave, extra carrier modulation/demodulation stages would be required. Low-frequency analog waveforms can be sent over the telephone network using PCM, with modems serving to modulate and demodulate audio tones.

The major advantage of digital versus analog communication lies in the apparent "ruggedness" of digital signals. Provided that a receiver or repeater station can recognize the 1 or 0 state of the signal, it can regenerate the bit pattern *perfectly*. It is not possible to eliminate noise and distortion from an analog signal in this manner. A further advantage of digital transmission is its compatibility with computer data and digital technology. Low-cost, reliable digital computer hardware can be used for storing, switching, and multiplexing the digitized signals.

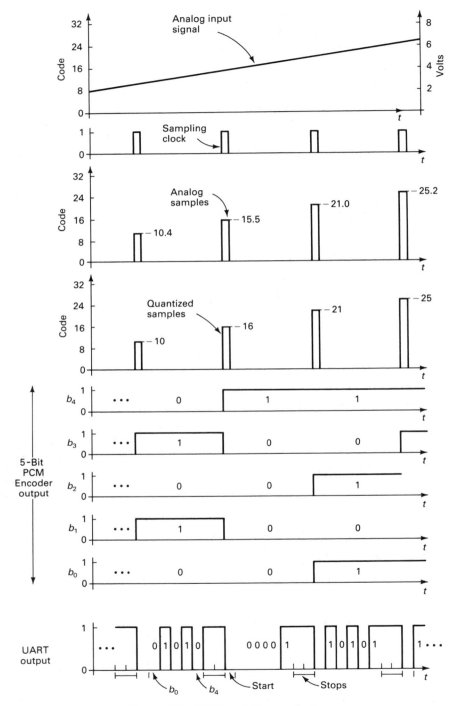

Figure 1.11 PCM transmitter waveforms

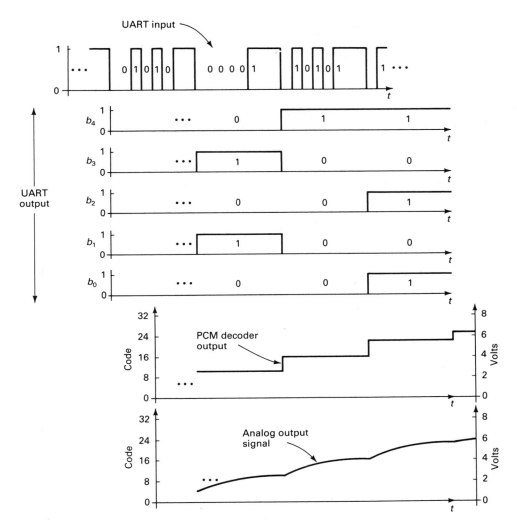

Figure 1.12   PCM receiver waveforms

PROBLEMS

1.1. Categorize the following as simplex, half-duplex, or full duplex.

   (a) Broadcast television

   (b) A telephone conversation

   (c) A conversation using an intercom

1.2. **(a)** If the signal power level at the input of a 15-dB attenuator is 3 mW, what is the output signal power level in milliwatts?

   (b) What are the input and output signal strengths in dB_m?

1.3. The voltage gain of an amplifier is 20. Its input resistance is 600 Ω and its output resistance (including the load) is 2kΩ. Express the amplifier power gain in decibels.

1.4. For an *LCR* tuned circuit, the bandwidth is BW $= f_r/Q$, where $f_r = 1/(2\pi\sqrt{LC})$. For a series resonant circuit, $Q = 2\pi f_r L/R$. For the parallel resonant circuit shown, $Q = R/(2\pi f_r L)$. Calculate the bandwidth for the two filter networks, and sketch their frequency response. Zero source impedance is assumed.

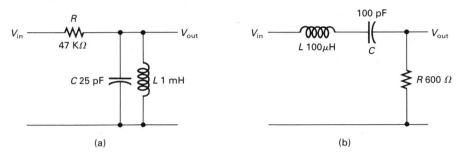

(a)   (b)

The cutoff frequency for an *RC* low-pass filter is that frequency where $X_c = R$. In this case, the cutoff frequency is the same as the -3-dB bandwidth. Calculate the bandwidth of the filter shown, and sketch its response.

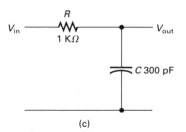

(c)

Figure P1.4

1.5. Using double-sideband AM and FDM, how many 4-kHz voice channels can be multiplexed onto a link that has a bandpass characteristic identical with that of the filter in problem 1.4(c)? An interchannel spacing of 5kHz should be provided.

1.6. Using a 4016 CMOS switch, design a TDM circuit to multiplex four analog signals together. Samples should be 25 μs wide, with an intersample guardband of 25 μs. Assume a TTL square-wave clock signal, having a 25-μs period, is available.
   The only inputs to your circuit should be the four analog signals and the clock.

1.7. Applying the sampling theorem, determine the maximum analog input frequency allowed for the circuit of problem 1.6.

1.8. A subset of the Chinese alphabet contains 300 characters. What width binary code would be required to encode each character uniquely?

1.9. Sketch the output waveform for a UART transmitting an ASCII "U."

1.10. Define the following terms.

    (a) Synchronous transmission   **(b)** Asynchronous transmission

    (c) Serial transmission   **(d)** Parallel transmission

    (e) Start bit   **(f)** Stop bit

    (g) Baseband link   **(h)** Modem

    (i) RS232 interface   **(j)** 20-mA loop

    (k) UART

1.11. Generally speaking, which provides faster data communication, and why?

    (a) Serial or parallel transmission

    (b) Synchronous or asynchronous transmission

1.12. List the advantages and disadvantages of digital versus analog communication for analog signals.

1.13. It is often said of digital communication that the received signal quality is independent of distance. Explain.

1.14. A television composite video signal is to be transmitted using 8-bit PCM, serially and synchronously. The maximum frequency component of the signal is 4.5 MHz (the sound FM carrier). Calculate each value.

    (a) The minimum sampling rate, f_s

    (b) The sample interval, T_s

    (c) The output bit rate, br

    (d) The bit time, T_b

    (e) The minimum link bandwidth required, assuming baseband transmission

2

Transmission Lines and Digital Signals

2.1 FREQUENCY COMPONENTS OF PULSE WAVEFORMS

The frequency spectrum of a square wave consists only of odd harmonics. Indeed, a square wave may be synthesized by the addition (in time) of all its odd-harmonic sine waves. The harmonic frequencies are odd multiples of the square-wave fundamental frequency, as shown in Figure 2.1. The harmonics must be combined using the correct relative amplitude and phase for each. Notice that the required amplitudes of the successive

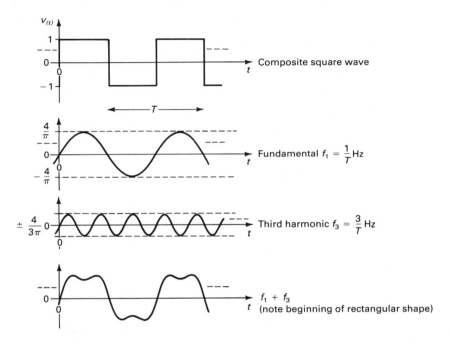

Fourier series for a square wave (as shown):

$$v_{(t)} = \frac{4}{\pi} \sin(2\pi f_1 t) + \frac{4}{3\pi} \sin(2\pi f_3 t) + \frac{4}{5\pi} \sin(2\pi f_5 t) + \ldots$$

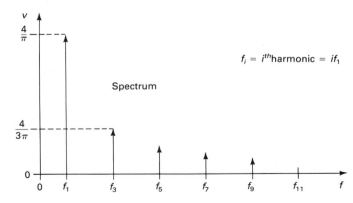

$f_i = i^{th}\text{harmonic} = if_1$

Figure 2.1 Harmonic content of a square wave

harmonics decrease exponentially. The expression shown in Figure 2.1 for $v(t)$, the instantaneous voltage of the square wave, expresses this fact mathematically, in a form known as the *Fourier series* for a square wave.

Baseband digital signals are, of course, also rectangular in waveshape. Their duty cycle is not 50 percent (usually), so they are not truly square waves, but their short rise and fall times cause a similarly high harmonic content. Furthermore, digital signals are usually not bipolar; they are usually unipolar (TTL levels of 0 V and 5 V, for example). This means that their DC or average voltage is greater than 0 V.

To carry such rectangular pulse signals over a communication link without introducing distortion, the link must attenuate all frequencies equally—from DC up to the highest harmonic frequency that is present in the pulse. Actually, even this strict requirement is not sufficient to avoid waveform distortion. The second requirement is that the transmission time, or delay, must be equal over the entire pulse bandwidth as well. If these two requirements of equal attenuation and delay are met, then the harmonics will combine properly at the receiver to produce the same waveform as was sent from the transmitter. The received waveform will be uniformly delayed and attenuated, but its shape will be preserved.

In terms of measurable transmission-line parameters, the preceding two requirements mean that the transmission line must have *attenuation constant* and *phase velocity* values that are constant ("flat") over the bandwidth of the signal. Otherwise, distortion will occur. These terms are explained in the next section. Such ideal lines are generally not possible, so compromises must be made among cost, distance, data speed, and allowed distortion in a practical system.

2.2 TRANSMISSION-LINE PARAMETERS AND DISTORTION

Equivalent circuit.   A two-wire transmission line exhibits resistance (R), capacitance (C), and inductance (L). Each is distributed along the entire length of the line. For analysis, the actual distributed line is approximated using an equivalent circuit. The equivalent circuit consists of a series of lumped, or discrete, R C, and L values, as shown in Figure 2.2. For convenience, the component values are chosen to approximate 1 meter

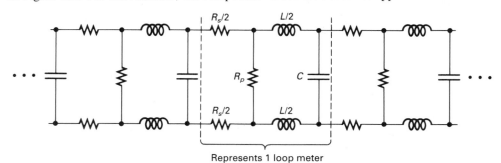

Figure 2.2   Lumped equivalent circuit of a two-wire line

of line. R_s represents the series resistance of 1 loop-meter of the conductors. R_p represents the leakage resistance of the insulation over 1 meter. C represents the capacitance formed between the two conductors per meter, and L is the small inductance of 1 loop-meter.

It is usually assumed that the R, C, and L values of the equivalent circuit are constant for any particular line; they are determined by the wire size, spacing, and type of insulation used. Typical values for a 22-gauge twisted-pair are as follows:

$$L = 2 \ \mu H/m$$
$$C = 50 \ pF/m$$
$$R_s = 0.1 \ \Omega/m$$
$$R_p = 800 \ M\Omega/m$$

In fact, these values are not really constant but do vary signficantly. They depend on such variables as temperature, moisture, and frequency. In particular, the phenomenon of *skin effect* causes R_s to increase in proportion to the square root of frequency. Skin effect is most important at higher frequencies. It is due to higher flux linkages that exist near the conductor center and that result in a larger back emf there, causing current flow to be "pinched" toward the conductor surface, effectively increasing the resistance.

The performance of a transmission line is expressed using three basic parameters: its phase velocity, V_p; its *attenuation* constant, α (alpha); and its characteristic impedance, Z_o.

Phase velocity.   *Phase velocity* is a measure of the speed of wave propagation along the transmission line, in meters/second. Ideally, we would like V_p to be constant for all frequencies. A constant speed of propagation would maintain the signal pulse frequency components in their original phase relationships and would avoid phase distortion.

Attenuation constant.   The *attenuation constant* is a measure of signal power loss per meter of line length. As with V_p, we would also like α to be constant for all frequency components to avoid amplitude distortion. (Recall from Section 2.1 that the relative amplitudes of the various harmonics that make up a rectangular pulse are critical in determining its waveshape.) α is usually expressed in nepers per meter. The neper is a logarithmic unit of power, as is the more familiar decibel; however, nepers use base e, or natural logarithms, instead of base 10 logs. To convert from nepers loss to decibels loss simply multiply by 8.686.

Characteristic impedance. Z_o is the inherent impedance that is presented to the signal by the transmission line. It is expressed in ohms. In general, Z_o will be complex, given by $Z_o = R_o + jX_o$. For a *reflectionless match* the source and load impedances should equal Z_o. Under these matched conditions, power losses and distortion due to waves reflected back from the load are avoided. Ideally, we would like the characteristic impedance of a line to be resistive (i.e., $X_o = 0 \ \Omega$) and constant over the signal bandwidth.

Based on the approximate equivalent circuit shown in Figure 2.2, general expressions for V_p, α, and Z_o may be developed. These expressions in their general form are rather unwieldy functions of R_s, R_p, C, L, and frequency; however, if consideration is restricted only to three frequency bands separately, useful expressions may be developed. When these three frequency regions are considered one at a time, a much-simplified equivalent circuit may be drawn for each. Equivalent circuits for the three bands—DC, low frequencies, and high frequencies—are shown in Figure 2.3. The three bands may be described as follows:

1. DC, where $X_L = 0$ and $X_C = \infty$.
2. low frequencies, where it is assumed that

$$X_L < R_s/10 \quad \text{and} \quad X_C < R_p/10$$

The assumption regarding inductive reactance establishes the upper-frequency boundary. The assumption regarding capacitive reactance establishes the lower-frequency limit.

$$(X_L = 2\pi f L \text{ and } X_C = 1/(2\pi f C).)$$

3. High frequencies, where it is assumed that

$$X_L > 10R_s \quad \text{and} \quad X_C << R_p$$

The assumption regarding X_L establishes the lower-frequency boundary of the high-frequency band.

EXAMPLE

For a line having parameters $R_s = 0.1 \ \Omega/m$, $R_p = 8 \times 10^8 \ \Omega/m$, $C = 50$ pF/m, and $L = 2 \ \mu H/m$, the boundaries of the three frequency bands may be calculated as follows:

The lower limit of the low band is the frequency at which $X_C = R_p/10$.

$$\frac{1}{2\pi f C} = \frac{R_p}{10}$$

$$f = \frac{10}{2\pi R_p C} = \frac{10}{2\pi(8 \times 10^8)(50 \times 10^{-12})} \approx 40 \text{ Hz}$$

The upper limit of the low band occurs where $X_L = R_s/10$.

$$2\pi f L = \frac{R_s}{10}$$

$$f = \frac{R_s}{(20\pi L)} = \frac{0.1}{20\pi(2 \times 10^{-6})} \approx 800 \text{ Hz}$$

The lower limit of the high band is where $X_L = 10R_s$,

$$f = \frac{10R_s}{2\pi L} = \frac{10(0.1)}{2\pi(2 \times 10^{-6})} \approx 80 \text{ kHz}$$

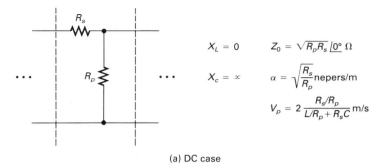

$$X_L = 0 \qquad Z_0 = \sqrt{R_p R_s}\ \underline{/0°}\ \Omega$$

$$X_c = \infty \qquad \alpha = \sqrt{\frac{R_s}{R_p}}\ \text{nepers/m}$$

$$V_p = 2\,\frac{R_s/R_p}{L/R_p + R_s C}\ \text{m/s}$$

(a) DC case

$$X_L < \frac{R_s}{10} \qquad Z_0 = \sqrt{X_c R_s}\ \underline{/-45°}\ \Omega$$

$$X_c < \frac{R_p}{10} \qquad \alpha = \sqrt{\frac{R_s}{2X_c}}\ \text{nepers/m}$$

$$V_p = 2\pi f \sqrt{\frac{2X_c}{R_s}}\ \text{m/s}$$

(b) Low-frequency case

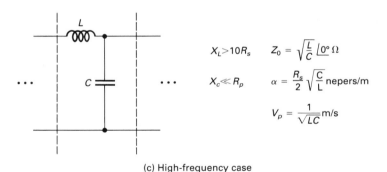

$$X_L > 10 R_s \qquad Z_0 = \sqrt{\frac{L}{C}}\ \underline{/0°}\ \Omega$$

$$X_c \ll R_p \qquad \alpha = \frac{R_s}{2}\sqrt{\frac{C}{L}}\ \text{nepers/m}$$

$$V_p = \frac{1}{\sqrt{LC}}\ \text{m/s}$$

(c) High-frequency case

Figure 2.3 Simplified equivalent circuits and equations (two-wire line)

The expressions for V_p, α, and Z_o as well as the equivalent circuits and assumptions for each band are shown in Figure 2.3.

At DC, Z_o is large and purely resistive. The attenuation, α, is low for DC, as one would expect, since X_L and X_C do not cause any loss at DC.

In the low-frequency range, Z_o is less than at DC and is complex (resistive-capacitive), decreasing in magnitude inversely as the square root of frequency. In this range, α and V_p both increase as the square root of frequency.

In the high-frequency band, Z_o becomes resistive again and minimum in magnitude—equal to the constant $\sqrt{L/C}$ ohms. This is the value usually referred to commercially as the line *characteristic impedance*. V_p and α approach constant values in this range as well. (This statement is somewhat misleading; in reality, skin effect causes α to increase continuously with frequency.)

Frequency plots for each parameter based on the expressions given in Figure 2.3 are shown in Figure 2.4. The frequency boundaries and parameter values shown in parentheses were calculated using the typical values given earlier for a 22-gauge twisted-pair line (i.e., $R_s = 0.1\ \Omega/\text{m}$, $R_p = 800\text{M}\ \Omega$, $C = 50\ \text{pF/m}$, and $L = 2\ \mu\text{H/m}$). Notice that the parameters vary most in the low-to-middle frequency portions of each plot. This range corresponds to the spectrum of a low-frequency rectangular pulse signal. Here there will inevitably be some distortion of the signal, and it will get worse as the line length is increased.

EXAMPLE

The approximate phase velocity for the line of Figure 2.4 may be calculated at a frequency of 400 Hz as follows:

400 Hz is in the low band for this line, and the appropriate expression for V_p is found from Figure 2.3 as follows:

$$V_p = 2\pi f\ \sqrt{\frac{2X_C}{R_s}}$$

$$X_C = \frac{1}{2\pi f C} = \frac{1}{2\pi(400)(50\ \times\ 10^{-1})} = 7.96\ \text{M}\Omega$$

$$V_p = 2\pi(400)\ \sqrt{\frac{2(7.96\ \times\ 10^6)}{0.1}} = 3.17\ \times\ 10^7\ \text{m/s}$$

Distortion.   The distortion effect on the received signal caused by the variation of phase velocity with frequency is known as *dispersion*. It causes the different components of the pulse to be received at incorrect relative times. This dispersion can actually cause the interference of later pulses by earlier ones—an effect known as *intersymbol interference*. Figure 2.5 illustrates these amplitude- and phase-distortion effects on the received signal waveshape. Notice that in many respects the result is similar to that of a low-pass filter on a pulse. High-frequency components (edges) are attenuated most, and the fundamental component is delayed most.

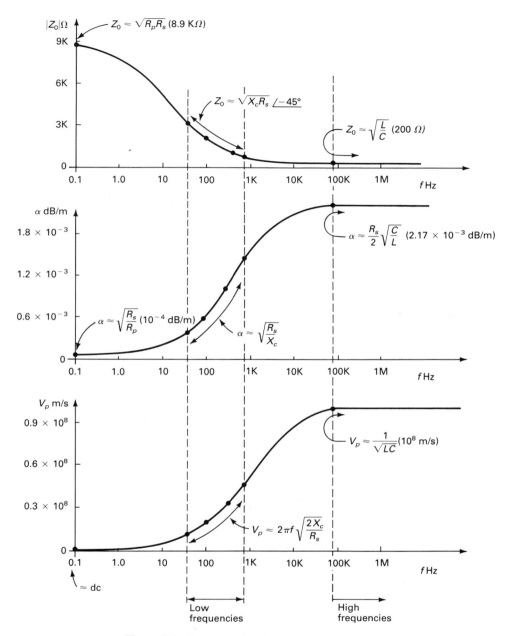

Figure 2.4   Frequency plots for Z_0, α, V_p for a two-wire line

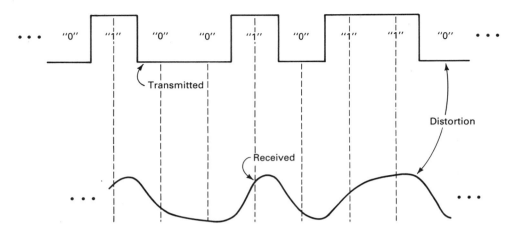

Figure 2.5 Waveform-distortion effects

2.3 PARALLEL VERSUS COAXIAL-CABLE LINES

Virtually all the characteristics discussed previously relating to parallel or twisted-pair lines also apply to coaxial cables. After all, a coaxial cable is a two-wire transmission line. The difference lies in the unique physical arrangement of the conductors of a coaxial cable: One forms an enclosure, or electromagnetic shield, for the other.

The outer shield is usually grounded. The shield almost totally eliminates one of the major disadvantages of an open unbalanced line—the pickup of unwanted electromagnetic interference, or noise. Similarly, the shield reduces signal loss due to electromagnetic radiation from the line.

A transmission line is said to be unbalanced when one conductor is grounded and the other is not. The ungrounded line carries the signal voltage (with ground as the reference). Because one conductor is grounded, a coaxial-cable link is inherently unbalanced and not suitable for use as the transmission line for a balanced system (although costly shielded-pair cable may be used.)

Local baseband links between terminals and the mainframe CPU of IBM systems historically have used coaxial cable.

Coaxial lines usually have higher capacitance-per-meter ratings (75 pF/m is typical); therefore, the characteristic impedance of coaxial lines is less (usually between 50 and 100 Ω) than that of parallel or twisted-pair lines. It is possible to calculate the approximate Z_0 for parallel and coaxial lines using their physical dimensions and the dielectric constant (ϵ) of their insulating material. Figure 2.6 shows the relationships involved and a plot comparing Z_0 for parallel versus coaxial cables.

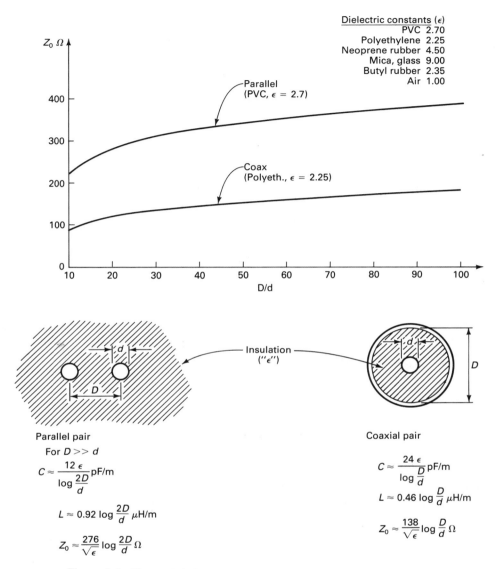

Figure 2.6 Characteristic impedance of lines: parallel versus coaxial

EXAMPLE

A parallel-pair transmission line is to have a characteristic impedance of 250 Ω. The diameter of the conductors to be used is 1 mm. If neoprene rubber is used for the insulation, what conductor spacing is required? Why is neoprene rubber a poor choice for this line? Explain.

From Figure 2.6, the dielectric constant for neoprene rubber is 4.5, and the required relationship is

$$Z_0 = \left(\frac{276}{\epsilon}\right)\log\left(\frac{2D}{d}\right)$$

$$\log\left(\frac{2D}{d}\right) = \frac{Z_0\sqrt{\epsilon}}{276} = \frac{250\sqrt{4.5}}{276} = 1.921$$

$$\frac{2D}{d} = \text{antilog } 1.921 = 83.46$$

$$D = \frac{(83.46)d}{2} = 4.17 \times 10^2 \text{ m} = 4.17 \text{ cm}$$

The spacing, D, is probably unacceptably wide. This is a consequence of the high dielectric constant of neoprene rubber—it increases the capacitance between the wires and reduces the line impedance; thus a large separation is necessary to achieve 250 Ω.

2.4 PRACTICAL LINE-INTERFACE CIRCUITS AND CAPABILITIES

The term *baseband link* refers to communication links that do not employ any modulation, by the data, of an analog carrier signal (such as AM or FM). Baseband transmission of data signals is more economical than use of a modulated carrier but must be limited to relatively short distances—usually between computer hardware within the same room or building.

To be specific, assume we have a need to communicate using a TTL-level signal (5 V for 1 and 0 V for 0) and to do so at typical TTL-gate impedances of a few kilohms to ground. Three different, basic approaches to designing the link interfaces may be used: A direct-TTL link, a TTL + driver-unbalanced link, or a TTL + driver-balanced link. These are illustrated in Figure 2.7 and are described below.

Direct-TTL link. This, the simplest method, uses no buffering of the TTL signal at all, as shown in Figure 2.7(a). The link is said to be unbalanced; that is, impedances to

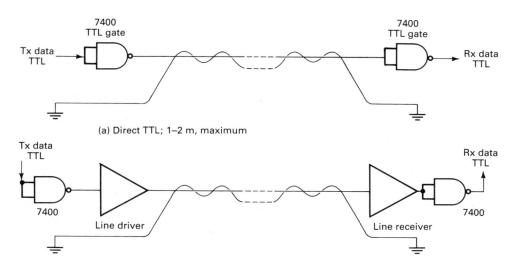

(a) Direct TTL; 1–2 m, maximum

(b) TTL + driver (unbalanced); ~ 10–100 m, maximum

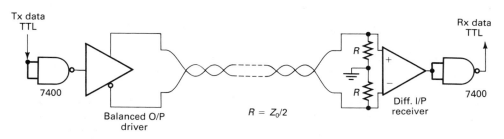

$R = Z_0/2$

(c) TTL + driver (balanced); ~ 100–1000 m maximum

Figure 2.7   General types of baseband data links

ground from either side of the transmission line are very different. One line is at a few kilohms above ground, and the other line is grounded directly.

Such a link suffers from three weaknesses in particular. The high-impedance side may act like an antenna because it is very prone to pick up unwanted interference. Also, the loading effect of the transmission-line capacitance on the TTL-gate output forms a low-pass filter and severely limits useful bandwidth (and, therefore, data speed). A third weakness of such an unbalanced line lies in the use of ground for the return signal path. There often are significant differences in equipment ground potentials, which can set up 60-Hz currents in the ground conductor. This current induces unwanted 60-Hz interference, or *hum*, in series with the signal. The preceding points are well worth remembering, since they highlight inherent weaknesses present in any high-impedance unbalanced communication link—digital or analog.

Direct-TTL connections must be used with much care and over very short distances (a few meters maximum). For example, they are sometimes used between a computer and its keyboard or printer.

TTL + driver-unbalanced links.

Most baseband data connections use some type of driver/receiver or buffer circuits. Drivers are used to condition the signal levels and to reduce the output impedance of the transmitter. Higher-voltage (and/or current) logic levels improve noise immunity. The low output impedance of the driver reduces the low-pass filtering effect of the line capacitance on the transmitted signal. Reducing the impedance to ground of the ungrounded line also reduces the antenna effect already mentioned.

This type of link, shown in Figure 2.7(b), can provide good baseband communication over distances up to approximately 100 m and at data rates up to several kilobits/second. The transmission line may use a parallel or twisted pair of conductors or a coaxial cable.

Common driver-receiver-pair ICs include the MC8T13/MC8T14 (for coax) and the MC1488/MC1489 (for parallel or twisted pair). Specifications for these ICs are provided in the appendix.

TTL + driver-balanced links.

The use of driver circuits having low-impedance balanced outputs with receivers having differential inputs provides the best baseband data link. External terminating resistors may be used, as shown in Figure 2.7(c), to match the line and to ensure equal resistance exists from each side of the line to ground. The driver outputs are complementary and may be bipolar (for example: -5 V for 1 and $+5$ V for 0).

Use of a balanced differential link can eliminate the two weaknesses, cited previously, of unbalanced links. Since the impedances from each line to ground are equal, interference pickup is equal in each line, and the resulting noise voltages cancel at the receiver differential input. Since ground does not form part of the signal path, 60-Hz noise, due to differences in ground potentials, is eliminated. Balanced links may provide reliable data communication over distances up to approximately 1 km.

The driver-receiver IC pair MC3487/MC3486 is typical for this type of interface. They are specified in the appendix. The MC3487 has three-state outputs, allowing half-duplex operation over a single transmission-line pair.

All the links shown in Figure 2.7 are simplex (one direction only). Full duplex requires a pair of such links: one for each direction.

PROBLEMS

2.1. **(a)** Describe in your own words the two basic requirements that an ideal transmission line should meet.

(b) What properties should the parameters V_p, α, and Z_o possess for an ideal line?

(c) What properties does a real line exhibit that make it not ideal?

2.2. A certain coaxial line has a capacitance of 66 pF/m and R_s equal to 0.05 Ω/m. Its leakage resistance, R_p, may be considered to be 10^{10} Ω. The commercial characteristic impedance of the line is 75 Ω.

    (a) What is the inductance per meter of the line?

    (b) Over what frequency band may the low-frequency approximations for its parameters be used?

    (c) Above what frequency may the high-frequency approximations be used?

    (d) Compare V_p in (b) and (c) with the speed of light in a vacuum by calculating the cable velocity factor, V_p/(speed of light), for each.

2.3. Assuming that the shield diameter for the coaxial cable of problem 2.2 is 0.5 cm and the insulation is polyethylene, calculate the diameter of the center conductor.

2.4. What would be the characteristic impedance of a parallel-pair line having the same D/d ratio as that of the coax of problem 2.3?

2.5. Why is a balanced two-wire line more resistant to interference pickup than an unbalanced line?

2.6. Draw a schematic for a full-duplex baseband link, using MC8T13 drivers and MC8T14 receivers.

2.7. Draw a schematic for a half-duplex baseband link, using MC3487 drivers and MC3486 receivers.

Use the tristate feature of the driver IC, and use only one two-wire transmission line.

2.8. Figure P2.8 shows a direct TTL link, with 3 m of coaxial cable as the transmission line. Assuming that the actual link can be approximamted by the equivalent circuit shown below it, calculate the link bandwidth.

Hint: Consider the circuit as an R-C low-pass filter with time constant equal to (R_o in parallel with R_{in})C.

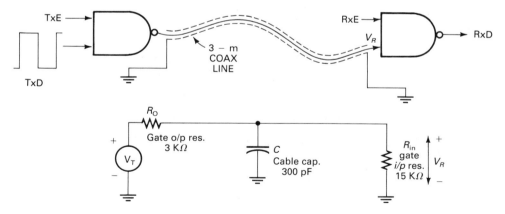

Figure P2.8

3

Serial Asynchronous Communications

3.1 ASYNCHRONOUS SERIAL PROTOCOL

Recall from Chapter 1 that the term *asynchronous* implies that the receiver and transmitter clocks are separate. Each clock is tuned to the same nominal frequency, which corresponds to the transmission bit rate, or *baud*. Also, over an asynchronous link, information is sent by way of separate, randomly spaced characters. Each character consists of its character code bits (such as ASCII) plus the necessary leading and trailing bits for time-framing the character. When 7-bit ASCII is used, an eighth bit, called the *parity bit*, is often appended for error checking. The link is held at a 1 state between characters, known as the *idle state*. The link voltage waveform for one character is shown in Figure 3.1. Data bits are usually sent LSB first, as shown.

In Figure 3.1, a shift register is the main hardware component of both the transmitter and receiver. The transmitter shift register serves as a parallel-to-serial converter. When the LOAD input is HIGH, the character code data bits are parallel-loaded into the register from the computer data bus (DATA IN). When LOAD is brought LOW, the character bits are shifted out in series to the communication link. The transmitter shift register includes logic that automatically adds the start and stop bits, as shown. The receiver detects the beginning of each character by sensing the 1-to-0 transition of the start bit. When the start bit is detected, the receiver control circuitry causes the shift register to start shifting bits in from the link. After 11 shifts (1 start + 8 data + 2 stops), the received character code may be read in parallel from the shift register (DATA OUT); thus, the receiver shift register performs serial-to-parallel conversion.

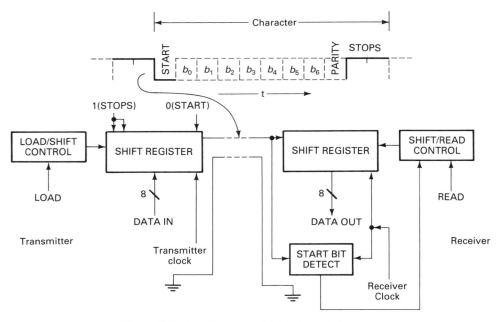

Figure 3.1 Asynchronous serial data transmission

When a parity bit is used, its logic state depends on the specific character code and on whether the agreed protocol specifies *even parity* or *odd parity*. The parity bit is simply made 1 or 0, as required, to make the total number of 1s in b_0–b_7 an even number (even parity) or an odd number (odd parity). Note that the parity bit itself is included in the count. The receiver then, by counting the total number of 1s in each character, can often detect bit errors. This method of error detection is far from 100 percent reliable, since errors involving an even number of bits will go undetected. In practice, however, errors usually occur in bursts, affecting several characters of information. The probability that some parity errors will be caught during such bursts is very high.

After detecting a start bit, the receiver shifts in the data bits, sequentially. Shifting is timed by the local receive clock. Since the receive clock cannot be tuned to exactly the same frequency as the transmit clock, some timing error (called *skew*) will develop as the successive bits are shifted in. This cumulative clock skew must not be so great as to cause an error in detecting the last bits of the character. The stop bits are always set to 1, and they can serve as a check on timing skew. If the stop bits are not read as 1, the receiver declares that a *framing error* has occurred. The stop bits also provide a minimum guardband between characters. The preceding protocol is not a rigid standard. In practice, variations are often used, such as

One stop bit instead of two

More or fewer than seven bits/character

Mark parity (parity bit always 1)

EXAMPLE

Sketch the serial-asynchronous link waveform for the character C. Assume ASCII code is being used, with even parity and two stop bits.

From the ASCII table (Table 1.1), the ASCII code for C is $43 = 100\ 0011_2$.

The ASCII code contains an odd number of 1s (three); therefore, for even parity we must set the parity bit to 1. The code, including parity, is $1100\ 0011_2 = \$C3$. Parity is always the most significant bit.

The waveform is shown in Figure E3.1.

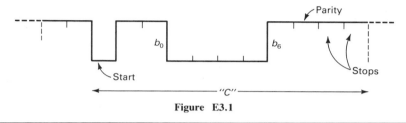

Figure E3.1

Space parity (parity bit always 0)

No parity bit

Implementing serial asynchronous protocol for data communication requires considerable overhead of system tasks, which must be repeated for each character and which involve critical timing. These tasks include adding or stripping start and stop bits, generating or checking the parity bit, shifting the bits in or out, and serial-to-parallel or parallel-to-serial conversion. These critical, repetitive tasks are often best done automatically by hardware (i.e., not done by the microprocessor software). Several LSI chips have been developooed for this purpose. They are referred to as universal asynchronous receiver transmitters (UARTs) or asynchronous communication interface adapters (ACIAs). The next section discusses these devices in some detail.

3.2 HARDWARE UARTs

Serial asynchronous receiver transmitters can, of course, be designed using SSI and/or MSI digital ICs, and several systems have been implemented this way in the past. For example, it is interesting to note how the parity bit can be generated or checked using simple exclusive-OR gates, shown in Figure 3.2. This circuit makes use of the fact that the output of an exclusive-OR gate is 1 only when its input data contains an odd number of 1s.

However, almost all current systems use one of the several low-cost LSI devices. Discrete SSI/MSI designs are used only when the protocol is unique or the data rate is too fast for LSI units (e.g., Megabits per second).

In this section, application guidelines for three of the more popular LSI UARTs/

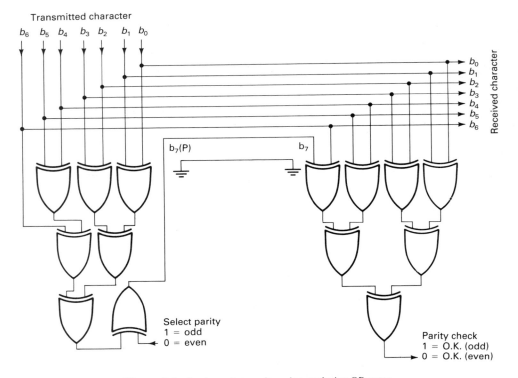

Figure 3.2 Implementing parity using exclusive-OR gates

ACIAs are given, including the microprocessor-bus interface connections. The ICs to be discussed were chosen to represent three general categories, as follows:

1. The Intersil 6402 UART: hardware programmable, CMOS.
2. The Intel 8251 USART: the S in USART indicates it can be used for synchronous or asynchronous communication. It is designed primarily to interface with Intel's 8080/8086 families of microprocessors, under software control.
3. The Motorola 6850 ACIA is designed to interface with Motorola's 6800/68000 families of microprocessors, under software control. The 6850 is also readily interfaced with the 6502 microprocessor.

3.2.1 The Intersil 6402 UART

Intersil's general description of the 6402 reads as follows:

> The 6402 is a CMOS/LSI UART for interfacing computers or microprocessors to asynchronous serial data channel. The receiver converts start, data, parity, and stop bits to parallel data, verifying proper code transmission, parity, and stop bits. The transmitter converts parallel data into serial form and automatically adds start, parity, and stop bits.

The data word length can be 5, 6, 7, or 8 bits. Parity may be odd or even. Parity checking and generation can be inhibited. The stop bits may be one or two (or one and one-half when transmitting 5-bit code).*

Figure 3.3 shows a programming model and pinout of the 6402. It is a most versatile UART, primarily because it uses a full 40-pin package. Separate pins are provided for the transmit data input, receive data output, and control word input. Because CMOS technology is used, power dissipation is extremely low (less than 15 mW!). Details of the protocol to be used are selected by the bit pattern loaded into the control register. Table 3.1 describes the effect of each control word bit.

Application of the 6402 is easily understood if it is considered under three topics: initializing, transmitting a character, and receiving a character. Refer to Figure 3.3 throughout the following description.

Initializing (6402).   To program the 6402 for proper operation, follow three steps:

Apply the control word to pins CR_4–CR_0.

Pulse CRL pin HIGH to load the control register.

Pulse MRST pin HIGH to reset the receiver and transmitter.

Transmitting a character (6402).   To load the character code into the transmitter buffer and transmit it, do the following:

Wait until TBRE pin is HIGH (indicating that the transmitter is ready).

Apply the character code to pins TBR_7–TBR_0.

Pulse TBRL pin HIGH to load the buffer register. (Transmission begins when TBRL returns LOW.)

Receiving a character (6402).   Read the received character from the receive buffer register. Read its error status from the status register: A 1 state of the PE (parity), FE (framing), or OVE (overrun) bits indicates an error was detected. An overrun error occurs when characters are received faster than they are being read from the buffer:

Wait for DR pin to go HIGH, indicating a new character has been received.

Read the character from buffer outputs RBR_7–RBR_0 (outputs enabled by $\overline{ROE}$ pin LOW).

Read the error status from outputs PE, FE, and OVE (enabled by $\overline{SOE}$ pin LOW).

Reset the receiver by pulsing $\overline{DRRST}$ pin LOW.

The transmit and receive bit rates are determined by the two clock inputs, on pins TC and RC. The 6402 contains fixed divide-by-16 circuits such that the input clock frequencies must be 16 times the desired baud. Speeds up to 250 kbits/s are possible.

*Reprinted courtesy Intersil, Inc.

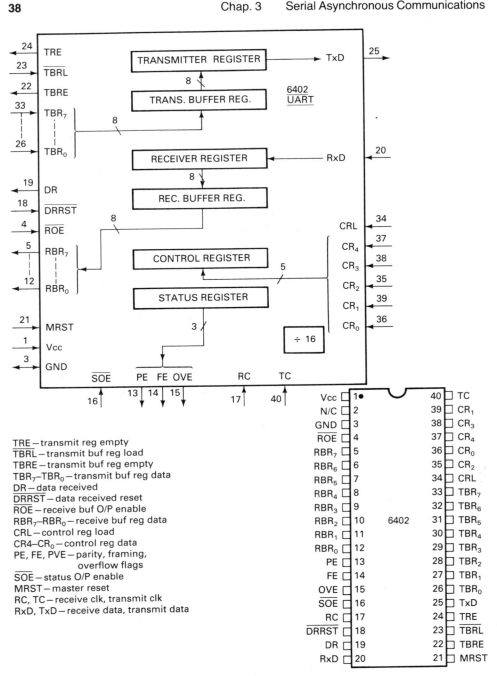

TRE – transmit reg empty
TBRL – transmit buf reg load
TBRE – transmit buf reg empty
TBR₇–TBR₀ – transmit buf reg data
DR – data received
DRRST – data received reset
ROE – receive buf O/P enable
RBR₇–RBR₀ – receive buf reg data
CRL – control reg load
CR4–CR₀ – control reg data
PE, FE, PVE – parity, framing,
          overflow flags
SOE – status O/P enable
MRST – master reset
RC, TC – receive clk, transmit clk
RxD, TxD – receive data, transmit data

Figure 3.3   Intersil 6402 UART

TABLE 3.1 6402 CONTROL WORD

CR$_4$	Character length select CLS$_1$	00 = 5 bits 01 = 6 bits
CR$_3$	 CLS$_0$	10 = 7 bits 11 = 8 bits
CR$_2$	Parity inhibit PI	1 = no parity bit and PE = 0 0 = parity enabled
CR$_1$	Even parity enable EPE	1 = even parity 0 = odd parity
CR$_0$	Stop bits select SBS	0 = 1 stop bits 1 = 1.5 (char. len. 5) 1 = 2 (char. len. 6, 7, 8)

3.2.2 The Intel 8251A USART

The 8251A is a USART, as opposed to a UART, indicating its capability to implement synchronous as well as asynchronous protocols. For now, only its use for asynchronous communication will be considered.

Intel describes their 8251A as follows:

> . . . designed for data communication with Intel's family of microprocessors . . . The USART accepts data characters from the CPU in parallel format and then converts them into a continuous serial data stream for transmission. Simultaneously, it can receive serial data streams and convert them into parallel data characters for the CPU. The USART will signal the CPU whenever it can accept a new character for transmission, or whenever it has received a character for the CPU. The CPU can read the complete status of the USART at any time. These include data transmission errors and control signals such as RxRDY (Receiver Ready) and TxRDY (Transmitter Ready).*

The 8251A uses NMOS technology in a 28-pin package. It is rated for data speeds up to 64 kbps. A programming model and pinout are shown in Figure 3.4. Unlike the 6402, all data to and from the CPU is via the data bus interface pins D$_7$–D$_0$. Use of the 8251A requires short software routines that program the mode and command control registers as well as periodically read the status register. Details of these three registers are given in Tables 3.2 and 3.3.

*Reprinted, courtesy Intel Corp.

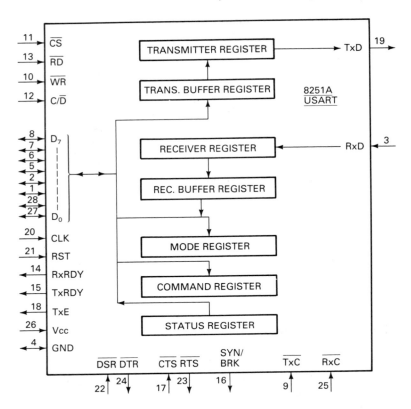

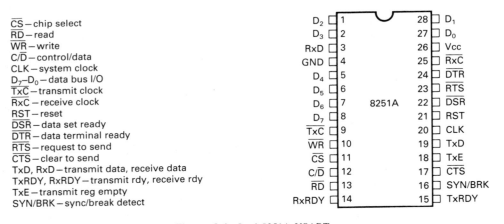

$\overline{CS}$ – chip select
$\overline{RD}$ – read
$\overline{WR}$ – write
$C/\overline{D}$ – control/data
CLK – system clock
D_7–D_0 – data bus I/O
$\overline{TxC}$ – transmit clock
$\overline{RxC}$ – receive clock
RST – reset
$\overline{DSR}$ – data set ready
$\overline{DTR}$ – data terminal ready
$\overline{RTS}$ – request to send
$\overline{CTS}$ – clear to send
TxD, RxD – transmit data, receive data
TxRDY, RxRDY – transmit rdy, receive rdy
TxE – transmit reg empty
SYN/BRK – sync/break detect

Figure 3.4　Intel 8251A USART

TABLE 3.2 8251A CONTROL AND COMMAND WORD BITS

	Mode-Control Word Bits *		Command Word Bits	
D_7	Stop bits* select S_1	00 = invalid 01 = 1 stop bit 10 = 1.5 11 = 2 11 = 2	Transmit enable Tx EN	1 = enabled 0 = disabled
D_6	S_0		Data term ready DTR	1 = $\overline{DTR}$ pin low 0 = HIGH
D_5	Even parity enable EP	1 = even 0 = odd	Receiver enable Rx E	1 = enabled 0 = disabled
D_4	Parity enable PEN	1 = parity enabled 0 = no parity bit	Send break character SBRK	1 = TxD pin low 0 = normal
D_3	Character length select L_1	00 = 5 bits 01 = 6 10 = 7 11 = 8	Error reset ER	1 = resets error flags PE, OE, FE to 0
D_2	L_0		Request to send RTS	1 = $\overline{RTS}$ pin low 0 = HIGH
D_1	Baud clock divisor select B_1	00 = synchron. mode 01 = ÷ 1 10 = ÷ 16 11 = ÷ 64	Reset RST	1 = returns 8251A to mode instruction format
D_0	B_0		Enter hunt mode EH	1 = enables search for sync character (synchronous mode)

*Asychronous mode shown

Register addressing is done using the C/D (control data) pin. HIGH selects the control group of registers (mode, command, and status registers). LOW selects the data registers (receive and transmit buffers). The transmit buffer, mode, and control registers are WRITE-only type, whereas the receive buffer and status registers are READ-only. The mode register may be accessed only immediately following a chip reset.

Application of this USART is best illustrated by describing the steps required for initialization of the 8251A, transmitting a character, and receiving a character. Refer to Figure 3.4 and Tables 3.2 and 3.3 throughout the following description.

Initializing (8251A).   Following a chip reset, write a byte to the mode register to select the desired protocol, as shown in Table 3.2. You may reset by using the RST pin (hardware reset during power up) or later by writing $D_1 = 1$ of the command register.

TABLE 3.3 8251A STATUS REGISTER

D_7	Data set ready DSR	1 = $\overline{DSR}$ pin is LOW 0 = HIGH
D_6	Sync. char. detect SYNDET	1 = sync character detected (Synchronous only)
D_5	Framing error FE	1 = framing error reset by writing ER = 1 (asynchronous only)
D_4	Overrun error OE	1 = overrun error
D_3	Parity error PE	1 = parity error
D_2	Transmit. reg. empty TxEMPTY	1 = empty 0 = busy
D_1	Receiver ready RxRDY	1 = ready with new character
D_0	Transmitter ready TxRDY	1 = ready for next character

After establishing the mode, maintain ongoing control of the receiver and transmitter by periodically writing to the command register. The steps involved are as follows:

Cause a chip reset (hardware or software).

Write the desired mode select word to the mode register.

Write the desired command word to the command register.

Transmitting a character (8251A).   For transmission to take place, the TxEN bit in the command register must be 1, and the $\overline{CTS}$ pin must be LOW:

Wait until the TxRDY pin is HIGH or until the TxRDY bit in the status register is 1.

Write the character to be transmitted to the transmit buffer register.

Receiving a character (8251A).   To receive a character and check its error status follow these steps:

Wait until the RxRDY pin is HIGH or until the RxRDY bit in the status register is 1.

Read the error status from the status register (may be combined with the previous step when RxRDY bit is read).

Read the character from the receive buffer register.

Reset the error status by writing bit ER = 1 in the command register.

The receive and transmit bit rates are determined by the clock frequencies applied to pins $\overline{RxC/TxC}$ divided by the factor (1, 16, or 64) selected with the mode word.

3.2.3   *THE MOTOROLA 6850 ACIA*

Motorola includes the following features in its ACIA specification:

Eight- or 9-bit transmission

Optional even or odd parity

Parity, overrun, and framing error checking

Optional divide-by-1, divide-by-16, or divide-by-64 clock modes

Up to 500 kbps transmission

Peripheral/modem control functions

One or two stop bit operation

Double buffered

The 6850 is software programmable, which makes it similar, in that respect, to the 8251A but somewhat less complex to apply. The 6850 does not provide for synchronous protocols, and it has only one control register. It is physically smaller than the 8251A, using a 24-pin package (also NMOS). A programming model and pinout are given in Figure 3.5. The 6850 is designed to interface directly with the Motorola microprocessor family bus.

Details of the protocol are selected by writing a byte to the control register (see Table 3.4). Receiver-transmitter status and error status are read from the status register (see Table 3.5).

Pin RS = LOW selects the control or status register, and RS = HIGH selects the receive or transmit data registers. The transmit data and control registers are WRITE-only type. The receive data and status registers are READ-only.

Typical application of the 6850 is illustrated by describing the procedure for initializing the chip, transmitting a character, and receiving a character.

Initializing the ACIA (6850).   Notice that the 6850 does not provide a pin for hardware reset. Reset the chip by writing to the control register (making bits $C_0 = C_1 = 1$):

Cause a chip master reset by writing to the control register.

Program the desired control word by writing to the control register again.

Transmitting a character (6850).   Once the 6850 has been initialized, only two steps are necessary to transmit each character. $\overline{CTS}$ pin must be LOW:

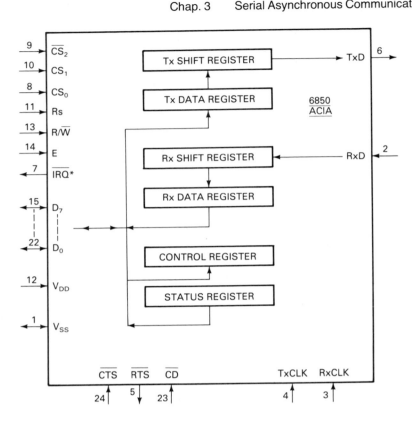

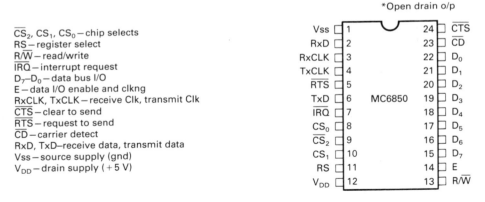

$\overline{CS}_2$, CS_1, CS_0 – chip selects
RS – register select
R/$\overline{W}$ – read/write
$\overline{IRQ}$ – interrupt request
D_7–D_0 – data bus I/O
E – data I/O enable and clkng
RxCLK, TxCLK – receive Clk, transmit Clk
$\overline{CTS}$ – clear to send
$\overline{RTS}$ – request to send
$\overline{CD}$ – carrier detect
RxD, TxD – receive data, transmit data
Vss – source supply (gnd)
V_{DD} – drain supply (+ 5 V)

Figure 3.5 Motorola 6850 ACIA

TABLE 3.4 6850 CONTROL REGISTER WORD BITS

D_7	Receive interrupt enable C_7	$1 = \overline{IRQ}$ low when Rx Data register full $0 = $ Receiver $\overline{IRQ}$ disabled
D_6 D_5	Transmit and transmit interrupt control C_6 C_5	$00 = \overline{RTS}$ low, Tx IRQ disabled $01 = \overline{RTS}$ low, Tx IRQ enabled $10 = \overline{RTS}$ High, Tx IRQ disabled $11 = \overline{RTS}$ Low, Tx IRQ disabled and transmit a break
D_4 D_3 D_2	Select character length, parity, stops C_4 C_3 C_2	$000 = 7$ bits $+$ even parity $+$ 2 stops $001 = 7$ bits $+$ odd parity $+$ 2 stops $010 = 7$ bits $+$ even parity $+$ 1 stop $011 = 7$ bits $+$ odd parity $+$ 1 stop $100 = 8$ bits $+$ 2 stops $101 = 8$ bits $+$ 1 stop $110 = 8$ bits $+$ even parity $+$ 1 stop $111 = 8$ bits $+$ odd parity $+$ 1 stop
D_1 D_0	Tx/Rx clock divisor select C_1 C_0	$00 = \div 1$ $01 = \div 16$ $10 = \div 64$ $11 = $ master reset

Wait until bit TDRE $= 1$ of the status register.

Write the character to be transmitted to the transmit data register.

Receiving a character (6850).   The $\overline{CD}$ pin should be LOW. There are three steps necessary to receive a character:

Wait until bit RDRF $= 1$ of the status register.

Read the error status from the status register.

Read the received character from the receive data register.

Transmitter and/or receiver interrupts may be enabled by the control word byte (see Table 3.4), in which case the $\overline{IRQ}$ pin will go LOW whenever status bits TDRE and/or RDRF become 1. While pin $\overline{IRQ}$ is LOW, status bit IRQ is 1.

Interpretation of the error status bits and use of the clock divisor in determining the bit rates is identical with that of the 8251A, described earlier.

TABLE 3.5 6850 STATUS REGISTER BITS

D_7	$\overline{IRQ}$ status IRQ	1 = $\overline{IRQ}$ low Reset by reading Rx data register or writing Tx data register
D_6	Parity error PE	1 = parity error occurred Set/reset during Rx data transfer
D_5	Overrun error OVRN	1 = overrun error holds RDRF = 1 Set/reset same as PE
D_4	Framing error FE	1 = framing error Set/reset same as PE
D_3	Clear to send $\overline{CTS}$	Follows $\overline{CTS}$ pin state $\overline{CTS}$ HIGH inhibits TDRE bit
D_2	Data carrier detect $\overline{CD}$	1 = $\overline{CD}$ pin HIGH (no carrier) (see note)
D_1	Transmit data register empty TDRE	1 = transmitter ready for character Reset by writing Tx data register
D_0	Receive data register full RDRF	1 = receiver ready with character Reset by reading Rx data register

Note: $\overline{CD}$ bit going to 1 causes an $\overline{IRQ}$ (LOW) when C_7 bit is set = 1. $\overline{CD}$ bit remains 1 after $\overline{CD}$ pin goes LOW until cleared by first reading the status register, and then the Rx Data Register, or until a MRST occurs.

3.3 UART-MICROPROCESSOR INTERFACES

Figures 3.6, 3.7, and 3.8 show typical microprocessor interface connections for the 6402 UART, the 8251A USART, and the 6850 ACIA, respectively.

The 6402 interface is slightly more complex than the others but requires less software for the transmitting and receiving functions. The control word is shown switch-selectable, and the error indicator is an LED. Programming the chip protocol and checking for errors requires no CPU time. Separate CPU interrupts are generated by the DR (data ready) and TBRE (transmitter buffer register empty) signals.

The 8251A interface uses the Intel 8085 *accumulator I/O* feature (as opposed to

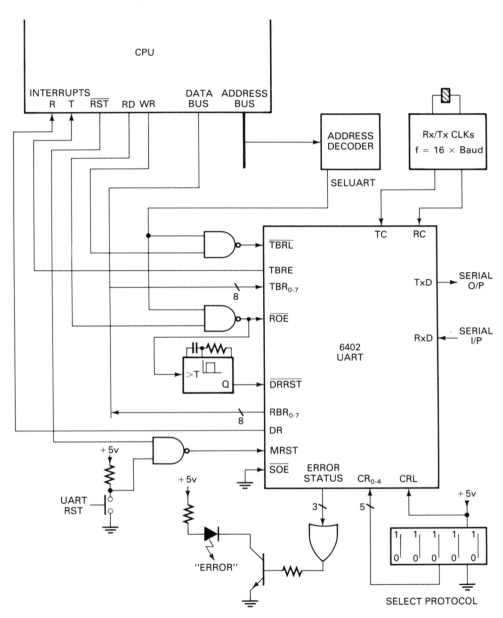

Figure 3.6 6402 UART microprocessor interface

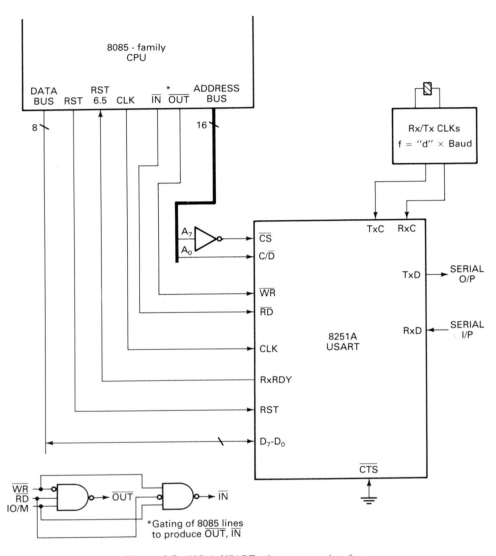

Figure 3.7 8251A USART microprocessor interface

memory-mapped I/O). Receiving a character is signaled to the CPU by an interrupt that is generated when the RxRDY (receiver ready) pin goes HIGH. The TxRDY (transmitter ready) pin is not used to generate an interrupt in this case—the CPU must poll the TxRDY status register bit before writing a new character for transmission.

The 6850 ACIA is shown interfaced with a 6800- or 6502-family processor. In this circuit, all address decoding is done externally—CS1 and CS0 (chip selects) are simply pulled HIGH. Interrupts ($\overline{\text{IRQ}}$) may be used to signal receiver ready and/or transmitter

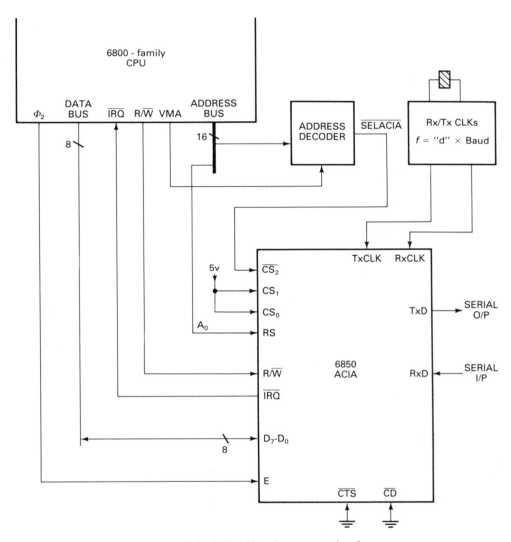

Figure 3.8 6850 ACIA microprocessor interface

ready. These are selected by proper programming of the interrupt enable bits in the ACIA control register.

Polling versus use of interrupts for I/O. Computer system I/O routines are often categorized as being either *polling* or *interrupt-driven*. Polling means that the CPU periodically stops other activity and asks the UART if it has any newly received data or if it is ready to transmit the next character. This polling usually takes the form of the CPU's reading the UART status register. An interrupt-driven routine, on the other hand, implies that the CPU carries on with its other activities, stopping them only in response to a UART-generated interrupt signal.

Polling to determine the UART status eliminates the need for interrupt hardware connections but is less efficient in the use of microprocessor time and software. Also, when polling is used to determine receiver status, care must be taken to ensure that overrun errors (missed characters) cannot occur. The decision to use interrupts or polling for I/O is made in each application by weighing such factors as hardware/software complexity and system task priorities.

3.4 SOFTWARE UARTs

In microprocessor-based systems, it is always possible to trade off software complexity for reduced hardware complexity, and the UART function is no exception. There is at least one very important limitation—that of speed. Replacing hardware with software almost always means that the related system task (such as transmitting or receiving a character) cannot be done as quickly.

Figure 3.9 shows a flowchart for a software transmit subroutine. Development of the receive subroutine is left as a problem exercise. Bit timing is controlled by software delay loops.

Real-time software of the type needed for such communication routines is usually written directly in assembly language to maximize speed and to perform efficiently the bit-level data handling needed.

With all the repetitive UART tasks performed by software, the required hardware interface reduces to a simple D-type latch, as shown in Figure 3.10.

3.5 BASEBAND INTERFACE STANDARDS

Computers and other data communication equipment that are located within the same room or building may be interconnected economically using baseband serial links or interfaces. The output impedance and TTL signal of a UART are not suitable to drive a twisted-pair or coaxial-cable transmission line directly. Driver and receiver circuits are required, which use voltage and/or current levels greater than those of standard digital ICs.

Standardization of such interfaces is required, if equipment made by different manufacturers is to be interconnected. The EIA standards are described in this section. An interface standard should include the signal electrical characteristics, circuit functions and names, as well as the connectors and pinout to be used.

3.5.1 20-mA Current Loop Interface

The 20-mA current loop interface uses a simple two-wire current loop for transmitting data serially. Logic 1 is represented as loop current $I = 20$ mA and logic 0 as $I = 0$ mA.

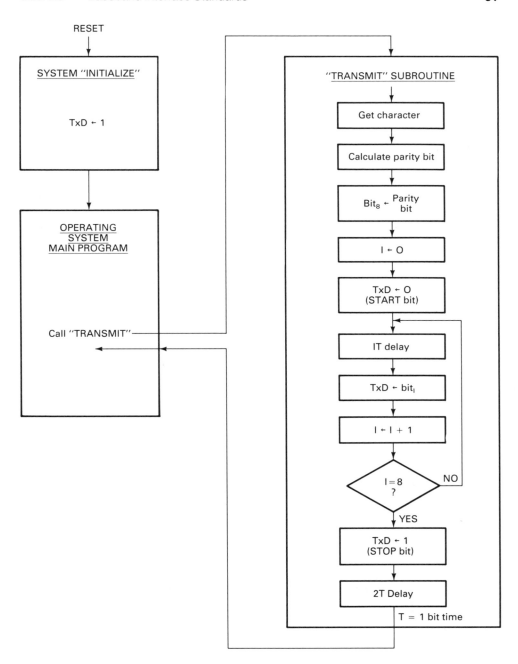

Figure 3.9 Software UART—T_x flowchart

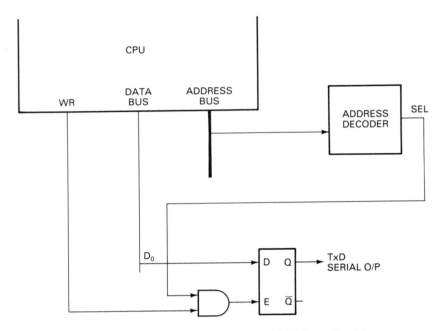

Figure 3.10   Interface for "software UART" (transmit only)

The loop current is sourced by the transmitter and detected by the receiver. The detection circuit must provide isolation of the loop from the receiver power supply and ground to prevent ground loop current from flowing across the loop. Also, the transmitter output circuit should approximate a switched 20-mA current source to minimize the effect of loop line length (resistance) on loop current. That is, the output resistance of the transmitter should be large compared with the line resistance.

The 20-mA current loop was first used as a standard interface between TTYs. The loop was "made" and "broken" by rotating switch contacts in the transmitting TTY and drove a printhead electromagnet in the receiving TTY. More modern implementations usually use an optocoupler as the receiver isolation device instead of an electromechanical relay. Figure 3.11 illustrates both relay and optocoupler circuits.

In designing the interface circuit of Figure 3.11(b), one must allow for the forward voltage drop of the LED (approximately 1.7 V) and ensure that both transistors are saturated when on.

The 20-mA loop interface is usually unbalanced, as shown. Its length should be limited to not more than a few tens of meters.

3.5.2 EIA RS232C Interface Standard

The RS232C standard was adopted in 1969 by EIA to specify the serial data and control line connections between a modem and a terminal or computer (see Figure 3.12(a)). The standard refers to the modem more generally as a DCE (data communication equipment)

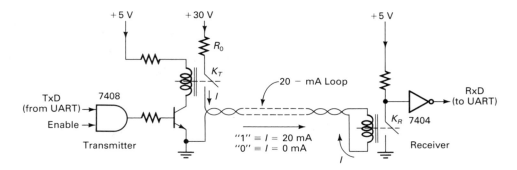

(a) 20 − mA loop using relays

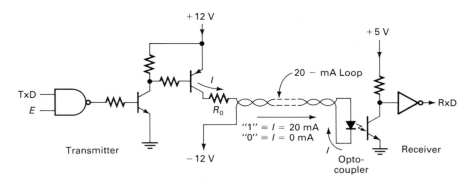

(b) 20 − mA loop using opto-coupler

Figure 3.11   20-mA current loop interface

and to the computer or terminal as a DTE (data terminal equipment). Standard RS232C applies to data rate–distance maximums of 20 kbps over approximately 15 m. It is an unbalanced-TTL-plus-driver category interface.

Description of the standard is broken into three sections: the electrical specifications, a description of the data and control lines, and the connector/pinout to be used.

RS232C electrical specifications.   RS232 logic voltages are bipotential, between $+15$ V and -15 V. Data lines use negative logic, such that logic 1 output is specified to be between -5 V and -15 V; logic 0 output is between $+5$ V and $+15$ V. However, the control lines (all lines except TDATA and RDATA) use positive logic; TRUE $= +5$ V to $+15$ V, and FALSE $= -5$ V to -15 V.

Ths standard includes a 2-V noise margin between the driver output and receiver input. Thus, the maximum receiver input threshold is ±3 V, as opposed to ±5 V for the driver output minimum. The absolute maximum driver output (i.e., unloaded) is ±25 V.

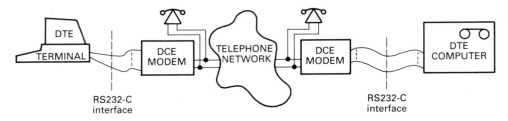

(a) Data communications over telephone network

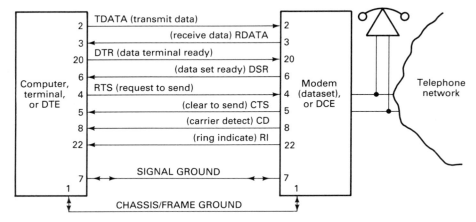

(b) RS232-C data and control lines

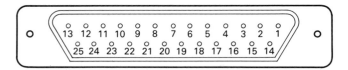

(c) DB-25 connector (female, front view)

Figure 3.12 EIA RS232-C interface standard

Other electrical specifications include:

R_L (load resistance) seen by the driver must be between 7kΩ and 3kΩ.

C_L (load capacitance) seen by the driver must not exceed 2500 pF.

To prevent excessive ringing, the voltage slew rate must not exceed 30 V/μs.

For the control lines, the signal transition time (from TRUE to FALSE, or FALSE to TRUE) must not exceed 1 ms. For data lines, the transition time (from 1 to 0 or 0 to 1) must not exceed 4 percent of one bit time or 1 ms, whichever is less.

RS232C data and control lines.   Figure 3.12(b) illustrates the most commonly used subset of RS232 lines. Their functions are best understood if they are grouped into one of four categories.

Data lines

    TDATA (transmit data): data to be transmitted by the modem over the telephone network.

    RDATA (receive data): data received by the modem over the telephone network.

Device ready lines

    DSR (data set ready): to signal that the data set (modem) is ready.

    DTR (data terminal ready): to signal that the terminal is ready.

Half-duplex handshake lines

    RTS (request to send): to signal a request to transmit data by the terminal.

    CTS (clear to send): modem response to the terminal's request to send, indicating that the channel is available for the terminal to transmit data.

Telephone signaling and carrier status lines

    CD (carrier detect): for the modem to signal the terminal that a valid carrier is being received from the network.

    RI (ring indicate): for auto-answer modems to signal detection of a ringing signal from the network.

Table 3.6 summarizes the signal lines and gives the EIA circuit two-letter designations for them. Note that two separate ground lines are provided: one for the power-line or chassis ground and one for signal-reference ground. These will be at the same nominal ground potential, but because they are separate, any 60-Hz currents or interference will not appear on the signal circuit. The specification recommends that the two grounds be isolated by 100-Ω resistance within the equipment.

RS232C connector.   A 25-pin connector is specified, and the de facto standard is the D-type, illustrated in Figure 3.12(c). Table 3.6 includes the pin allocation.

RS232C Null Modem.   Although the EIA RS232C standard is meant to apply specifically to a modem-terminal connection, a subset of the standard is often used when two terminals are directly connected together—or a computer and a printer, for example—without the use of modems. In such cases, the TDATA and RDATA lines must be crossed, and the necessary control lines must be wired TRUE or suitably "swapped" within the connecting cable. An RS232 cable assembly, which has this swapping of lines built in, is referred to as a *null modem*. Such a cable provides a convenient means of directly connecting two DTE devices via their RS232 ports. Two possible interconnection schemes are shown in Figure 3.13. Note that in the simplest case only four interconnecting wires are needed. In practice, the two grounds (SIG GND and CHAS GND) are often combined as well, although this is not recommended.

TABLE 3.6 EIA RS232C SIGNALS

Symbol	EIA circuit designation	Pin number	Name	Description
TDATA	BA	2	Transmit data	Serial data from DTE
RDATA	BB	3	Receive data	Serial data to DTE
DTR	CD	20	Data terminal ready	Ready signal from DTE to DCE
DSR	CC	6	Data set ready	Ready signal from DCE to DTE
RTS	CA	4	Request to send	Request to transmit, DTE to DCE
CTS	CB	5	Clear to send	OK to transmit, DCE to DTE (half-duplex turnaround)
CD	CF	8	Carrier detect	DCE signals receive carrier present
RI	CE	22	Ring indicate	DCE signals ring present (for auto-answer DCE)
SIG GND	AB	7	Signal ground	Common signal ground
CHAS GND	AA	1	Chassis ground, or frame ground	Power line ground return

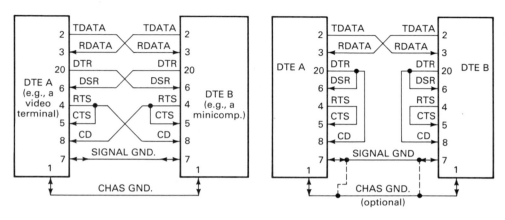

(a) "Null modem" DTE - DTE interface   (b) Simplest interface of two DTEs

Figure 3.13 Interfacing DTEs directly via their RS232-C ports using "null modem" cables

RS232 driver and receiver ICs.   Due to the popularity of the RS232 interface, custom IC drivers and receivers have been developed. Two such devices are the Motorola MC1488 driver and MC1489 receiver quad packages. Figure 3.14 shows an RS232 port for the 6850 ACIA, using the MC1488 and MC1489.

Each 1488 driver accepts a TTL-level input signal and translates it to an RS232-compatible output signal. The 1489 receivers detect RS232 input levels and translate them to TTL outputs.

3.5.3 EIA standards RS449, RS423, and RS422

As popular as RS232 is, it has several limitations:

Application of the RS232C standard is limited to signaling rates of 20 kbps maximum, over distances of 15 m or less.

Since RS232 circuits are unbalanced, noise immunity is less than optimum.

RS232 voltages are too high for the circuit density of modern IC technology.

In some applications, there is a need for additional modem-DTE lines for remote testing, and so forth.

In 1977–78, the EIA issued three new interrelated standards that were meant to overcome the shortcomings of RS232C and eventually replace it. RS449 is the umbrella document. RS449 specifies the functional and physical aspects of the new interface, and it refers to electrical standards RS422A (balanced) and RS423A (unbalanced)—the choice between balanced and unbalanced is to be determined by the signaling bit rate. A balanced interface is specified for most circuits when the bit rate exceeds 20 kbps.

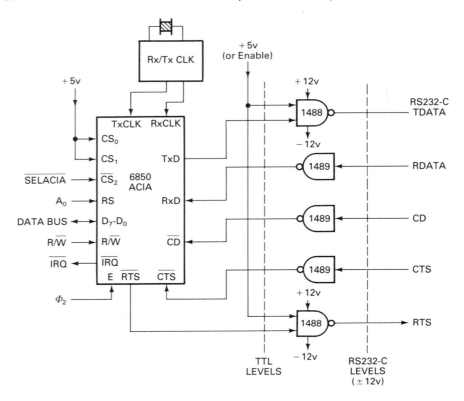

Figure 3.14 Application of RS232-C drivers and receivers

RS449 interface standard. RS449 requires use of 37-pin connectors plus optional use of additional 9-pin connectors (46 altogether!) for the DTE-DCE interface. The
additional 9-pin connections are required only when so-called secondary data channels are
used.

The basic 37 lines include all the previously described RS232 functions and introduce 10 new circuits for the following:

DCE (modem) testing

Selecting DCE standby mode

A terminal-in-service signal

Selecting optional modem carrier-frequency bands

Separate grounds (returns) for receive and transmit

A line designated "new signal"

See Table 3.7 for designations of the most common RS449 lines and for a partial cross-
reference to RS232 signals.

RS449 classifies each of the interface circuits as being either type I or type II. Type I

TABLE 3.7 EIA RS449 SIGNALS

EIA Cicuit Designation	Pin Number	Name	RS232 Equivalent	Circuit Type
SD	4,22	Send data	TDATA	I
RD	6,24	Receive Data	RDATA	I
TR	12,30	Terminal ready	DTR	I
DM	11,29	Data mode	DSR	I
RS	7,25	Request to send	RTS	I
CS	9,27	Clear to send	CTS	I
RR	13,31	Receiver ready	CD	I
IC	15	Incoming call	RI	II
SG	19	Signal ground	SIG GND	I
RC	20	Receive common		II
SC	37	Send common		I
SHIELD	1	Shield	CHAS GND	
IS	28	Terminal in service		II
LL	10	Local loopback		II
RL	14	Remote loopback		II
TM	18	Test mode		II
SS	32	Select standby		II
SB	36	Standby indicator		II
NS	34	New signal		II
SF or SR	16	Select frequency or select rate		II
SI	2	Signal rate indicator		II

circuits are considered most critical, and the standard specifies use of balanced links for these circuits (electrical standard RS422) when the bit rate exceeds 20 kbits/s. Otherwise, unbalanced links are allowed, as described in standard RS423 (differential receivers are used, even for the unbalanced link, as described below).

The physical configuration specified for the 37-pin and 9-pin connectors is the D-type, which is similar in construction to the RS232 DB-25 connector.

RS423A and RS422A electrical standards. RS423 is not a balanced interface but does include two improvements over RS232. First, separate send and receive ground lines are used (send common, receive common), which are connected to receivers having differential inputs. This excludes ground-potential differences (between the DTE and DCE) from the input signals of each receiver. Second, the logic voltage levels are reduced to $\pm$ 6 V maximum for improved compatibility with IC voltage restrictions.

RS422 is a fully balanced interface, using a separate balanced driver and differential receiver pair for each circuit. As mentioned earlier, RS449 requires use of an RS422 interface for all type I signals when the data bit rate exceeds 20 kbps.

Figure 3.15 presents a summary and comparison of the RS422 and RS423 electrical standards. Note the differences in the maximum distance and speed guidelines given for each.

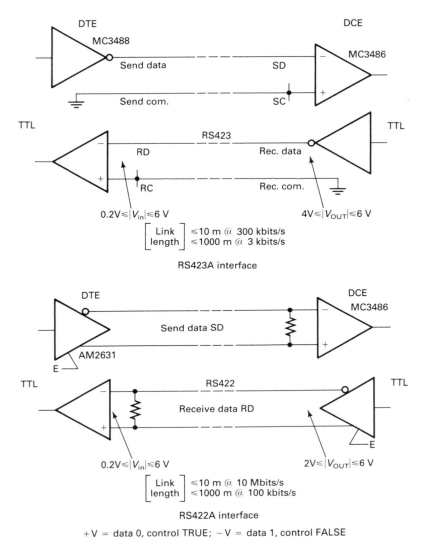

Figure 3.15 RS422A and RS423A standards

Recall that the RS232 standard specifies performance up to only 15 m distance. RS423 and RS422 standards specify performance up to 1 km for 3 kbps and 100 kbps, respectively.

3.6 FLOW CONTROL

In many practical cases, it is necessary for a receiving unit to exercise some control over the flow of data to it. Printers, for example, process (print) data relatively slowly. There is a real danger that the printer receive buffer will overflow and data will be lost when a large file is to be printed. Means must be provided for the printer to signal the CPU to suspend data transmission temporarily when the printer buffer is full and to restart transmission when the printer has caught up. This *feedback* may be provided using hardware handshaking; the printer could control the computer CTS (clear to send) signal, for example.

Another approach that is quite common is to use ASCII device-control characters DC1 and DC3. The ASCII codes for these two control characters are shown in Table 1.1, of Chapter 1. In such applications, DC1 is called XON (turn transmitter on), and DC3 is called XOFF (turn transmitter off). By sending these control characters to the transmitting equipment, the receiving unit can control the flow of data. When the transmitter receives an XOFF, it stops transmission and waits for an XON character before restarting transmission. Of course, such a procedure requires a full-duplex communication link.

PROBLEMS

3.1. **(a)**   Sketch the waveform at the TxD pin of a UART when the ASCII code for C is being transmitted. The protocol includes two stop bits and odd parity.

   (b)   Label your sketch to show one bit time for 300-bps transmission.

   (c)   Sketch one cycle of the waveform when the character string ABC is being continuously transmitted.

3.2. Design a receiver, using a 6402 CMOS UART, to receive the waveform of problem 3.1. Your circuit should display the received ASCII code, using seven LEDs. Error status should be displayed using an eighth LED (on indicates an error).
   The display should be updated each time a new character is received (i.e., each time DR (data received) goes HIGH).

3.3. The subroutine TRANSMIT, when called, is to initialize an 8251A USART and asynchronously transmit a string of 10 characters. The string of characters is stored in a RAM buffer, beginning at address TBUF.
   Draw a flowchart for the TRANSMIT subroutine.

3.4. Repeat problem 3.4 for the case of a 6850 ACIA instead of the 8251A.

3.5. Figure 3.9 shows a flowchart for a software transmitter. Draw a flowchart for a software asynchronous serial receiver.

3.6. **(a)**   Design a hardware RxD (receive data) interface for your software receiver of problem 3.5.

   (b)   Add a provision for an RS232 RDATA input, using an MC1489 receiver.

3.7. What is the purpose of the THLD input on the 1489 receiver?

3.8. The terminal-modem pair at site A in Figure P3.8 is communicating asynchronously over the telephone network with a similarly equipped site B.

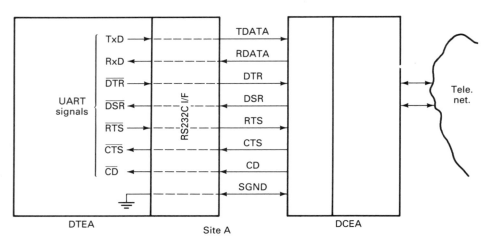

Figure P3.8

The link is half-duplex, and currently site A is transmitting the character ''F'' (ASCII). Give typical voltages (with respect to ground) you would expect to measure on each RS232 line. Include the waveform for one character on the TDATA line.

3.9. A serial-input printer and a computer terminal are to be interfaced, using the RS232 port on each, as shown in Figure P3.9.

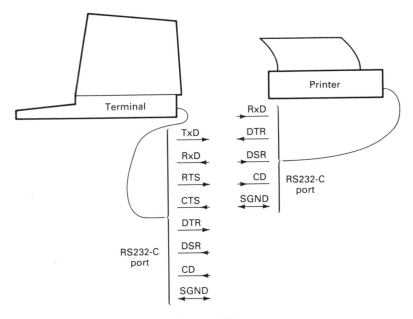

Figure P3.9

Besides the serial data connection, handshaking is required for flow control, since the terminal would otherwise output characters at a rate faster than the printer can print.

The printer makes DTR TRUE when it is ready to accept a character. Its receiver is enabled only when DSR and CD are TRUE.

Devise a suitable null-modem interconnecting scheme. Remember, the terminal will normally require certain of the RS232 lines be TRUE for it to transmit.

3.10. Revise the UART serial port interface circuitry of Figure 3.14 to meet RS449. The data rate is to be 50 kbps. Use AM2631 drivers and MC3486 receivers.

4

The Telephone Network

4.1 NETWORK HIERARCHY AND SWITCHING

It is not practical to have direct lines between each telephone and all others. Fortunately, this is not necessary, because most telephones are unused most of the time. By applying estimated probabilities of usage, the telephone companies have developed a sophisticated network of shared trunk lines and tiered switching offices. This network serves as a practical solution to the interconnection problem.

The North American telephone network uses five major levels, or classes, of switching centers, or offices. These are listed in Figure 4.1(a). The highest level, known as class 1, is the regional center. Twelve such centers serve all North America. Two are located in Canada, in Montreal and Regina. The lowest level office, class 5, is the end office, where the individual subscribers' loops terminate.

In some areas, tandem offices are installed to provide additional local switching among several end offices.

Private branch exchanges, or PBXs, are small in-house switches used by business.

In general, each class of office needs to connect only to the centers directly above and directly below, as shown by the solid lines in Figure 4.1(b). However, for more efficient servicing of higher-traffic patterns, additional direct lines are often provided between nonadjacent centers. These are shown by the dashed lines in Figure 4.1(b). At each office, calls are switched to the next-higher-level center only when it has been established that all the more direct lines (routes) are busy. The maximum number of intermediate links between subscribers is seven (the solid lines), but by far the majority of calls are completed using fewer. During exceptionally busy periods, such as Christmas, some call blocking does occur because even the highest level routes are busy.

An end office may handle up to 10,000 lines. Thus, the subscribers connected to each end office can be uniquely identified by a four-digit decimal number—the last four digits of their telephone numbers. The first three digits of each telephone number identify the particular end office. An area containing up to 1000 end offices is designated by a three-digit area code number.

The term *loop* refers to a two-wire link associated with one customer, or subscriber. Lines that are shared by several subscribers are referred to as *trunks*. Trunk lines are usually four-wire in nature. That is, separate circuits or channels are provided for each direction of communication.

Higher-level trunks usually employ some form of modulated-carrier method to multiplex several voice channels together onto wideband coaxial, optical fiber, or microwave links. These links often include appropriately spaced repeater amplifiers. For example, several hundred voice channels are multiplexed onto a single coaxial cable, using single-sideband AM and frequency-division multiplexing (FDM). Repeaters are required approximately every 10 km on such a line.

A subscriber lifting the handset of a telephone to place a call closes the telephone hook switch, causing current to flow in the subscriber's loop. The end-office equipment senses the off-hook condition, and a line-finder switch connects to the line, provides a dial tone, and becomes ready to receive the customer-dialed number. The switching equip-

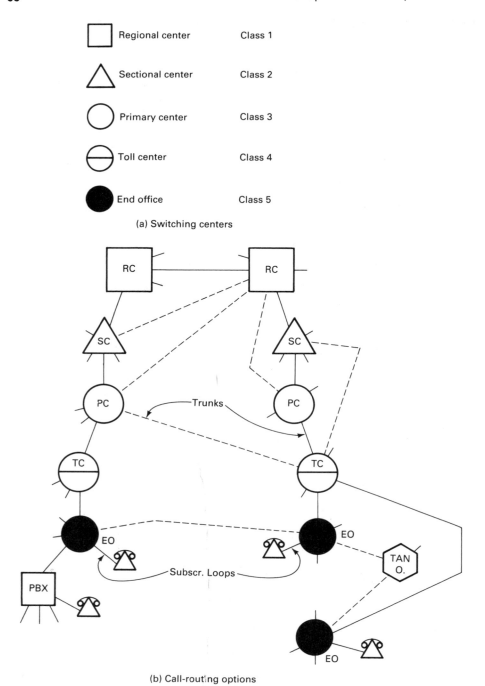

(a) Switching centers

(b) Call-routing options

Figure 4.1 Switching hierarchy and routing

ment must then take over and connect the subscriber to the line addressed by the dialed telephone number. The final stage in the switching sequence must include a test for busy and must supply a ringing signal to the called subscriber's loop.

Since the first manually operated patch-cord panels, the technology of telephone-exchange switching has progressed dramatically, through several phases.

The first automatic exchange used step-by-step electromechanical switches. The *stepper switch,* sometimes referred to as a Strowger switch after its inventor, is shown in Figure 4.2. It is a multilevel rotary switch, having a common wiper contact. The wiper is positioned vertically, corresponding to one dialed digit (by dial pulses), to select among the 10 stacked stators. The wiper is then rotated to select an available line among the 10 pairs of contacts located on each wafer or level.

Next came the electromechanical *cross-bar switch.* The cross-bar switch contacts are arranged in a matrix, with each group of contacts located at a row-column junction. A typical switch consists of 10 rows of 20 columns each. There is a set of 4 contacts at each

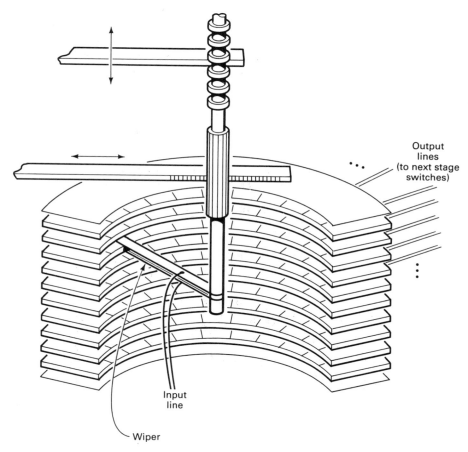

Figure 4.2 Step-by-step switch

crosspoint, as illustrated in Figure 4.3. Two groups of electromagnets allow the sequential selection of the desired row and column. Thus, up to 20 separate closures may be maintained. The cross-bar switch made it possible to centralize the switch-control equipment—a process known as *common control*. Common control was not as readily possible using step-by-step switches.

The next major development, in the early 1970s, introduced *stored-program* computer control of exchange switches. The first such systems used cross-bar-type switches. Later stored-program systems used matrices of smaller, faster, *reed relays*. Figure 4.4 illustrates a reed relay, or reed switch. The contact reeds are made of ferromagnetic material and are, therefore, mutually attracted (closed) when subjected to the magnetic field created when the surrounding coil is energized. The reeds are sealed in a nitrogen-filled glass tube.

Meanwhile, the immense strides being made in the field of IC technology were closing in on telephone switching. The developments of special field-effect transistor (FET) analog switches, A/D and D/A converters, and microprocessors were the most instrumental in the birth of digital switching. The first all-digital electronic switching systems were introduced around 1975. In digital systems, analog voice signals are sampled

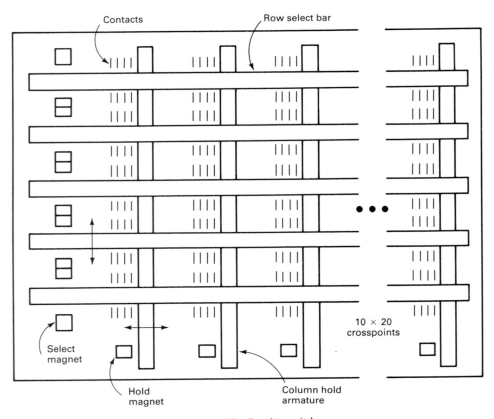

Figure 4.3 Crossbar switch

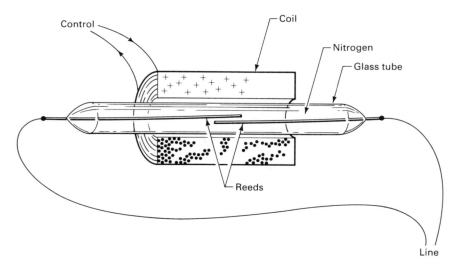

Figure 4.4 Reed switch

and digitally encoded using 8-bit PCM. The 8-bit samples from several subscribers are time-division multiplexed into *frames* and carried on common buses within the switching equipment.

Digital switching introduces the need for *time switching* in addition to the customary physical switching, or *space switching*. Time switching refers to the delaying or buffering in random access memory (RAM) of samples from one subscriber in order to match the TDM time slot of a second subscriber. This concept is illustrated in Figure 4.5. The digi-

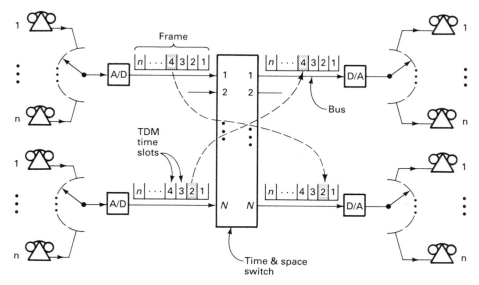

Figure 4.5 TDM switching

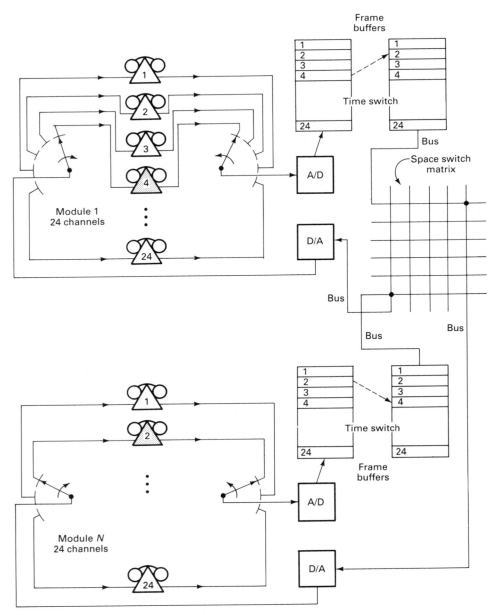

Figure 4.6   Digital switching between phone 4 module 1, and phone 2 module *N*

tal switch provides the time and space switching necessary to service *N modules;* each module contains *n* telephones, or *channels*. In the public network, *n* is usually 24. In Figure 4.5, channel 4 of module 1 is connected with channel 2 of module *N*. In general, digital switching requires both time switching to match up TDM-bus time slots and space switching to connect subscribers on different buses.

Figure 4.6 provides a more detailed look at the switching of Figure 4.5. Each module of 24 channels (each frame) is cyclically read into a frame buffer memory. Similarly, each module is cyclically written to from a second frame buffer. The time and space switching to connect phone 4 of module 1 with phone 2 of module *N* is shown. System software provides the time translation required by reading data from one time slot from each input buffer and writing it to a different time slot in each output buffer, as shown. Physical or space switching is used to interconnect the two module buses.

PCM and TDM are discussed much more completely in Chapter 8.

4.2 TRANSMISSION CHARACTERISTICS OF THE NETWORK

4.2.1 Echo

Hearing a delayed echo of one's own voice while using the telephone can be very annoying. Echos result from signal reflections, which occur at points of mismatch along the network. In general, the longer the echo delay time and the stronger the received echo signal, the more disturbing is the effect for the talker.

Transmission-line impedance matching is usually poorest on the subscribers' loops and at the end-office interface. Here, matching is difficult to control, because loop lengths and subscriber apparatus are so variable.

Fortunately, the echo heard by the talker is doubly attenuated on the network, because the echo signal must traverse the network twice—from the talker, to the point of reflection, and back. For short delays, attenuation is added to the network, which sufficiently reduces the echo level.

Over long routes, special *echo suppressors* must be used, as illustrated in Figure 4.7. The voice signal from either talker is sensed and activates a 60-dB attenuater in the return path. The suppressor deactivates a few milliseconds after the talker stops speaking. An activated suppressor can also be turned off if the far-end party interrupts loudly.

In North America, echo suppressors are used in circuits when round-trip delays can exceed 45 ms. Calls between network regional centers and some other long routes fall in this category. For example, propagation delays over satellite links can be several hundred milliseconds, making it mandatory to use echo suppressors.

Echo suppressors must be disabled during data communication calls. The several-millisecond interruption while the suppressor for one direction was turned off and the other turned on would be catastrophic for data! Modems attenuate their own echo within the input filter of each receiver. This is possible because the carrier frequencies used for the transmit and receive channels of each modem are different.

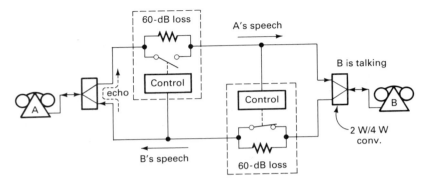

Figure 4.7   Echo suppressor concept

A disabler feature is provided by the network, which allows the echo suppressors to be automatically disabled. The disabler is triggered when either party transmits a 2025-Hz or 2100-Hz tone. The tone must last for at least 300 ms, and its level should be -5 dB$_m$. A no-signal interval of 100 ms or more will cause the echo suppressors to be switched back in circuit. The task of controlling the echo suppressors is accomplished by the user's modem (DCE) and must take place between the RTS (request to send) asserted by the terminal (DTE) and the CTS (clear to send) granted by the modem.

4.2.2 Bandwidth

The bandwidth of the telephone network is from approximately 300 Hz to 3400 Hz. This range corresponds to the spectrum of speech signals for which the network was designed. A representative frequency response is shown in Figure 4.8(a).

Recall also from Chapter 2 that any practical transmission system containing transmission lines and/or filters will have amplitude-response and delay characteristics that vary with frequency. The variable delay is caused by the variation in propagation time with frequency. Figure 4.8(b) shows a representative delay curve.

As also discussed in Chapter 2, these varying amplitude- and delay-versus-frequency plots give rise to amplitude distortion and phase distortion.

4.2.3 Loading Coils

Figure 2.3 presented approximate equations for calculating α, the attenuation constant for a two-wire line. A detailed analysis shows that the attenuation of a line may be reduced and made more constant in the voice-frequency range if its inductance, L, is increased. To achieve the desired effect, L must be increased substantially—by much more than could be realized by any practical line itself. To reduce the attenuation, discrete or "lumped" inductors, called *loading coils*, are placed in series with the line. The coils are located at regularly spaced points to achieve the desired effect. A typical arrangement uses 88-mH coils at 1.8-km spacing. Figure 4.9(a) shows the configuration of a loading coil.

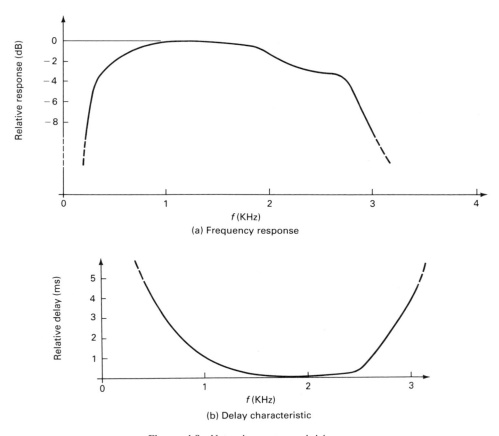

Figure 4.8   Network response and delay curves

When loading coils are used, the attenuation is reduced and remains relatively constant up to a critical cutoff, above which the attenuation rises rapidly. This is shown in Figure 4.9(b).

The propagation velocity of a loaded line is also made more constant and is less than that for an unloaded line. Making V_p more constant reduces phase distortion. However, the absolute delay is increased, which aggravates echo problems somewhat.

Loading coils must be removed from loops in order for frequencies above the cutoff value to be carried—for example, for dedicated high-speed data lines.

4.2.4 Loss, Levels, and Noise

Over the switched telephone network, the loss of signal power between subscribers varies dramatically, ranging approximately from 10 dB to 25 dB. The variation with time between any two subscribers is normally less than ±6 dB.

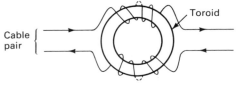

(a) Loading coil configuration

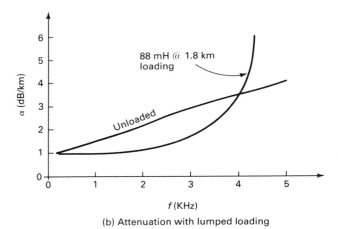

(b) Attenuation with lumped loading

Figure 4.9 Loading coil and effect on loop attenuation

The received signal-to-noise ratio S/N is as important as the received signal strength. For reliable reception, the S/N voltage ratio should be at least 30:1 (29.5 dB). Most noise contributed by the network may be broken into three categories:

1. Thermal and shot noise is broadband random noise due to the motion and fluctuation of charge carriers within the various components of the network.
2. Intermodulation and cross-talk noise results from interference with the desired signal by other signals on the network. The interfering signals may use a cable pair that is adjacent to that used by the desired signal, or the signals may be modulated onto adjacent-frequency carriers, in an FDM system.
3. Impulse noise consists of voltage spikes or transients that are caused primarily by mechanical switching in the exchange office, power-line surges, or lightning.

To minimize the effects of noise on the received signal, it is desirable to use transmission power levels that are as high as possible; however, higher signal levels on the network increase intermodulation and cross-talk problems. A compromise is necessary in establishing the transmit level. The maximum allowed power level is strictly controlled by the network authority. Published regulations set maximum levels allowed, depending on the type of signal being sent (for example, on the duty cycle and frequency). Generally, the specifications call for transmit power levels to be less than 0 dB_m (1 mW).

Random-noise power levels measured at subscribers' terminals are typically in the -40-dB$_m$ range.

Impulse noise is the most catastrophic for data transmission and the least predictable. When a noise pulse occurs, an error burst, or *hit*, results, and several bits are lost. This illustrates the need for error-detection schemes, such as parity checking. Many protocols require the receiver to acknowledge the error-free reception of each data block before the next block is sent.

4.3 THE LOCAL LOOP AND SIGNALING

The subscriber's local loop is a balanced two-wire line to the end office. Its characteristic impedance is between approximately 500 and 1000 Ω (nominally, 600 Ω).

A common *battery* at the end office supplies 48 V DC to power each subscriber's loop. The two loop conductors are referred to as *tip* and *ring*—a carry-over of the terminology used to describe the historic telephone jack. Figure 4.10 illustrates the local loop and jack. Ring is at -48 V DC, relative to tip. Tip is grounded (for DC only) at the end office.

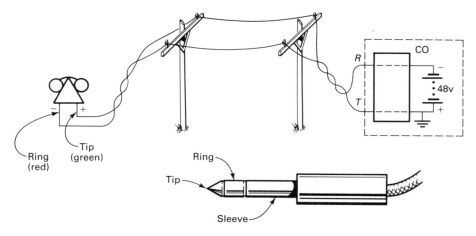

Figure 4.10   Local loop tip-ring designation

When a subscriber goes *off hook,* usually by lifting the telephone handset, the telephone hook switch closes, causing approximately 20 mA DC to flow in the loop. In the off-hook mode, the tip-to-ring DC potential falls to around 4 V at the subscriber's terminals.

The audio voice signals are conveyed in either direction on the loop as small variations in the loop current. The current variations comprise an AC signal superimposed on the DC loop current.

Figure 4.11 shows a common loop-trunk interface method used at the end office. The audio signal is transformer-coupled between the loop and trunk circuits. The office

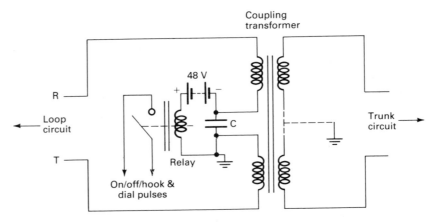

Figure 4.11   End office loop-trunk interface

loop-relay coil senses the average loop current and conveys off-hook–on-hook status to the office by opening or closing its contacts. Capacitor C bypasses the AC signal around the relay coil.

It is important to understand that for AC signals and AC impedances to ground, the loop *is balanced*, although the two conductors are at DC potentials of −48 V (off hook) and ground, respectively.

When the office detects an off-hook condition, dial tone is applied to the loop, and the exchange is ready to receive the dialed telephone-number digits. Signaling for customer dialing may use loop-current pulsing (rotary dial), or each digit may be frequency-encoded, using specific pairs of tones. The latter method is referred to as *touch-tone* dialing, or DTMF (for dual-tone multiple frequency).

In pulse or rotary dialing, the loop circuit is "broken" and "made" by a switch connected to the rotary dialing mechanism. A unique series of current pulses is created, corresponding to the digit being dialed, as illustrated for the digit 3 in Figure 4.12. The period of each pulse cycle is nominally 100 ms, having a 40-percent duty cycle. Being manually controlled, the time between successive digits may vary from 0.5 s to a few seconds.

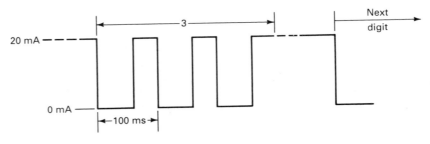

Figure 4.12   Loop dial pulses for the digit 3

When DTMF dialing is used, digits are selected by push-button switches, and a specific pair of frequencies is transmitted simultaneously for each digit. Figure 4.13 shows the allocation of frequency pairs. Each tone pair is present for 40 ms, minimum. The interdigit time is 60 ms, minimum. Touch-tone dialing may be 10 times faster than rotary dialing.

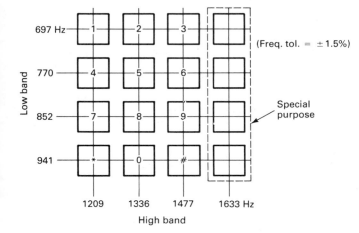

Figure 4.13 DTMF frequencies

To cause a subscriber's telephone to ring, a ringing signal of approximately 90 V rms AC (20 Hz) is applied to the loop at the called end office.

For satisfactory signaling of hook status, dialing, and ringing, the series resistance of the loop circuit must not exceed approximately 1300 Ω (including the resistance of the loop, the telephone, and any loading coils). A 7-km loop, using 24-gauge wire has a resistance of 1200 Ω.

Allowable signal loss between the subscriber and the end office is about 9 dB maximum, with 4 dB being typical. The loss for an unloaded 24-gauge loop is approximately 1.4 dB/km.

The subscriber loop interface IC (SLIC).   The local subscriber loop uses a balanced two-wire line. The same pair of wires is used for transmission in both directions between the telephone set and the central telephone office. Interfacing the office with the loop requires two-wire to four-wire conversion so that the receive and transmit signals can be separate, on separate two-wire circuits. Many trunk circuits use four-wire transmission lines—one pair for each direction between offices.

In the past, two wire to four-wire conversion was accomplished by special audio transformers called *hybrids*. In its simplest form, a hybrid transformer couples a single winding on the loop side to two separate windings on the trunk or office side. In practice, the transformers are more complex in order to accommodate connections for line matching impedance networks and call signaling.

In the late 1970s, semiconductor manufacturers developed the first subscriber loop interface circuit (SLIC) ICs, which were designed to replace the bulky hybrid transformers.

An interface circuit, using Motorola's MC3419 SLIC, is shown in Figure 4.14. The circuit provides conversion between a two-wire balanced loop and four-wire unbalanced central-office circuits. Provision is made on the office side for the common analog ground line to be floating—that is, not connected to the -48-V power supply ground.

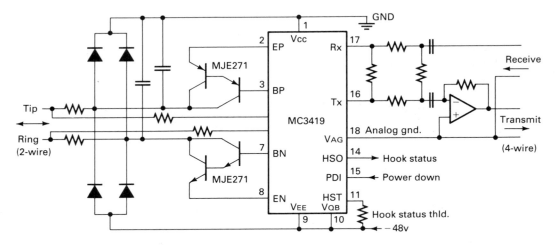

Figure 4.14 SLIC application circuit (Adapted; courtesy Motorola, Inc.)

Besides two-wire to four-wire conversion, the circuit shown provides the 48-V battery feed for the local loop and an on/off hook status output signal. The external darlington power transistors provide current gain to drive the loop. The external op-amp circuit drives the transmit pair on the office side.

The various resistors and capacitors are chosen to provide for correct signal levels, loop resistance, and impedance matching in each application. The design procedure is detailed in Motorola's specification for the MC3419.

4.3.1 The Telephone Set

Figure 4.15 shows a schematic for the common passive telephone set, often referred to as a 500 *set,* after its model type, 500D. An electric bell serves as the ringer, which is activated directly by the 90-V, 20-Hz ringing signal from the end office. The receiver is essentially a small, permanent magnet-moving-armature speaker. Sound is generated by vibrations of an aluminum diaphragm. The diaphragm moves in correspondence to the AC fluctuations in the loop current. The transmitter is a carbon microphone; sound pressure on its diaphragm compresses granules of carbon. The resistance of the contained carbon granules changes with pressure variations. The carbon resistance is connected in series with the loop, and the loop current is modulated by the changes in resistance.

The hook switch has three sets of contacts: S_1, S_2, and S_3, as shown. Lifting the

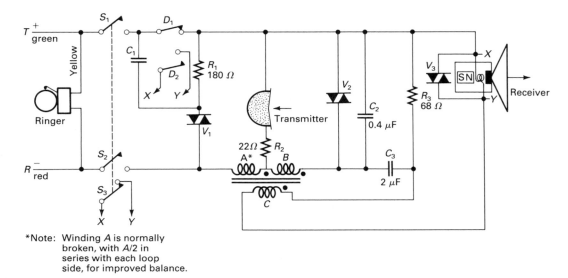

*Note: Winding *A* is normally
broken, with *A*/2 in
series with each loop
side, for improved balance.

Figure 4.15 The 500D telephone

telephone handset causes S_1 and S_2 to close and S_3 to open. This connects the receiver and transmitter circuits to the telephone line; direct current flows in the loop. S_3, when closed, serves as a protective shunt across the receiver. The shunt is removed while the telephone is off hook.

Loop current is interrupted for pulse dialing via switch D_1, which is operated by the rotary dial mechanism. Dial switch section D_2 is kept closed while dialing takes place to prevent objectionable dial-pulse noise in the receiver. C_1 and R_1 form a resistance-capacitance low-pass filter to suppress the radiation of electromagnetic interference that would result when D_1 opened and closed during dialing.

The three-winding transformer, known as a hybrid, provides directional coupling between the telephone receiver and the loop. Phasing of the transformer windings is such that currents through windings A and B are magnetically aiding for incoming signals and coupling of the signal to the receiver is maximum; however, outgoing AC signal currents generated by the transmitter flow in opposite directions through windings A and B. This makes transmitter-generated signal currents magnetically opposing within the hybrid transformer, and coupling to the receiver is minimum.

The term *sidetone* is used to describe the portion of the transmitter signal that is heard by the user through the receiver. The level of sidetone determines how loud the user will hear his or her own voice from the receiver. The design objective is to set the sidetone level to equal the level of the received signal, as heard through the receiver. The strength of the sidetone signal is controlled by adjusting the turns ratios of the hybrid, and by the sidetone-balancing network: C_2, C_3, R_3, and V_2.

The components that affect the level of sidetone also affect the AC impedance of the telephone, which should match the loop impedance (approximately 600 Ω) to minimize reflections. The DC resistance of the telephone, as seen by the loop, is from 50 to 90 Ω.

Varistors V_1 and V_2 perform a loop-equalizing function to compensate for differences in lengths of subscribers' loops. The resistance of a varistor decreases as its current increases. Short loops have less resistance, causing the loop current to be higher (50 to 90 mA) and the signal strength to be higher compared with long loops; thus, the increased shunting effect of the varistors (due to their lower resistance) compensates by reducing the received and transmitted signals when connected to a short loop. Varistor action actually causes the resistance of the telephone to vary in such a way as to equalize loop currents and signal strengths.

Telephones using DTMF dialing often use a pair of transistor or op-amp oscillator circuits to generate the tones. The required oscillator inductances (for L-C oscillators) or capacitances (for R-C oscillators) are selected for each digit, using the dial keypad switches.

Electronic telephones.   The popularity of the 500 set is giving way to all-electronic designs, using ICs. The IC phones are smaller and less expensive and offer many popular new features. They use active circuitry for ringing, impedance matching,

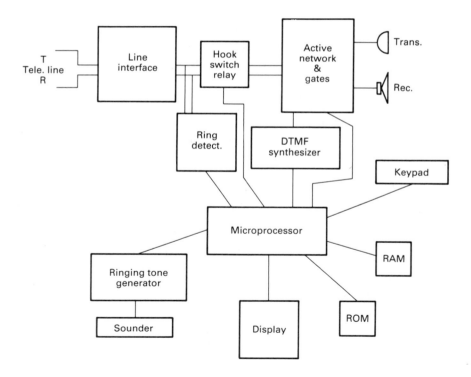

Figure 4.16 Microprocessor-controlled telephone

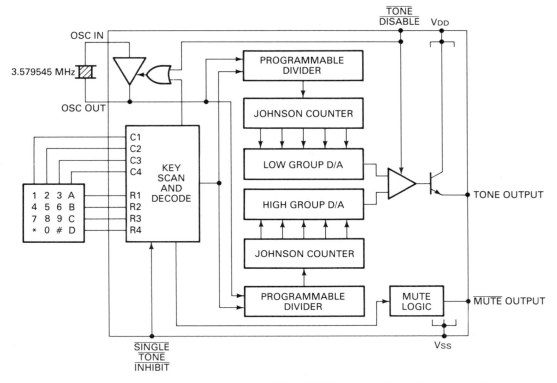

Figure 4.17 National Semiconductor's TP5089 DTMF generator IC (Reprinted courtesy National Semiconductor Corp.)

filtering, amplification, and so forth. Some include microprocessors for number storage, automatic dialing, and other features. Figure 4.16 shows a representative block diagram for a microprocessor-controlled telephone. Notice that the DTMF tones are synthesized digitally instead of being produced by analog oscillator circuits.

Figure 4.17 shows the block diagram for a DTMF tone generator IC manufactured by National Semiconductor, the CMOS TP5089. Depression of a digit key pulls the corresponding row (R1–R4) and column (C1–C4) inputs LOW, and the TP5089 generates the correct DTMF dual-tone signal at the tone output pin. An external 3.58-MHz crystal is required, as shown. The tone disable input is used to enable or disable the tone generator. The single tone disable pin is normally held LOW to ensure that only valid dual-tones are produced (in the event that more than one key is pressed at once). Mute output goes HIGH whenever a key is pressed.

Figure 4.18 shows a block diagram of a *single-chip telephone* using the MC34010/11 Electronic Telephone Circuit IC from Motorola. The MC34010/11 uses integrated-injection logic (I^2L) and may be powered completely from the telephone loop, as shown. The microprocessor interface is optional, to provide automatic dialing features, and so forth.

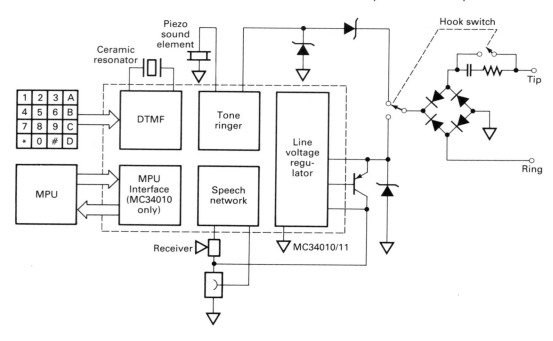

Figure 4.18 Motorola's MC34010/11 electronic telephone circuit IC (Reprinted, courtesy Motorola, Inc.).

PROBLEMS

4.1. How many lines would be needed to interconnect directly each of the following?

  (a) Three telephones

  (b) Ten telephones

  (c) *N* telephones

4.2. List the five classes of switching-center offices.

4.3. What is a PBX?

4.4. List the sequence of events that take place in the local switching office in setting up a telephone call. Begin with a subscriber lifting a telephone handset to place a call.

4.5. Distinguish between space switching and time switching.

4.6. What causes disturbing echos in a telephone network? How do echo suppressors alleviate this problem?

4.7. Sketch the frequency response curve for a typical voice-grade telephone network.

4.8. What are loading coils, and for what are they used?

4.9. **(a)** Sketch the waveform of local loop current when the digit 4 is being dialed using a rotary system. (Refer to Figure 4.12.) Label the on and off time intervals.

  (b) What two tones are transmitted when the digit 4 is dialed using DTMF?

4.10. What are the functions of a SLIC IC?

4.11. Where are hybrid transformers used in a telephone network, and what are they for?

4.12. What is sidetone?

4.13. What are the approximate on-hook and off-hook voltages and currents of the local loop?

5

Modems

5.1 NETWORK ATTACHMENT AND REGULATIONS

Since the telephone companies are held responsible for the quality of their service, they must exercise control over the type of equipment and signals their customers are allowed to connect to the network. More than two-thirds of the North American telephone network is operated by AT&T (United States) or Bell Canada.

Historically, attachment regulations were documents that were developed and kept internal to AT&T or Bell. They were used primarily by their respective manufacturing arms, Western Electric and Northern Telecom. The attachment of equipment manufactured by anyone else was aptly discouraged. Modems, for example, were seldom connected directly to the network. Instead, a data coupler unit, or DAA (for data access arrangement), was installed by the telephone company to interface the modem with the network local loop, as shown in Figure 5.1.

Two types of DAAs are used: the CBS, which has RS232C-level control signals, and the CBT, for which the control signals are contact closures or relay coil currents.

Recently, this direct control by telephone companies over loop attachment has changed considerably. Attachment regulations are now published and administered by agencies of the federal government: the FCC (Federal Communications Commission) in the United States, and the DOC (Department of Communications) in Canada. The role of the telephone company has been reduced to that of influencing the technical content of these regulations, through periodic review and consultation with the government agency. The regulations are readily available to all, and any manufacturer can submit equipment to be certified for direct attachment to the telephone network. This fundamental change in authority has fostered the growing *interconnect* industry for such products as phones, modems. security systems, and small PBXs for the home. Direct connection of these units

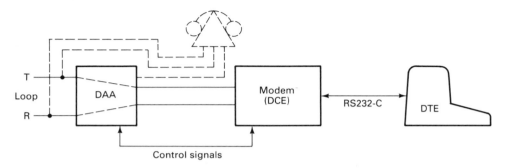

Figure 5.1   Modem-loop interfacing via a DAA

to the customers' loop terminals has been made easier through use of the miniature plug-and-jack assembly, shown in Figure 5.2.

The FCC and DOC regulations cover such items as transmitted signal levels, pulse dialing signals, DTMF frequency tolerances, surge protection, impedances, balance, sensitivity, spurious signal levels allowed, and connector types to be used.

Transmitted signal power for attachment to the switched network is specified to not exceed -9 dBm (at 600 Ω), averaged over any 3-s period, in the frequency band below 3995 Hz.

Besides direct connection or connection via a DAA, modems can be connected to the network acoustically, using transducers to transmit and receive modulated audio tones in the form of sound to or from a telephone handset. Acoustic coupling is illustrated in Figure 5.3.

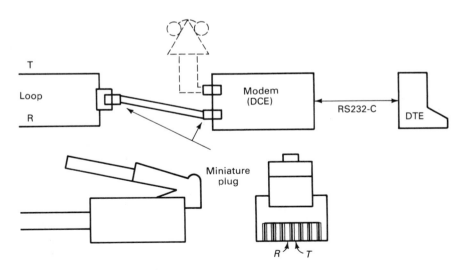

Figure 5.2   Direct modem-loop connection

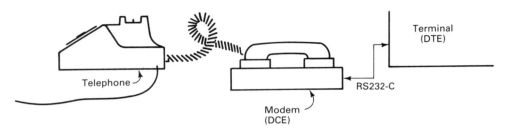

Figure 5.3 Acoustic or indirect modem-loop coupling

When indirect or acoustic coupling is used for data signals, performance is inferior, so use of such coupling must be limited to slower data rates (usually 300 bits/s). The -9-dB$_m$ maximum transmitted signal power applies here as well, but it is measured at the tip-ring terminals of the telephone.

5.2 LINE CONDITIONING AND LEASED LINES

The telephone company makes specially conditioned lines available by lease, which can be customer-dedicated for point-to-point data communication.

The special conditioning uses equalizing networks, which flatten the delay and frequency response characteristics, compared to the characteristics of an unconditioned line. (Refer back to Figure 4.8 for typical curves for unconditioned lines.) Also, the route through the network is more permanently fixed and is not determined randomly by the exchanges during call setup. Signal-to-noise ratio and harmonic distortion are also controlled in some cases.

Higher data rates and improved error performance are possible when conditioned lines are employed. Also the time for signaling and call setup is much reduced.

Conditioning for improved amplitude and delay versus frequency characteristics is known as *C conditioning,* and it is available in several grades—from C1 to C5, the latter being best.

D conditioning controls *S/N* and harmonic distortion and is being introduced for 9600 bps operation.

5.3 MODEMS

The frequency spectrum of baseband data signals can extend from dc upward to include the higher harmonics of the bit rate. For transmission over the telephone voice network, the digital signal is modulated onto an audio sinewave carrier, producing a modulated tone signal, the frequency of which is chosen to be well within the telephone band (approximately 300 Hz to 3300 Hz). The transmitting modem modulates the audio carrier with the TxD (transmit data) signal, and the receiving modem demodulates the tone to recover the RxD (receive data) signal.

The modem serves as the interface between the UART or ACIA of each end and the local loop. If synchronous protocol is being used, a USART or SSDA is used instead of a UART or ACIA, and each modem must recover the bit-timing information besides the RxD signal.

Usually the modem (DCE) is separately contained and connected to the computer or terminal (DTE) using an RS232C or RS449 EIA interface, as shown in Figure 5.4(a). Some microcomputers and special-purpose terminals have integrated, or built-in, modems including an autodialer, which eliminates the EIA interface, as shown in Figure 5.4(b).

The baseband TxD signal may be used to modulate either the amplitude, the frequency, or the phase of the audio carrier, depending on the data rate required. These three types of modulation are known as amplitude shift keying (ASK), frequency shift keying (FSK), and phase shift keying (PSK), respectively. In its simplest form, the modulated carrier takes on one of two states—that is, one of two amplitudes, one of two frequencies,

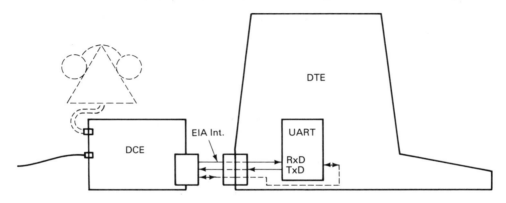

(a) Separate modem

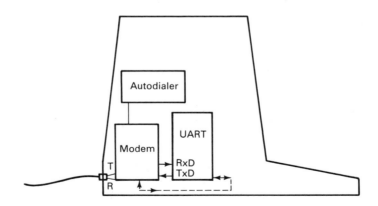

(b) Integrated modem

Figure 5.4   Separate and integrated modems

or one of two phases, as illustrated in Figure 5.5. In each case, the two states are referred to as *mark* and *space* and correspond to the 1 and 0 logic states of the TxD signal.

Low- to medium-speed data links usually use FSK and asynchronous communication up to 1200 bps. Multiphase PSK and synchronous protocol are used for 2400 bps and 4800 bps links. PSK utilizes bandwidth more efficiently than FSK but is more costly to implement. ASK is least efficient and is used only for very low speed links (less than 100 bps). For 9600 bps, a combination of PSK and ASK is used, known as quadrature amplitude modulation (QAM).

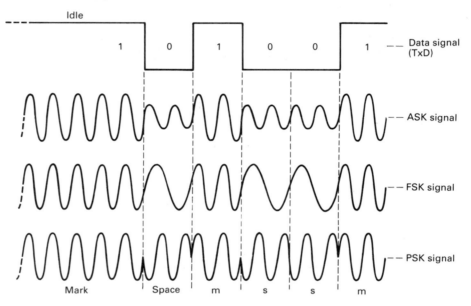

Figure 5.5 Types of modulation

5.3.1 FSK Bandwidth

Figure 5.6 shows the frequency spectrum associated with an FSK signal.

Referring to the figure, the data bit rate is br bits per second, giving the time for 1 bit, T_b, to be $T_b = 1/br$ seconds.

The data signal changes state most frequently when it consists of alternate 1s and 0s; it then becomes a square wave, having a fundamental frequency $f_f = 1/(2T_b) = br/2$ hertz. The maximum fundamental frequency of the baseband data signal is one-half the bit rate. Being a rectangular signal, the odd harmonic components are also present—the third harmonic frequency is $3f_f$, the fifth is $5f_f$, and so on.

The instantaneous FSK signal can be written as

$$v_{FSK} = v_b\sin(2\pi f_m t) + \overline{v}_b\sin(2\pi f_s t)$$

where v_b is the data-bit variable and may be only 1 or 0, depending on the state of the modulating data signal, and the f_m/f_s are the mark-space tone frequencies.

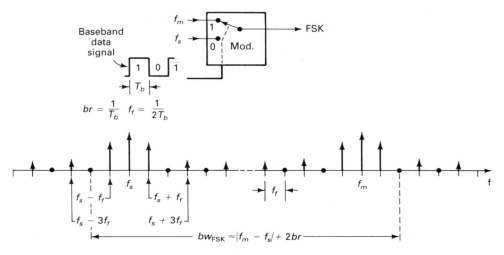

Figure 5.6 Approximate FSK bandwidth

The spectrum for each term in the v_{FSK} equation consists of the carrier surrounded by pairs of sidebands. There is a sideband pair for each harmonic present in the digital signal. The illustration in Figure 5.6 assumes $f_m > f_s$, which is purely arbitrary.

To estimate the minimum system bandwidth required to transmit the FSK signal satisfactorily, the range between the two outer frequencies located midway between the first and third harmonic sidebands is usually taken. This gives the bandwidth as

$$\text{BW}_{FSK} = (f_m + 2f_f) - (f_s - 2f_f) = f_m - f_s + 4f_f \text{ Hz}$$

$$\text{BW}_{FSK} = |f_m - f_s| + 2br \text{ Hz}$$

The last relationship says that the approximate bandwidth of the FSK signal is equal to the difference between the mark and space frequencies plus twice the bit rate.

For the demodulator design to be reasonably economical, guidelines for choosing the FSK center frequency and the mark-space difference are often given as follows:

$$f_{FSK} = \frac{(f_m + f_s)}{2} > 3br$$

$$|f_m - f_s| > \frac{2br}{3}$$

Modems can be designed to provide simplex, half-duplex, or full-duplex communication. The latter requires two separate FSK channels, one for each direction, in which case all four tones and their sidebands must fit within the telephone bandwidth. This will become clearer when the Bell 103 modem is examined in the next section.

EXAMPLE

(a) A 600-bps FSK modem uses a mark frequency of 1500 Hz and a space frequency of 2000 Hz. Calculate f_{FSK} and the bandwidth of the FSK channel.

f_{FSK} is the center frequency between f_m and f_s:

$$f_{FSK} = \frac{1500 + 2000}{2} = 1750 \text{ Hz}$$

BW may be estimated from

$$BW_{FSK} = (2000 - 1500) + 2(600) = 1700 \text{ Hz}$$

(b) Do these values of f_m and f_s meet the guidelines given above for economical demodulator design?

The first guideline suggests that $f_{FSK} \geq (3br)$. This is not quite met by the frequencies given—1750 Hz is less than 1800 Hz.

The second guideline suggests that $(f_s - f_m) \geq 2br/3$. This requirement is met, since the 500-Hz separation is greater than two-thirds of 600 Hz (400 Hz).

5.3.2 The Bell 103 Modem

The Bell 103 modem provides 300 bits/s asynchronous full-duplex communication over a voice grade line using FSK modulation. The result is an economical data link, which is suitable for keyboard applications.

Assuming 7-bit ASCII and 4 bits/character overhead (start, parity, and two stop bits), 300 bits/s translates to approximately 27 characters/second. This is faster than a person can type but is too slow for transferring large files or for many applications requiring graphics.

High-band and low-band FSK channels are provided, each including mark and space frequencies to allow the simultaneous transmission of data in both directions over a single line. The spectrum allocation is shown in Figure 5.7.

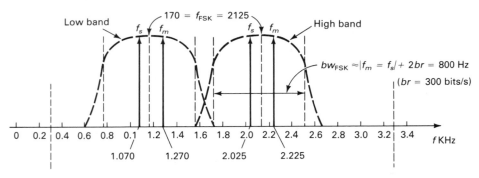

Figure 5.7 Bell 103 modem spectrum

The mark-space frequencies for the low and high bands are 1270 Hz and 1070 Hz and 2225 Hz and 2025 Hz, respectively. The center frequencies (f_{FSK}) are 1170 Hz and 2125 Hz, and the mark-to-space difference is 200 Hz in each case. The approximate bandwidth required for each channel is calculated to be 800 Hz, using the expression given in Section 5.3.1. Both bands fit well within the telephone voice bandwidth, but separation between the two is small (around 150 Hz).

Before communication can take place, the parties must agree on who will transmit and receive on which bands—the high or the low. This is resolved by designating one party as the call originator and the other as the call answerer; the former's modem is configured as an *originate modem* and the latter's as an *answer modem*. The originate modem transmits on the low band and receives on the high band. The arrangement is opposite for the answer modem.

Historically, the originate end has been associated with a remote terminal, accessing a mainframe computer by placing a data call, the answer end being the computer end. However, the call could just as well take place between two microcomputer users, in which case the originate-answer modem configuration should be selectable (manually or automatically) at each end, depending on which party places the call.

Figure 5.8 shows functional block diagrams for both the originate and answer

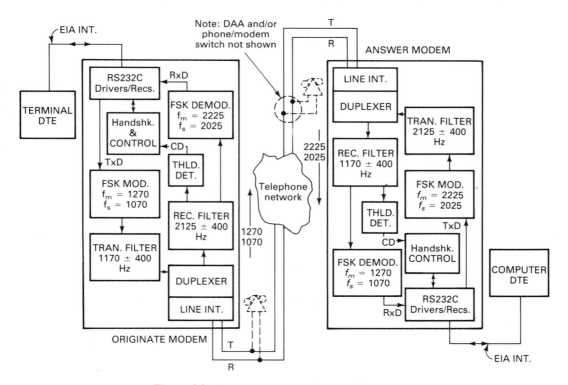

Figure 5.8 Block diagrams: originate and answer Bell 103 modems

modems. A pushbutton data-talk switch is usually provided and is located on the modem or on a special dataset telephone, used to transfer the line between the telephone and modem. When installation is by the telephone company, a dataset telephone is used in conjunction with a DAA.

Many recently introduced modems for microcomputers include autodialers, a relay-controlled hookswitch, and ring detector circuits. Such modems directly connect to the line, and do not require use of a telephone for originating or answering calls.

The following text reviews the operation of each modem block shown in Figure 5.8.

Line interface.   The line-interface circuitry must provide impedance matching for the local loop (nominally 600 Ω) and signal conversion between the balanced line and unbalanced modem circuitry. A small transformer is usually the main component of the interface block (referred to as a *hybrid*).

The interface block in a direct-connect modem must also provide such features as surge protection needed to meet federal agency regulations.

Duplexer.   The duplexer provides directional coupling and isolation among the telephone line, the FSK transmitter, and the FSK receiver signals. The signal from the Tx filter must be coupled to the loop but not to the Rx filter input. The signal received from the loop is coupled to the Rx filter input and provided with a few decibels of gain as well.

The heart of the duplexer is usually an op-amp connected as a differential amplifier, feeding the received signal to the Rx filter and rejecting the transmitted signal.

Rx Filter.   The Rx filter provides modem sensitivity through amplification and selectivity through bandpass filtering. The response should match that shown for the appropriate band in Figure 5.7—passing frequencies up to around 400 Hz above and below the center frequency, also indicated in Figure 5.8.

The circuitry of the Rx filter consists of from four to seven active filter stages using op-amps and RC networks. The circuitry forms a multiple pole Chebyshev filter with 20-dB to 30-dB gain.

This frequency selectivity of the receiver is important, to reject unwanted out-of-band signals and noise.

Demodulator.   An FSK demodulator is essentially a simplified FM detector using a frequency discriminator or phase-locked loop circuit to provide a shift in output voltage, corresponding to a shift in input signal frequency. The output is the RxD digital signal.

The demodulator mark-space frequencies are 2225 Hz and 2025 Hz for the originate modem and 1270 Hz and 1070 Hz for the answer modem.

Threshold detector.   This circuit uses a comparator, whose output toggles HIGH or LOW, depending on the level of the received signal. When the level is too weak for reliable demodulation, the RxD line is clamped HIGH and carrier detect (CD) is held FALSE.

Modulator. FSK modulators use some form of voltage controlled oscillator (VCO) having the TxD signal as the controlling voltage, such that either the mark or space frequencies are output corresponding to a HIGH or LOW state of the data input.

The modulator mark-space frequencies are 1270 Hz and 1070 Hz for the originate modem and 2225 Hz and 2025 Hz for the answer modem.

Better-quality modulators generate what is known as *coherent* FSK—that is, the output voltage transition is smooth and continuous when the frequency changes without any erratic transients. Transmitting coherent FSK reduces jitter of the demodulator output in the receiving modem and improves performance.

Tx filter. The Tx filter should bandlimit the transmitted FSK signal, eliminating spurious and harmonic signals beyond $f_{\text{FSK}} \pm 400$ Hz that may be generated by the demodulator circuit.

The active filter circuit used also sets the transmitted signal level to keep the output near, but not above, the -9-dB_m allowed on the telephone line.

Bandlimiting the transmitted signal is particularly important in the Bell 103 originate modem, because any second harmonic of the mark-space frequencies present falls within the passband of the Rx filter and will interfere with the desired signal, degrading performance.

Handshake or control. This logic block controls modem operation and conveys modem status from or to the DTE using the RTS, CTS, and DTR, DSR, and CD lines.

5.3.3 The Bell 202 Modems

Many applications involve a remote terminal accessing the database of a host computer. Such applications require a high-speed channel from the host to the terminal, but the reverse channel, used for infrequent keyboard entries, can be lower speed.

Bell 202 modems provide this characteristic, known as *asymmetrical* full-duplex communication, where the upstream and downstream data rates are different but can be used simultaneously. Often the two channels are referred to as *primary* (the host-to-terminal higher-speed channel) and *secondary* (the lower-speed terminal-to-host channel).

The Bell 202 system provides a 1200-bits/s FSK channel from the answer modem to the originate modem and a 75-bits/s channel in the reverse direction using ASK modulation. Figure 5.9 shows the utilization of the telephone band. The mark-space frequencies for the primary channel are 1200 Hz and 2200 Hz (note that $f_m < f_s$ here.), and the amplitude-modulated carrier for the secondary channel is at 387 Hz.

The Bell 202C modem. A typical application for which asymmetrical full duplex is suitable is videotex. Remote videotex terminals call in to a host database computer, from which files of text and encoded graphics must be transmitted downstream to the terminals. The files are organized to form individual videotex pages and are requested by each user inputting page numbers and other commands via a small keypad. A low-

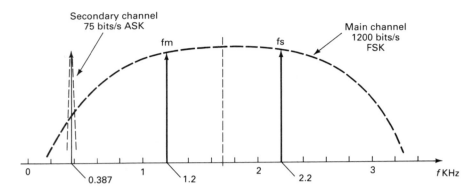

Figure 5.9 Bell 202 modem spectrum utilization

speed channel can be used to convey the user commands to the host, whereas the file transfers require the higher-speed primary channel.

Upgrading the videotex user input device from a keypad to a full ASCII keyboard makes the interactive aspect of videotex more powerful but requires a secondary channel bit rate greater than 75 bits/s for best results. The Bell 202C modem was developed for this need, retaining the 1200-bits/s primary channel but providing a 150-bits/s FSK secondary channel instead of the 75-bits/s channel of the basic Bell 202.

The spectrum utilization of the Bell 202C is shown in Figure 5.10. The mark-space frequencies for the 150-bps reverse channel are 390 Hz and 490 Hz.

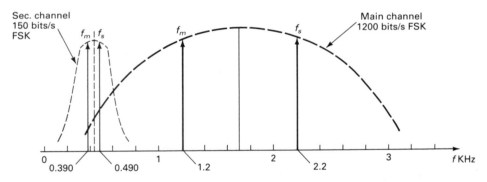

Figure 5.10 Bell 202C modem spectrum utilization

Because of the potential overlap of energy from the sidebands of each channel, as seen from Figure 5.10, bandlimiting and selectivity filters are particularly important in the Bell 202C system.

5.3.4 PSK Modulation

Assuming equal data rates, PSK requires less bandwidth for transmission than FSK, but PSK modulator-demodulator circuitry is more costly. Consequently, PSK is used by

2400-bits/s and 4800 bits/s modems, where use of FSK would not be possible within the telephone network bandwidth.

The simplest form of PSK, known as binary PSK (BPSK), was illustrated in Figure 5.5. The carrier phase is shifted between 0° and 180°. The instantaneous PSK voltage can be written as

$$v_{PSK} = v_b\sin(2\pi f_c t) + \bar{v}_b\sin(2\pi f_c t + 180°)$$

where v_b is the logical variable representing the 1 or 0 state of the baseband data signal.

This expression for v_{PSK} is very similar to that given for v_{FSK} in Section 5.3.1, except in this case, the frequency of both terms is f_c, whereas for FSK, the frequencies were f_m and f_s. Referring to Figure 5.11, the bandwidth required for the PSK signal is approximately equivalent to that of one of the v_{FSK} terms:

$$BW_{PSK} = (f_c + 2f_f) - (f_c - 2f_f) = 4f_f\,Hz$$

f_f is the fundamental frequency of the modulating square wave and equals one-half the bit rate, br. This gives,

$$BW_{PSK} = 2br$$

Contrast this with the expression given previously for BW_{FSK}.

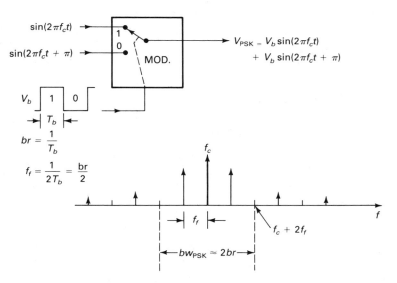

Figure 5.11   Approximate PSK bandwidth

Multiphase PSK.   Common 2400-bps modems use four-phase PSK and 4800 bits/s modems use eight-phase PSK, as illustrated in Figure 5.12. These are multiphase systems, as opposed to two-phase, or BPSK.

When the carrier can take on one of four states (phases), data bits are grouped in

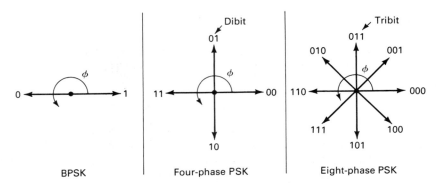

Figure 5.12 PSK phasor diagrams

pairs (dibits) in determining the phase of the modulated carrier. Four-phase PSK is some-times known as quadrature PSK (QPSK). Effectively, having four carrier states allows the sending of 2 bits at once. Similarly, eight-phase PSK allows the sending of data bits in groups of three (tribits).

Notice also, referring to Figure 5.12, that the order of dibits or tribits around each phasor diagram forms a Gray code sequence (only 1 bit changes between any two adjacent codes). This serves to reduce the effect of carrier phase jitter and noise on the demodu-lated data.

Table 5.1 lists several Bell modems that use PSK modulation. Data communication at rates of 2400 bps and faster usually uses synchronous protocol, and these modems in-clude circuits to recover the bit timing from the received PSK signal and to generate the RCLK (receive clock) signal for the DTE.

TABLE 5.1 PSK Modems

Type	Line	Modulation	Rate	Mode
201C	2-wire switched	4-phase PSK	2400 bits/s	Half-duplex/synchronous
	4-wire private	4-phase PSK	2400 bits/s	Full-duplex/synchronous
208A	4-wire private	8-phase PSK	4800	Full-duplex/synchronous
208B	2-wire switched	8-phase PSK	4800	Half-duplex/synchronous
212A	2-wire switched	4-phase PSK	1200	Full-duplex/syn-asyn
		FSK	300	Full-dup/asyn

The Bell 212A is a popular modem, since it provides 1200-bits/s full-duplex com-munication over the switched network. Custom LSI devices being developed for the 212A are reducing its cost dramatically, making it a practical alternative for videotex and pro-viding improved performance over the Bell 202C.

5.3.5 QAM and the Bell 209A Modem

QAM combines PSK and ASK to give 16 carrier states, illustrated by the phasor diagram in Figure 5.13. Data bits are grouped in fours, to modulate the carrier.

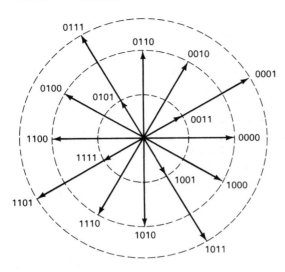

Figure 5.13 QAM phasor diagram

The Bell 209A modem uses QAM and provides 9600-bps full-duplex synchronous communication using a four-wire dedicated line with D1 conditioning.

5.3.6 Bits/s versus Baud

Baud is a unit to indicate the actual signaling rate on a communication link; it refers to the rate at which changes in carrier states occur, or the modulation rate.

In previous sections, the terms bits/s (bit rate) and baud have been used interchangeably. If a carrier having just two states is modulated by binary data, the bit rate and signaling rate are equal (i.e., the number of bits per second equals the number of baud), since the carrier is modulated using just one bit at a time. FSK systems, which use two frequencies, and BPSK fall in this category. When the data bit rate is faster than the rate of change in modulation of the carrier, a distinction must be made between the bit rate in bits per second and the signaling rate in baud.

In multiphase PSK and QAM systems, where the number of carrier states is 4, 8, or 16, the signaling rate is one-half, one-third, or one-quarter the bit rate. For example, the Bell 209A modem transmits and receives data at the rate of 9600 bits/s using a signaling rate of 9600/4 = 2400 baud.

5.3.7 Differential PSK

Demodulation of PSK requires the generation or extraction of a reference signal having a known absolute phase within the receiver. It may be necessary for the transmitter periodically to send a carrier burst of reference phase to accomplish this.

This need for absolute phase detection by the receiver can be eliminated by using differential PSK (DPSK) modulation. Only changes in the data signal, instead of the data stream itself, are used to modulate the carrier phase.

When the current data bit is the same as the last encoded data bit sent, one carrier phase is transmitted. When the current data bit is different from the last encoded data bit sent, the other carrier phase is transmitted (for a two-phase system).

Providing the transmitter and receiver "agree" always to precede the data stream with a known reference bit (1 or 0), then the receiver need only detect phase changes, not absolute phase, to reconstruct the data.

The DPSK modulation concept is illustrated by the circuit in Figure 5.14, for a two-phase system.

Referring to Figure 5.14, the D-latch provides a delay of 1 bit time, and the ENOR gate compares each data bit with the previous bit of the encoded data. The encoded data modulates the carrier phase by selecting between the 0° and 180° (π radians) sine waves. The OR gate and S-C flipflop force the encoded data signal to reference one state during idle periods.

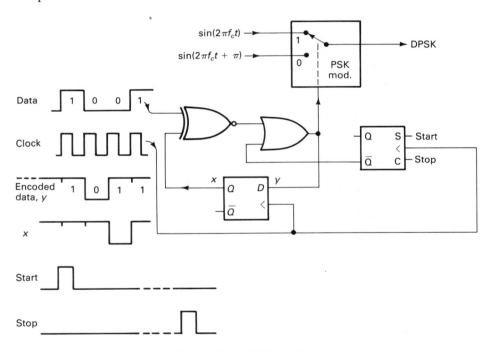

Figure 5.14 DPSK modulation

5.4 MODEM CIRCUITS AND IC APPLICATIONS

5.4.1 MSI Modem Circuits

A functional block diagram for the Bell 103 modem was presented in Figure 5.8. The duplexer, filters, modulator, and demodulator circuits are often implemented using small- or medium-scale ICs. An example for each is described next.

Duplexer.   Figure 5.15 shows a simplified duplexer circuit using an audio op-amp. The duplexer must provide good coupling of the FSK signals to and from the telephone line, while rejecting the transmit carrier from the receive filter input. The op-amp is connected as a differential amplifier. The transmit signal is connected equally to both inputs and is therefore rejected by the amplifier. The output of the transmit filter (V_{TF}) is coupled directly to the telephone line via R_s and the transformer. The receive FSK signal is applied to the noninverting input of the amplifier, as shown, and is coupled to the receive filter input with some voltage gain. The transformer matches the modem to the 600-Ω impedance line.

It should be noted that the rejection of the transmit signal by the amplifier requires that the reflected line impedance R_o, equal the feedback resistor, R_f. Although the line impedance is nominally 600 Ω, in reality it is highly variable, and the rejection of V_{TF} by the amplifier is less than ideal (10 dB to 15 dB is typical).

Filters.   Modem filters can be implemented using active filter stages, which use op-amps and RC networks. A typical bandpass filter stage is shown in Figure 5.16. Such

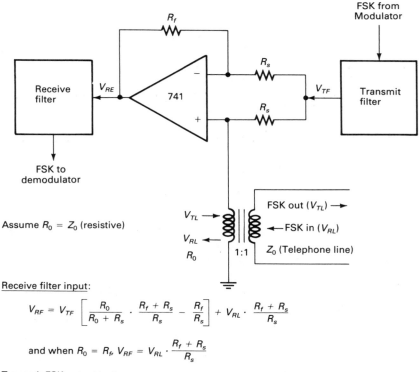

Receive filter input:

$$V_{RF} = V_{TF} \left[\frac{R_0}{R_0 + R_s} \cdot \frac{R_f + R_s}{R_s} - \frac{R_f}{R_s} \right] + V_{RL} \cdot \frac{R_f + R_s}{R_s}$$

and when $R_0 = R_f$, $V_{RF} = V_{RL} \cdot \dfrac{R_f + R_s}{R_s}$

Transmit FSK output to line:

$$V_{TL} = V_{TF} \cdot \frac{R_0}{R_s + R_0}$$

Figure 5.15   Duplexer circuit using op-amp

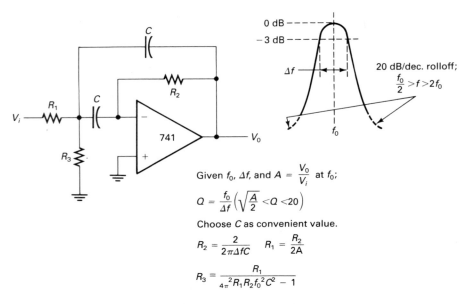

$$Given\ f_0,\ \Delta f,\ and\ A = \frac{V_0}{V_i}\ at\ f_0;$$

$$Q = \frac{f_0}{\Delta f}\left(\sqrt{\frac{A}{2}} < Q < 20\right)$$

Choose C as convenient value.

$$R_2 = \frac{2}{2\pi\Delta fC} \qquad R_1 = \frac{R_2}{2A}$$

$$R_3 = \frac{R_1}{4\pi^2 R_1 R_2 f_0^2 C^2 - 1}$$

Figure 5.16 Active bandpass filter stage

circuits provide gain as well as selectivity and require no LC tuned circuits. Typically, a receive filter might use four to six such stages cascaded, with each providing 5-dB to 7-dB gain. The overall response of a receive filter must provide 60 dB to 70 dB attenuation at the transmit frequencies but have sufficient bandwidth to pass the receive mark and space frequencies (including, at least, the first sidebands; see Figure 5.6).

Cascading n filter stages, each having the same center frequency f_o and bandwidth Δf, results in an overall bandwidth of

$$BW_{ov} = \Delta f \sqrt{2^{1/n} - 1}$$

Modulator. FSK modulator circuits often make use of VCO (voltage-controlled oscillator) chips, such as the XR2206 shown in Figure 5.17. The VCO is made to toggle between the mark and space frequencies by using the TTL data signal as the VCO control voltage, as shown. C_T, R_{MARK}, and R_{SPACE} are chosen to provide the desired FSK output frequencies. The XR2206 also has provision for external adjustment of the output waveshape and amplitude (gain).

Demodulator. PLL (phase-locked loop) chips, such as the LM565 shown in Figure 5.18, make convenient FSK demodulators. The phase detector generates an error voltage (V_o), which is proportional to the difference in frequencies between the FSK and VCO signals. This error voltage is amplified, filtered by the 3.6-kΩ/0.001-μF low-pass filter, and applied to the VCO control input. The varying error voltage causes the VCO frequency to "follow" that of the FSK input and serves as the demodulated data signal at pin 7. The output from the PLL is filtered further by the RC ladder network to remove the

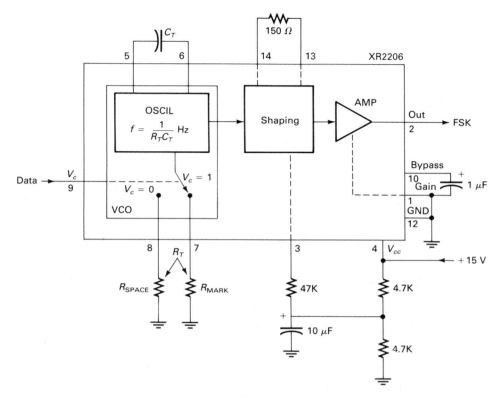

Figure 5.17 FSK modulator

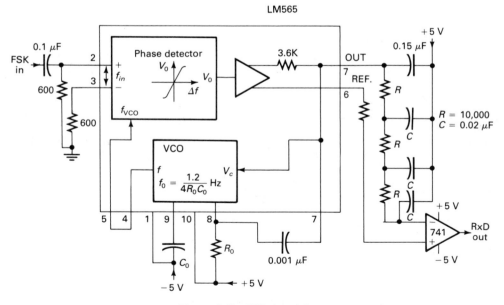

Figure 5.18 FSK demodulator

FSK carrier component and applied to the 741 comparator circuit. R_o and C_o are chosen to make the free-running frequency of the VCO equal to the FSK center frequency (midway between the mark and space frequencies).

5.4.2 LSI Modems

IC manufacturers have developed several LSI devices, which combine many of the modem circuit functions in one package. NMOS and CMOS chips are available that contain the modulator, demodulator, and control logic for various low- to medium-speed modems. Quite recently, CMOS switched-capacitor filter chips were introduced to provide complete receive or transmit filters in an IC. Three representative ICs from Motorola are described next: the MC6860 modem, the CMOS MC14412 modem, and the MC145440 switched-capacitor filter.

The MC6860 digital modem. The 6860 is optimized for 300-bits/s or 600-bits/s data communication using FSK modulation. It is fully compatible with the Bell 103 full-duplex standard. It uses NMOS technology in a 24-pin package and includes the modulator, demodulator, and the necessary control logic to interface directly with a UART chip and data coupler. The receive filter, transmit filter, duplexer, and a 1-MHz crystal must be provided externally.

Figure 5.19 shows a block diagram for a Bell 103 originate modem, using the MC6860 interfaced to an 8251A USART. Taking the $\overline{\text{SH}}$ (switch hook) input LOW places the 6860 in originate mode and ready to receive the 2225-Hz (mark) tone from the remote

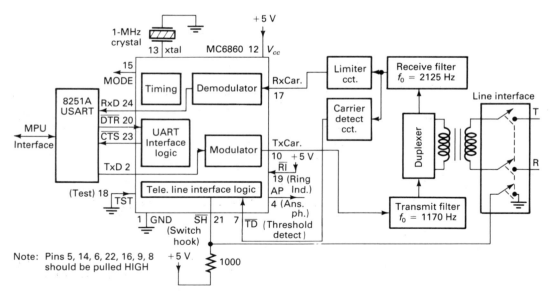

Figure 5.19 Application of MC6860 in Bell 103 originate mode

answering modem. At 450 ms after receiving the mark signal, the 6860 begins transmitting its mark tone (1270 Hz). At 750 ms after first receiving the 2225-Hz tone, $\overline{\text{CTS}}$ (clear to send) is taken LOW, and data can be transmitted as well as received. After $\overline{\text{SH}}$ goes LOW, the mark carrier from the remote modem must be received within 17 ms maximum.

A function similar to that of the RS232 carrier detect control line is performed by the $\overline{\text{TD}}$ (threshold detect) input. Insufficient carrier level results in the carrier detect circuit taking $\overline{\text{TD}}$ HIGH, which causes the 6860 to make $\overline{\text{CTS}}$ HIGH and turn off the Tx car (transmit carrier) signal.

The FSK carrier output is synthesized by a D/A converter within the 6860, and its waveshape is a "stairstep" approximation of a sine wave, rich in undesirable harmonics. The transmit filter must attenuate these harmonics to prevent their interfering with the received FSK carrier; harmonics of the transmit frequencies (1070 Hz to 1270 Hz) fall within the receive band (2025 Hz or 2225 Hz) in the originate modem.

The $\overline{\text{RI}}$ (ring indicate) input is meant to be driven from a ring-detector circuit when used. A LOW on $\overline{\text{RI}}$ places the 6860 in answer mode and causes the AP (answer phone) output to go HIGH, which is normally used to cause a switch-hook relay to close (answering the phone).

The MODE output indicates the modem state: HIGH indicates originate mode and LOW indicates answer mode. Mode can be used to switch (transpose) the receive and transmit filters in auto-originate-answer modems.

The MC145440 switched-capacitor filter.   The MC145440 is a CMOS IC in an 18-pin package. It contains both the high- and low-band filters for a Bell 103 modem, plus the switching required to transpose the filters between the transmit and receive paths for selecting originate or answer configuration. In originate mode, the high-band filter is placed in the receive channel and the low-band filter is placed in the transmit channel; the opposite is done for answer mode. Figure 5.20 shows a simplified block diagram for the MC145440, including the frequency response curves for the two filters. The filter response curves are very unsymmetrical compared with those of conventional filters, but the attenuation by each of the other-band carriers is adequate (approximately 50 dB). Notice also that each filter provides some 10-dB midband voltage gain.

The logic level of the originate/answer ($O/\overline{A}$) input controls the internal CMOS switches in selecting between originate and answer modes.

V_{LS} (logic select) input is used to select between TTL levels (V_{LS} LOW) and CMOS levels (V_{LS} HIGH) for the digital input and ouput signals.

Input ST (self-test) places the chip in a self-test loopback mode, when HIGH.

The CLK SEL (clock select) input controls internal frequency dividers to allow use of either a 1-MHz or 4-MHz crystal: CLK SEL LOW or HIGH, respectively. The crystal circuit is connected to the CLK1 and CLK2 pins. The 1-MHz clock output is available from CLK OUT, which normally supplies the modulator/demodulator chip (such as the MC6860).

The MC145440 also includes an extra op-amp, as shown, which can be used for the duplexer circuit.

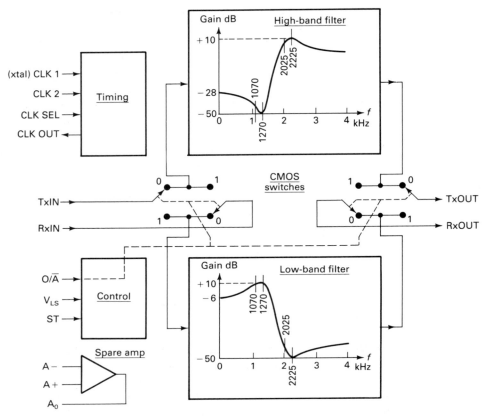

Figure 5.20 MC145440 switched-capacitor filter

The MC14412 CMOS modem. Figure 5.21 shows the schematic for a complete Bell-103 modem, using the MC14412 modem chip and the MC145440 switched-capacitor filter. Notice that the entire modem requires only three ICs (U1 is optional) and, except for the op-amps, is entirely CMOS using a single 5- to 12-V supply.

The MC14412 is similar in its functions to the MC6860 NMOS modem but includes less interfacing and control logic—it is essentially an FSK modulator and demodulator housed in a 16-pin package. Following is a brief description of its pins and signals:

Pin 1—RxCar: Receive FSK input from a limiter stage.

Pin 9—TxCar: Transmit FSK output.

Pin 14—Type: Selects Bell-103 (HIGH), or CCITT (LOW) frequencies.

Pin 15—Echo: When HIGH, in CCITT/answer mode, causes transmission of a 2100-Hz tone to disable echo suppressors.

Pin 10—Mode: Selects originate (HIGH) or answer (LOW) mode.

Pin 12—TxE: HIGH to enable transmitter.

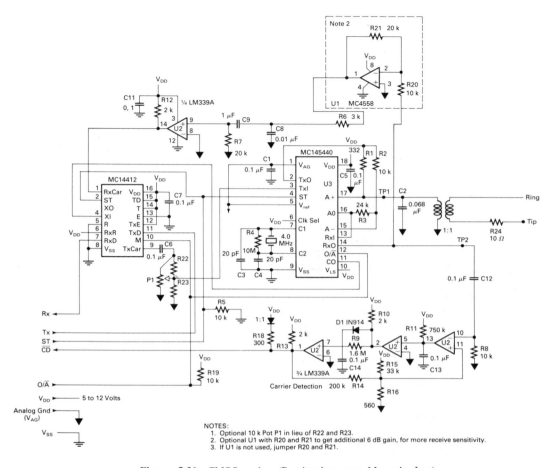

Figure 5.21   CMOS modem (Reprinted courtesy Motorola, Inc.)

Pin 11—TxD: Transmit data from UART.

Pin 7—RxD: Receive data to UART.

Pins 4 and 3—XI and XO: Oscillator in and out. A 1-MHz crystal or external oscillator may be used.

Pin 5—Reset: HIGH disables demodulator.

Pin 2—Self-test: HIGH selects loopback for testing.

Pin 15—TTL disable: LOW for TTL; HIGH for CMOS levels.

Pins 16 and 8—V_{DD} and V_{SS} connections, respectively.

Referring to the modem schematic, note the distinction between analog ground (V_{AG}) and digital ground. This makes it possible to use a single-polarity supply for the op-amps. The MC145440 provides $V_{ref} = V_{DD}/2$, a regulated DC output, which can be used as the V_{AG} potential, as shown. If a split supply is used (e.g., ± 5 V), V_{ref} is left open.

PROBLEMS

5.1. What is a DAA and where is it used?

5.2. What are the three main methods used to connect a modem to the telephone loop?

5.3. Why is the quality of the transmit filter circuit particularly critical in the originate-mode Bell 103 modem?

5.4. Calculate the approximate bandwidths of the primary and secondary FSK channels for the Bell 202C modem. Can its total bandwidth fit within that of the telephone network?

5.5. Receive filters for full-duplex FSK modems are often designed to have a bandwidth of only $f_m - f_s + $ br, which is less than the signal bandwidth ($BW_{FSK} = f_m - f_s + 2$br). This results in a design trade-off of sensitivity for improved selectivity.

Assuming this to be the case, sketch the frequency response characteristics for Bell 202C receive filters.

5.6. In checking out a modem installation, a technician measures the output as 0.52 V at the MARK frequency and 0.4 V at the SPACE frequency. Measurements are RMS voltages, taken directly across the telephone line.

Are these levels within the maximum limit specified by the Telco of -9 dB$_m$? Assume the line impedance is 600 Ω.

5.7. What is the signaling rate in baud when a Bell 208A modem is being used to transmit data at 4800 bits/s?

5.8. Refer to the duplexor circuit of Figure 5.15:

The FSK output (V_{TL}) on the telephone line is to be 200 mV.

The circuit sensitivity is to be -30 dB$_m$ (V_{RL} across Z_0).

The receive filter input must be at least 60 mV.

If $R_0 = Z_0 = R_f = 600$ Ω, specify appropriate values for the series resistor, R_s, and the transmit filter output, V_{TF}.

5.9. The receive filter for a Bell 103 modem consists of three stages. Each stage uses the circuit shown in Figure 5.16. The overall filter bandwidth is 500 Hz, its center frequency is 2125 Hz, and the total voltage gain is 3.

(a) What is an appropriate design bandwidth for each filter stage?

(b) Design one stage of the filter.

5.10. Of all the functions shown in the block diagram for a Bell 103 modem (Figure 5.8), what functions may be accomplished on-chip using a 6860 LSI modem chip?

6

Synchronous Serial Communication

6.1 INTRODUCTION

Asynchronous serial protocols are simple and inexpensive to implement. Asynchronous communication is particularly suitable when messages consist of short, randomly spaced bursts of a few characters each. On the other hand, for transmitting long preformatted files of data, the high bit overhead required for asynchronous communication can be prohibitive. Synchronous transmission is much more efficient. Messages are sent in *blocks*. Each block consists of a sequence of characters. Start and stop bits with each character are not required. Each block is synchronized as an entity rather than character by character. Error checking is also done over an entire block at once.

In synchronous systems, two levels of synchronization are required. First, the receiver bit-shift clock must be synchronized with the received bit timing for proper sampling of the serial input signal. Secondly, the *character* boundaries must be established.

A separate clock signal can be sent from the transmitter to the receiver in parallel with the data signal, which can be used to clock the receive shift register directly. This method is practical when the two stations are quite close physically. In particular, it is often used between a terminal (DTE) and a synchronous modem (DCE).

When it is not practical to send a separate clock signal from the transmitter to the receiver, the receiver must contain circuitry to extract the bit timing from the actual data signal itself. This increased complexity partially accounts for the higher cost of a synchronous receiver versus an asynchronous one. The synchronizing circuitry makes use of a PLL. A specially suited binary code is sometimes used for the data signal, which ensures voltage transitions occur often enough (even during long strings of 1s or 0s) for the receiver to maintain synchronization.

Once bit synchronization is achieved, the receiver must locate the character bit boundaries. To facilitate this, the transmitter sends one or more identifiable *sync* characters, or *flags,* at the beginning of each transmission.

Most synchronous networks use one of the protocols developed by IBM—either binary synchronous communication (BISYNC) or synchronous data-link control (SDLC). Both are described in this chapter.

6.2 SYNCHRONOUS DTE-DCE INTERFACE

When network data speeds exceed approximately 1200 bps, communication is usually synchronous. If a synchronous modem is used, it generates a receive clock signal, which is automatically synchronized with the received bit stream. The RS232 and RS449 interface standards include lines for the clock signals to be passed between the terminal and modem pairs. The signal designations and pins are listed in Table 6.1.

TABLE 6.1   RS232/RS449 CLOCK CIRCUITS

	RS232			RS449	
Symbol	Pin	Name	Symbol	Pins	Name
TCLK	15	Transmit clock (from DCE)	ST	6 & 23	Send timing
RCLK	17	Receive clock (from DCE)	RT	8 & 26	Receive timing
ETCLK	24	External transmit clock	TT	17 & 35	Terminal timing (from DTE)

When a synchronous modem is used, the receiver timing is usually supplied by the modem to the computer terminal. The transmit clock may originate from either the modem or the terminal. Further, the master clocking for a two-station link may be shared between the two stations (with each station generating the clock for one direction). Figure 6.1 shows the four possibilities and the RS449 circuits involved.

6.3 BISYNC OR BSC PROTOCOL

Data communication protocols (rules of procedure) are categorized in *levels*. BISYNC is a level 2 protocol. Level 2 protocols describe the procedures for controlling the data-link information flow. Level 1 protocols describe the physical and electrical characteristics used. RS449 is an example of a level 1 protocol.

The term BISYNC (or BSC) stands for binary synchronous communication. It is a *byte-controlled* protocol, since several special-purpose control characters (bytes) are used to control the link. The transmission of start and stop bits with each character is not required. BISYNC messages are sent in continuous blocks and each block is several characters long. The character boundaries within each block are established by prefixing each block with two or more synchronizing characters (SYN characters), which the receiver recognizes.

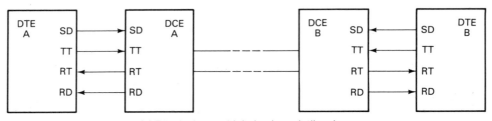

(a) Terminals control timing in each direction

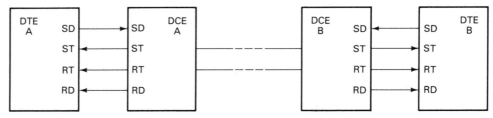

(b) Modems control timing in each direction

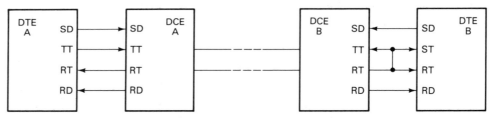

(c) Terminal A controls timing in both directions

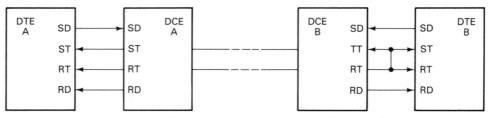

(d) Modem A controls timing in both directions

Figure 6.1 RS449 synchronous interface options

The various control characters used for BISYNC are from the ASCII code table, and they include the following ($ denotes hexadecimal ASCII code):

SYN	Synchronizing character	$16
SOH	Start of header character	$01

STX	Start of text character	$02
ETX	End of text character	$03
EOT	End of trans. character	$04
ETB	End of trans. Block character	$17
ENQ	Enquiry character	$05
ACK	Acknowledge reception character	$06
NAK	Negative acknowledge character	$15
NUL	Null character	$00
DLE	Data-link escape character	$10
CAN	Cancel character	$18

A typical BISYNC message block is structured as follows:

	SYN	'SYN	SOH	header	STX	text	ETX	BCC	
— —									— —
(first)								(last)	

The text string portion of the block contains the message. The header portion usually contains the destination address and an ACK/NAK response if required.

The BCC character is the block check character byte. This byte is unique to the block and is generated to form an error check over the entire block. The BCC is often a simple parity *checksum* as illustrated:

STX	T	E	S	T	ETX	BCC	
0	0	1	1	0	1	1	b_0
1	0	0	1	0	1	1	b_1
0	1	1	0	1	0	1	b_2
0	0	0	0	0	0	0	b_3
0	1	0	1	1	0	1	b_4
0	0	0	0	0	0	0	b_5
0	1	1	1	1	0	0	b_6
1	1	1	0	1	0	0	$b_7 (P)$

The transmitted bit stream for this would be as follows:

STX	T	E	S	T	ETX	BCC
-01000001	00101011	10100011	11001010	00101011	11000000	11101000-
(first)						(last)

In this example, even parity is used, and the BCC includes only characters from STX to ETX. Normally, the checksum is formed over an entire block (from SOH to ETX).

Upon receipt of a block, the receiver performs the checksum calculation and compares the result with the received BCC; then it responds accordingly with an ACK or NAK. The transmitter should not send another block until it has confirmation that the previous block was received correctly. Thus, BISYNC is said to be a half-duplex protocol.

Transparent mode.   The foregoing description is workable providing the TEXT portion of the block does not contain BISYNC control codes as part of the message (such as the same code as ETX, for example). To accommodate this possibility, the link may be switched into *transparent* mode, using the character DLE. Preceding the first STX by a DLE shifts the receiver into transparent mode and preceding the final ETX by a DLE terminates transparent mode. To allow for possible occurrences of DLE codes in the transparent message, the transmitter automatically doubles all such occurrences. Thus the receiver, when in the transparent mode, must ignore all double occurrences of DLE codes, except to remove one of each DLE code pair before passing the message on.

The IBM corporation, developer of BISYNC, uses EBCDIC (extended BCD information code) instead of ASCII. Also, in such cases the BCC character is a 16-bit cyclic redundancy check (CRC) code instead of a single checksum byte. EBCDIC and CRC codes are detailed in Chapter 7.

6.4 IBM 360/370 ELECTRICAL INTERFACE

The level 1 protocol, or electrical interface, specified for IBM 360/370 computer systems uses 96-Ω terminated coaxial cable and line drivers having emitter-follower outputs. Figure 6.2 gives the main characteristics of the IBM interface and shows the SN75123/SN75124 driver-receiver pair.

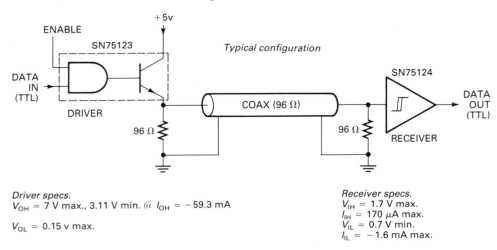

Driver specs.
V_{OH} = 7 V max., 3.11 V min. @ I_{OH} = −59.3 mA

V_{OL} = 0.15 v max.

Receiver specs.
V_{IH} = 1.7 V max.
I_{IH} = 170 μA max.
V_{IL} = 0.7 V min.
I_{IL} = −1.6 mA max.

Figure 6.2 IBM 360/370 interface-electrical (Adapted; courtesy Texas Instruments, Inc.)

Line length is specified indirectly in terms of the maximum allowed noise voltage, which is not to exceed 400 mV.

6.5 LSI APPLICATIONS FOR BISYNC

Three examples of using LSI for asynchronous serial link-to-MPU interfaces were given in Chapter 3: Intersil's 6402 UART, Intel's 8251A USART, and Motorola's 6850 ACIA.

The 8251A USART may be used for synchronous protocols (i.e., BISYNC) as well. Motorola's equivalent chip for synchronous use is the 6852 SSDA (synchronous serial data adapter). Application of these two devices for BISYNC is described below.

6.5.1 The 8251A USART—Synchronous Mode

Chapter 3 dealt with application of the USART for asynchronous protocol, much of which is applicable here as well. When used in its asynchronous mode, the 8251A is rated for data speeds up to 19.2 kbps. In synchronous mode, Intel rates it for speeds up to 64 kbps.

The block diagram of the 8251A and its register bit tables are reprinted here for convenience; see Figure 6.3, and Tables 6.2 and 6.3. Note the redefinition of control register bits 6 and 7 for synchronous mode (compare Tables 3.2 and 6.2). Synchronous mode is selected by programming bit 0 and bit 1 of the mode register to 0.

In synchronous mode, the USART transmitter automatically inserts SYNC (sychronizing) characters, preceding each block. Start and stop bits are not sent. The SYNC character to be used is programmed into the chip during initialization; it is normally the ASCII SYN character.

The receiver section of the USART automatically hunts for an incoming SYNC character, and it signals the MPU when character synchronization has been achieved (SYN pin goes HIGH).

The receiver bit-shift clock must be supplied externally (pin $\overline{RxC}$). This clock signal must be externally synchronized with the incoming data bit stream. The $\overline{RxC}$ signal is often supplied by the local synchronous modem, which contains a PLL synchronizing circuit. The 8251A internal transmit-receive clock divisor is fixed at $\div 1$ in synchronous mode.

Making pin $C/\overline{D}$ (control/$\overline{data}$) HIGH selects the control or status registers. Making pin $C/\overline{D}$ LOW, selects the receive buffer or transmit buffer data registers. Thus $C/\overline{D}$ is normally connected to address line A_0. The control and transmit buffer registers are WRITE-only, whereas the status and receive buffer registers are READ-only.

8251A initialization.   The procedure is similar to that for asynchronous mode, except the specific SYNC character code must be programmed as well:

Reset the chip using the RST pin (hardware) or the RST bit of the command word (software).

Write the mode word.

Write the SYNC character code.

Write the command word.

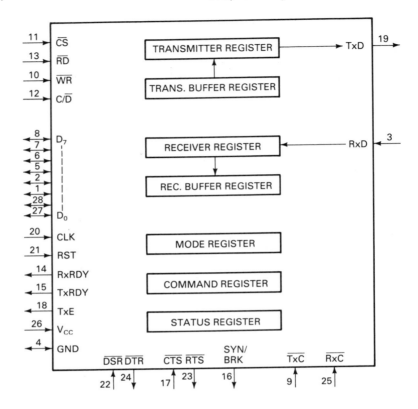

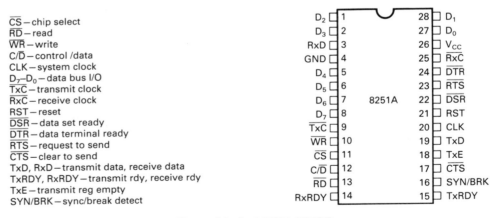

CS — chip select
RD — read
WR — write
C/D — control /data
CLK — system clock
D7–D0 — data bus I/O
TxC — transmit clock
RxC — receive clock
RST — reset
DSR — data set ready
DTR — data terminal ready
RTS — request to send
CTS — clear to send
TxD, RxD — transmit data, receive data
TxRDY, RxRDY — transmit rdy, receive rdy
TxE — transmit reg empty
SYN/BRK — sync/break detect

Figure 6.3 Intel 8251A USART

TABLE 6.2 8251A CONTROL AND COMMAND WORD BITS

D_7	Single character SYNC * SCS	1 = single 0 = double	Transmit enable Tx EN	1 = enabled 0 = disabled
D_6	External sync. detect ESD	1 = SYNDET an Input 0 = SYNDET an Output	Data Term ready DTR	1 = $\overline{DTR}$ pin LOW 0 = HIGH
D_5	Even parity enable EP	1 = even 0 = odd	Receiver enable RxE	1 = enabled 0 = disabled
D_4	Parity enable PEN	1 = parity enabled 0 = no parity bit	Send break character SBRK	1 = TxD pin low 0 = normal
D_3	Character length select L_1	00 = 5 bits 01 = 6	Error reset ER	1 = resets error flags PE, OE, FE to 0
D_2	 L_0	10 = 7 11 = 8	Request to send RTS	1 = $\overline{RTS}$ pin LOW 0 = HIGH
D_1	Baud clock divisor select B_1	00 = synchronous mode 01 = ÷ 1	Reset RST	1 = returns 8251A to mode instruction format
D_0	 B_0	10 = ÷ 16 11 = ÷ 64	Enter hunt mode EH	1 = enables search for SYNC character (synchronous mode)
	Mode Control Word Bits*		Command Word Bits	

*Synchronous mode.

The C/$\overline{D}$ pin should be HIGH for all three WRITE operations. The byte written between the mode and command words will be latched into the USART as the SYNC character code.

Transmitting a character (8251A).   As for the asynchronous case, $\overline{CTS}$ (clear to send) must be LOW, and the TxEN bit must be set for transmission to take place:

TABLE 6.3 8251A STATUS WORD BITS

D_7	Data set ready DSR	$1 = \overline{DSR}$ pin is LOW $0 = $ HIGH
D_6	SYNC character detect SYNDET	$1 = $ SYNC character detected (synchronous only)
D_5	Framing error FE	$1 = $ framing error reset by writing ER $= 1$ (asynchronous only)
D_4	Overrun error OE	$1 = $ overrun error reset by writing ER $= 1$
D_3	Parity error PE	$1 = $ parity error reset by writing ER $= 1$
D_2	Transmit register empty TxE	$1 = $ empty $0 = $ busy
D_1	Receiver ready RxRDY	$1 = $ ready with new character reset by reading receive register
D_6	Transmitter ready TxRDY	$1 = $ ready for next character reset by writing (see note) transmit register

Note: TxRDY has a different meaning from the TxRDY pin. The latter is conditioned by the $\overline{CTS}$ pin state and TxEN bit.

TxRDY bit is 1 whenever the transmit buffer register is empty.

Wait for the TxRDY bit to be set or for the TxRDY pin to go HIGH.
Write the next character to the transmit buffer register.

When the transmission of the last character of a block is completed, the TxE (transmitter empty) pin goes HIGH, and the TxE bit is set. The USART automatically transmits SYNC characters during idle periods (if the transmitter is enabled).

Bits are shifted out coincident with the falling edge of the $\overline{TxC}$ signal.

Character reception (8251A).   To receive a character in synchronous mode

Write an Enter Hunt command word as part of the first command word written to the command register.
Wait for the SYN pin to go HIGH.
Wait for the RxRDY pin to go HIGH or for the corresponding status bit to be set.
Read the character from the receive buffer register.
Read the error status from the status register.

The status register error bits must be reset by writing a command word having the ER (error reset) bit set. Data bits are shifted in coincident with the rising edge of the receive clock ($\overline{\text{RxC}}$).

8251A modem interface.   Figure 6.4 shows a typical modem interface for the USART. The EIA RS449 (unbalanced) standard interface is shown. The receive and transmit clock signals are supplied by the modem in this case. Connections for the microprocessor side of the USART are given in Figure 3.7.

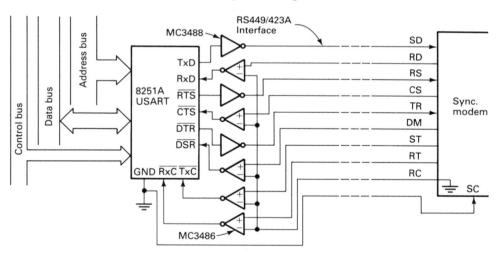

Figure 6.4   USART to synchronous modem interface (RS423A)

6.5.2 The Motorola 6852 SSDA

The block diagram or model of the synchronous serial adapter is shown in Figure 6.5. The 6852 is an NMOS device in a 24-pin package. The MPU interface lines are configured for direct connection to the 6800-family bus—similar to the connection in Chapter 3 for the 6850 ACIA chip.

Being a synchronous-only device, the SSDA provides some features not available using the 8251A USART. In particular, note the 3-byte receiver and transmitter first-in-

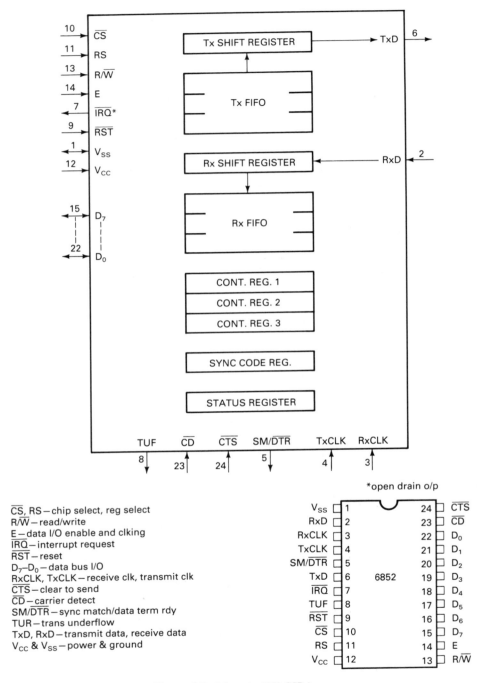

Figure 6.5 Motorola 6852 SSDA

first-out (FIFO) buffers! Using these buffers, the 6852 can be operated in a *double-byte* mode, where two characters may be written or read consecutively by the MPU with no waiting between them (for transmission or reception to take place).

Selection of the operating mode and ongoing control of the SSDA is via the MPU writing to the three control registers. Error and handshake statuses are read from the status register. The bit allocation for these four registers is given in Tables 6.4 and 6.5.

To the MPU, the 6852 appears as only two address locations (i.e., pin RS HIGH and RS LOW—usually connected to address line A_0). There are, in fact, seven registers accessible to the MPU, as seen from the block diagram. All registers, except for control register 1, are either READ-only or WRITE-only, as their functions require. The state of the R/$\overline{W}$ line is used on-chip to select automatically between the READ-only and WRITE-only groups. Also, notice from Table 6.4 that the two most significant bits of control register 1 are used to address other registers.

Addressing may be summarized as follows:

Pins		Control Register 1		
RS	R/$\overline{W}$	b_7	b_6	Register selected
0	1	X	X	Status
0	0	X	X	Control register 1
1	1	X	X	Rx FIFO Register
1	0	0	0	Control Register 2
1	0	0	1	Control Register 3
1	0	1	0	SYNC Code register
1	0	1	1	TxFIFO register

In scanning the bit allocations of the control and status registers, shown in Tables 6.4 and 6.5, it is seen that many of the flags and options are similar to those described with reference to the 8251A USART chip. Each time the SSDA receiver detects a sync code match in the received data, a 1-bit pulse is output on pin SM (sync match).

6852 initialization.   Initializing the SSDA involves the following steps:

Write to control register 1 to cause a chip reset and to address control register 3 next.

Write the desired control word to control register 3.

Write to control register 1 to maintain the chip reset and to address control register 2 next.

Write the desired control word to control register 2.

Write to control register 1 to maintain the reset condition and to access the sync code register next.

Write the desired code to the sync code register.

Write the desired control word to control register 1 (including enabling the receiver and/or transmitter).

TABLE 6.4 6852 CONTROL REGISTER WORDS

	bit 7	bit 6	bit 5	bit 4
	NOT USED	NOT USED	NOT USED	NOT USED
	Error interrupt enable — EIE: 1 = enables PE, Rx, Ovrn, TUF, $\overline{CTS}$, $\overline{CD}$ interrupts	Transmit sync on underflow — Tx Sync: 1 = Transmit Sync Character on underflow + enables TUF; 0 = Transmit mark on underflow	Word length select — WS3: 000-6 + even parity, 001-6 + odd parity, 010-7 bits, 011-8 bits, 100-7 + even parity	
	Address control bits — AC2: 00-Select control Register 2, 01-Select Control Register 3, 10-Select Sync Code Register, 11-Select Tx FIFO Register —when RS = 1 + $R/\overline{W}$ = 0 also	AC1 ; 1	Receiver Interrupt enable — RIE: 1 = enable $\overline{IRQ}$ on RDA	Transmitter interrupt enable — RIE: 1 = enable $\overline{IRQ}$ on TDRA

Bit	Control Register 3 (CR3)	Control Register 2 (CR2)	Control Resiger 1 (CR1)
bit 3	CLR Trans. underflow — CTUF; 1 = clears TUF	WS2; 101-7 + odd parity, 110-8 + even parity, 111-8 + odd parity	TIE — CLR sync; 1 = clears receiver character synchronization
bit 2	CLR $\overline{CTS}$; 1 = clears $\overline{CTS}$	WS1; 1-1 Byte Data I/O, 0-2 Byte Data I/O mode	strip sync characters — strip sync; 1 = strips all sync codes from the received data stream
bit 1	One sync character two sync character select — 1 sync/2sync; 1 = one sync character, 0 = two sync characters	Peripheral control bits — PC2; 00-$\overline{DTR}$/SM = 1, 10-$\overline{DTR}$/SM = 0	Transmitter reset — Tx Rs; 1 = resets and inhibits transmitter section
bit 0	External/ internal sync select — E/I sync; 1 = external, 0 = internal	PCI; 01-$\overline{DTR}$/SM = pulse on synchronization, 11-$\overline{DTR}$/SM = 0, synch match inhibited	Receiver reset — RxRs; 1 = resets and inhibits receiver

TABLE 6.5   6852 STATUS REGISTER WORD BITS (SR)

bit 7	Interrupt request IRQ	1 = IRQ active source determined by CR bits TIE, RIE, EIE. Cleared when source of interrupt cleared.
bit 6	Parity error PE	1 = error detected Reset by READ of RxFIFO or a WRITE of CR3 with RxRS = 1
bit 5	Receiver overrun Rx OVRN	1 = overrun occurred Reset by READ of Status Reg. followed by READ of RxFIFO, or a WRITE of CR with RxRS = 1
bit 4	Transmitter underflow TUF	1 = underflow occurred Reset by a WRITE of CR with CTUF and/or TxRS = 1
bit 3	$\overline{\text{Clear to}}$ $\overline{\text{Send}}$ $\overline{\text{CTS}}$	1 = $\overline{\text{CTS}}$ ↑ occurred since last clear or reset. Reset by a $\overline{\text{WRITE}}$ of CR with clr $\overline{\text{CTS}}$ and/or TxRS = 1
bit 2	$\overline{\text{Carrier}}$ $\overline{\text{Detect}}$ $\overline{\text{CD}}$	1 = $\overline{\text{CD}}$ ↑ occurred since last reset Reset by READ of Status Reg. followed by a READ of RxFIFO, or a WRITE of CR with RxRS = 1
bit 1	Transmitter data register available TDRA	1 = available Reset by a WRITE of TxFIFO
bit 0	Receiver data available RDA	1 = unread data available Reset by a READ of RxFIFO

6852 character transmission. $\overline{\text{CTS}}$ (clear to send) must be LOW, and the transmitter reset bit (TxRS) must be cleared for transmission to take place:

Wait for the TDRA (transmit data register available) status register bit to be set. Write the character code to be transmitted to the TxFIFO buffer.

This cycle is repeated until the entire block has been sent. If the MPU does not provide characters fast enough to sustain transmission, the transmitter underflow (TUF) bit and pin will go HIGH, and SYNC characters are sent automatically by the SSDA. The TUF flag must be reset by writing $b_3 = 1$ in control register 1.

Bits are shifted out (LSB first) coincident with the falling edge of the TxCLK input signal.

6852 character reception.   The $\overline{\text{CD}}$ input must be LOW, and the RxRS bit must be cleared to enable the receiver.

Incoming bits are compared with the programmed sync code until a match is detected. Each sync code match is indicated by a 1-bit-wide pulse on the SM pin:

Wait for the RDA bit to be set.

Read the error status from the status register.

Read the character code from the Rx FIFO buffer.

Data bits are sampled on the rising edge of the RxCLK signal.

6.6 SYNCHRONOUS DATA-LINK CONTROL (SDLC)

BISYNC or BSC is categorized as a byte-controlled protocol. The operation of a BISYNC link is controlled by several control characters or bytes (SOH, STX, and so on). BISYNC is a half-duplex protocol, since the receiver must acknowledge reception of each block as it is received before the transmitter may send the next block of data.

In the middle-1970s, IBM introduced an improved protocol for synchronous data communication; synchronous data-link control, or SDLC. SDLC is a bit-oriented protocol rather than byte-controlled. It is much less dependent on the use of special control characters. Also, acknowledgements of reception by the receiver may be postponend until the message is completed or until the receiving station is ready to transmit.

With fewer characters reserved for link control, SDLC is more easily made transparent to user data. BISYNC requires use of complex escape procedures if the user data contain link control character codes.

SDLC information is sent in frames, as shown in Figure 6.6. Each frame is bracketed by two (identical) 8-bit flag bytes, which are the only special-purpose characters used. The bit pattern of the flag is 01111110. The flag serves to establish synchronization and to mark the beginning and end of each frame. Any number of flags may be transmitted between frames to maintain synchronization of the receiver.

Flag	Address	Control	User data	FCS	Flag

Figure 6.6 SDLC frame format

The transmitter uses a technique called *bit stuffing,* to eliminate all occurrences of the flag pattern from the remainder of the frame. The data between the flags is monitored, and a 0 is inserted after all occurrences of five consecutive 1s. The receiver then can identify the beginning and end flags (six consecutive 1s), and it removes one 0 after all occurrences of five consecutive 1s elsewhere in the frame to restore the data. This procedure insures total transparency to user data.

The address field is normally 1 byte long. SDLC assumes an arrangement whereby one primary station (for example, a host mainframe) is networked with several secondary stations (terminals). The address field is used to identify the secondary station, whether it is transmitting or receiving data. One address ($FF) is reserved as a broadcast address, which the host uses to direct a transmission to all terminals on the network.

The 8-bit control field identifies the frame type; there are three basic types: unnumbered (U), supervisory (S), and information (I). U frames are used to control receiving stations—such as to cause initialization, disconnect, station testing, and so on. S frames are used for the frame counts (sent and received), ACK/NAK responses, to report busy/ready status, and the like. The I frames are used to convey the user data or messages. Further detail of the control-field bit patterns is given later.

The user data field may be any length but is usually limited to an agreed-upon maximum number of bytes in each SDLC application.

The FCS, or frame-check sequence, field is a 16-bit CRC computed over the address, control, and user data fields of the frame.

Bytes are transmitted beginning with the leftmost, as shown in Figure 6.6. Each byte is sent least significant bit first.

6.6.1 The SDLC Control Field

Table 6.6 details the makeup of the control field bit pattern. The least significant bits indicate the broad classification of the frame type: 0 for I, 01 for S, and 11 for U frames. SDLC allows for any station to be in one of three modes: initialization mode, normal response mode, or normal disconnected mode. Each station maintains two frame counts. N_r is the number of frames received and N_s is the number of frames sent. The transmitting station counts the number of frames sent and transmits N_s in the control field. Each time the receiving station receives an error-free frame, it increments N_r and transmits back an ACK response that includes N_r. This technique, used for data flow control, is sometimes referred to as a ''sliding-window'' method.

TABLE 6.6   SDLC CONTROL FIELD BITS

Name	Type	Bit Pattern			Comments
I	I	Nr	P/F	Ns 0	
REJ	S	Nr	P/F	1001	No I field
RNR	S	Nr	P/F	0101	No I field
RR	S	Nr	P/F	0001	No I field
TEST	U	111	P/F	0011	
UP	U	001	P	0011	No I field
XID	U	101	P/F	1111	
RD	U	010	F	0011	No I field
CFGR	U	110	P/F	0111	
BCN	U	111	F	1111	No I field
FRMR	U	100	F	0111	
UA	U	011	F	0011	No I field
DISC	U	010	P	0011	No I field
DM	U	000	F	1111	No I field
SNRM	U	100	P	0011	No I field Resets Nr and Ns
SIM	U	000	P	0111	No I field Resets Nr and Ns
RIM	U	000	F	0111	No I field
UI	U	000	P/F	0011	

The P/F (poll/final) bit, shown in the control field in Table 6.6, is set to 1 by the primary station when it polls a secondary station. It is set to 1 by a secondary station to indicate the final frame of a transmission.

The various command and response frames are described as follows:

I (information): For user data and ACK/NAK response.

REJ (reject): requests retransmission of a frame.

RNR (rec. not ready): Indicates station is busy. Frame may include ACK/NAK response.

RR (rec. ready): Indicates station is ready to receive. It may include ACK/NAK response.

TEST (Test): To request a test response from a secondary station.

UP (unnumbered poll): Used by the primary station for polling terminals on a network loop. Stations may respond or pass the poll to the next terminal.

XID (exchange station identification): Requests identification response from a secondary station.

RD (request disconnect): Used by a secondary station to request disconnect.

CFGR (configure): This command is used to configure a secondary station in a predefined manner.

BCN (beacon): Causes a secondary station to turn a test carrier on or off for network troubleshooting.

FRMR (frame reject): Used by a secondary station to reject a frame other than for an incorrect FCS.

UA (unnumbered acknowledgment): Serves as an ACK to an SNRM, DISC, or SIM frame.

DISC (disconnect): Transmitted by the primary station to cause a secondary station to enter normal disconnected mode.

DM (disconnect mode): Transmitted by a secondary station to indicate it is in the normal disconnected mode.

SNRM (set normal response mode): Places a secondary station in response-only mode (normal response mode).

SIM (set initialization mode): Used to initialize an exchange session between primary and secondary stations.

RIM (request initialization mode): Used by a secondary station to request that the primary station transmit a SIM command.

UI (unnumbered information): Allows user data to be transmitted in an unsequenced manner.

6.6.2 SDLC Abort Character

SDLC includes a provision for the transmitting station to signal the receiver to abort a frame in process. The transmitter ''violates'' bit stuffing and sends eight consecutive 1s;

the receiver interprets this as an abort character. Reception is terminated (awaiting the next flag), and the data of the frame are discarded.

6.7 HDLC PROTOCOL

SDLC is very similar to high-level data-link control (HDLC), adopted as a standard protocol for synchronous data networks by the International Standards Organization (ISO). HDLC is the link protocol used on CCITT-standard X.25 packet-switching networks. X.25 network protocol is described in the appendix.

There are three significant differences between HDLC and SDLC. HDLC offers extended (beyond 8 bits) address and control fields, and the HDLC abort character is seven continuous 1s, as opposed to eight continuous 1s.

The address and/or control field is extended by making the LSB of each byte 0, except for the last byte. The last byte in the address and control fields have the least significant bit set to 1 to indicate the end of the field.

6.8 LSI DEVICES FOR SDLC/HDLC

Intel's 8273 Programmable HDLC/SDLC Protocol Controller and Motorola's 6854 Advanced Data-Link Controller (ADLC) are examples of ICs designed to transmit and receive serial data using SDLC or HDLC protocol. Each provides complete full-duplex interface between an MPU bus and the serial port.

Motorola's 6854 is the smaller of the two ICs and uses a 28-pin package. Intel's 8273 uses a 40-pin package; it contains a digital PLL circuit, which the 6854 lacks. The PLL may be used to automatically synchronize the receiver with the received bit stream. Operation of the PLL requires application of an external clock signal of frequency 32 times the bit rate, and it requires that the data be NRZI (nonreturn to zero-invert on 0) encoded.

NRZI encoding of a standard NRZ (nonreturn to zero) data signal is illustrated in Figure 6.7. Transitions are used to encode the data bits rather than the voltage level. A transition (HIGH-to-LOW or LOW-to-HIGH) at a bit boundary indicates that the next bit is a 0. No transition at a bit boundary indicates the next bit is a 1. Use of NRZI encoding ensures the signal contains at least one voltage transition every five bits; recall that five is the maximum number of contiguous 1s allowed within a frame. If this was not the case, the receiver could lose synchronization during long strings of 0s.

The 6854 ADLC has an NRZI mode, but the PLL circuitry must be provided externally. Either device can be used with a synchronous modem, in which case the modem's synchronizing circuitry generates the receive clock signal. Refer to Figure 6.8 for three possible arrangements.

Features that are common to both the 8273 and 6854 include the following:

HDLC or SDLC implementation
Automatic FCS generation and checking
NRZ or NRZI modes

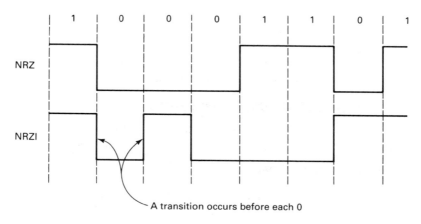

Figure 6.7   NRZI versus NRZ line coding

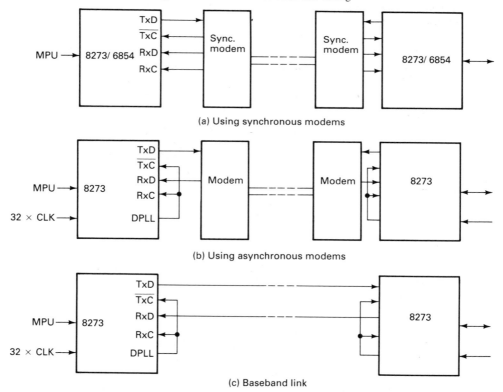

(a) Using synchronous modems

(b) Using asynchronous modems

(c) Baseband link

Mnemonics: TxD/RxD—transmit/receive data
TxC/RxC—transmit/receive clock
DPLL—digital phase-locked loop

Figure 6.8   8273 and 6854 link interface options

automatic flag detection and character synchronization

automatic zero insertion and deletion

automatic detection and deletion of abort character

modem interface (RTS, CTS, and so on)

6.9 TESTING DATA COMMUNICATION SYSTEMS

Analog tests, digital tests, and protocol tests are performed on data communication systems. Some of the more popular techniques are described in this section.

6.9.1 PAR Analog Test

The distortion of a pulse waveform transmitted over a line is caused by variations in amplitude response and delay over the bandwidth of the signal. This was explored in Chapter 2. Direct measurement of attenuation and delay are complex and very time-consuming. The peak-to-average ratio test provides a relatively simple alternative that indirectly provides a measure of the quality of analog performance.

A signal generator drives one end of the transmission line with a repetitive burst waveform. The signal bursts consist of audio sine waves. The bursts are spaced approximately 4 ms apart. The signal is chosen so that its spectrum covers the 300 Hz to 3400 Hz range. A receiver is used to make measurements on the waveform received at the far end of the line. The amplitude and delay distortion introduced directly affect the received waveform.

At the receive end, a factor is calculated that relates the peak burst voltage (v_p) to the full-wave rectified DC value (v_{DC}) of the signal:

$$PAR = \left(\frac{2v_p}{v_{DC}} - 1 \right) 100\%$$

Acceptable values for the PAR range from 45 for an unconditioned line to 95 for a C5-conditioned line.

6.9.2 The Eye Diagram

An *eye diagram,* or *eye pattern,* on an oscilloscope screen is often used to evaluate the digital performance of a line. A random sequence of 1 and 0 bits is transmitted over the line under test. The received signal bits are then superimposed on an oscilloscope, to create the eye pattern.

The oscilloscope is triggered horizontally using the bit clock, and the received signal is applied to the vertical input. Near perfect input pulses and zero distortion results in a nearly rectangular display pattern, since all transitions overlap and between transitions the signal is either HIGH or LOW. This is a fully "open" eye pattern, shown in Figure 6.9(a).

In practice, distortion introduced by the line will cause the eye pattern to "close," as shown in Figure 6.9(b). The horizontal variation of the 1/0 crossover points is sometimes referred to as *jitter.*

Thus the size of the open area in the eye's center is a measure of the quality of digital transmission on the line.

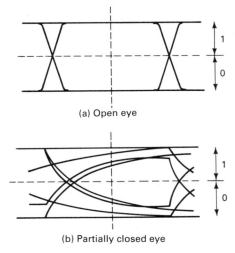

(a) Open eye

(b) Partially closed eye

Figure 6.9   Eye patterns

6.9.3 EIA-Interface Monitors

Many commercial "breakout" and/or monitor boxes are available for RS232/RS449 interfaces.

These devices may be conveniently connected in series with the interface cable at either the DTE or DCE end. They include access terminals for each signal line and/or colored LEDs for each line, which indicate HIGH, LOW, or FAULT voltage levels.

6.9.4 Bit-Pattern Generators

The bit-error performance of systems is often evaluated using a pattern generator and receiver. The generator and receiver are available in a single unit, which also compares the received data stream bit by bit with that transmitted and logs the resulting bit-error rate (the number of bit errors compared to the total number of bits sent). A common sequence length used for each test is approximately 65,000 bits.

Long-term, average bit-error rates of the order of 10^{-6} to 10^{-9} (from one error in 1 million bits to one error in 1 billion bits) are typical (excluding error-correcting protocols).

6.9.5 Loopback Testing

The components of a communication link are often tested using loopback methods. Test data is transmitted and *looped back* at various points so that the data may be received at the transmitting site, where it is compared with the data sent.

Most modems may be switched into a loopback mode using a switch on the modem or over the EIA interface from the DTE. Recall that RS449 has provision for this.

6.9.6 Protocol Testing

Protocol testing involves exercising the link DTEs by transmitting particular test-bit sequences and monitoring results. Various protocol testers are available commercially that emulate a variety of protocols. Such instruments have built-in facilities for diagnostic testing and display the data streams as characters on a CRT. The instrument is attached to the link as a special purpose DTE.

PROBLEMS

6.1. Explain what is meant by the statement, in synchronous systems, two levels of synchronization are required.

6.2. Is it true that in synchronous systems there is always a separate clock signal sent from the transmitter to the receiver? Explain.

6.3. Using ASCII codes and even parity, give the complete bit sequence for the BSC data block below. Write your answer in shorthand by using a two-digit hexadecimal number for each character.

SYN SYN SOH ACK 0 2 0 9 STX P A G E 0 7 CR ETX BCC

6.4. List the major differences between the 8251A USART (in synchronous mode) and the 6852 SSDA.

6.5. A subroutine labeled SYNTX, when called, is to initialize a 6852 SSDA and synchronously transmit a BSC data block. The characters that make up the data block are previously stored in a RAM buffer. The buffer starts at address ''SYNBUF'' = $0300. The first two characters stored in the buffer are SYN characters; the last two characters are always ETX or ETB, followed by the proper BBC.

   (a) Draw a flowchart for the SYNTX subroutine.

   (b) If you are familiar with 6800-family assembly language, write the program. Assume the SSDA $\overline{CS}$ pin goes LOW for addresses $8000 and $8001 only and that RS pin is driven from address line A_0.

6.6. A subroutine labeled TRANSMIT, when called, is to initialize an 8251A USART and synchronously transmit a BSC data block. The characters that make up the data block are previously stored in a RAM buffer. The buffer starts at address ''TXBUF'' = $F000. The first two characters stored in the buffer are SYN characters; the last two characters are always ETX or ETB, followed by the proper BCC.

   (a) Draw a flowchart for the TRANSMIT subroutine.

   (b) If you are familiar with 8080-family assembly language, write the program. Assume the hardware configuration is as shown in Figure 3.7.

6.7. List the advantages of SDLC protocol compared with BISYNC.

6.8. Explain bit stuffing as it relates to SDLC.

6.9. Why is bit stuffing not required when BISYNC protocol is used?

6.10. Draw the voltage waveform for the bit sequence 1 1 0 1 1 0 0 1 0 0:

   (a) Using NRZ coding

   (b) Using NRZI coding

6.11. What is the advantage of NRZI coding compared with NRZ?

7

Data Coding Methods

7.1 ALPHANUMERIC BINARY CODES

Sets of binary codes used to represent the letters of the alphabet and numerals are called *alphanumeric* codes. An *n*-bit binary code set can represent 2^n different characters or elements. The most popular codes used for data communication are Baudot, ASCII, and EBCDIC.

Baudot code. The Baudot code, shown in Table 7.1, is an early 5-bit code used with teletype or teleprinter terminals. Since there are only 32 different codes (2^5), several of the codes must represent either of two characters—a letter or a figure—one of which is selected by a preceding FIGS or LTRS shift character. For example, the following format is used to encode NO. 27:

LTRS	N	O	FIGS		SPC	2	7
11111	00110	00011	11011	00111	00100	11001	11100

When Baudot codes are sent using serial asynchronous transmission, the stop pulse is usually 1.5 bits in width instead of the 1- or 2-bit times used for ASCII transmission.

ASCII code. ASCII is the most popular alphanumeric code used for data communication. The ASCII table was given in Table 1.1, and the ASCII control characters were described as they relate to BISYNC protocol in Section 6.3. The table and control codes are summarized again in Table 7.2. ASCII is a 7-bit code, and it is customary to append an eighth bit in the most significant position, as an even- or odd-parity check bit, when using ASCII for data communication.

EBCDIC code. EBCDIC is an 8-bit alphanumeric code widely used by IBM computer communication systems. The EBCDIC chart and control codes are given in Table 7.3. Since each character code requires the full 8-bit field, a ninth bit is required if parity is used. Since much of the code table is uncommitted, it is possible to assign codes for special-purpose control functions or graphics in a particular application.

7.2 ERROR DETECTION

Adding bits to a data stream for the purpose of error detection is referred to as *redundancy error-check method*. The check bits are considered redundant because they are not part of the message being sent. The simplest redundancy method is the addition of a parity bit to

TABLE 7.1   THE BAUDOT CODE SET

	Character	
Code	Letter	Figure
11000	A	-
10011	B	?
01110	C	:
10010	D	$
10000	E	3
10110	F	!
01011	G	&
00101	H	#
01100	I	8
11010	J	'
11110	K	(
01001	L	)
00111	M	.
00110	N	,
00011	O	9
01101	P	0
11101	Q	1
01010	R	4
10100	S	BELL
00001	T	5
11100	U	7
01111	V	;
11001	W	2
10111	X	/
10101	Y	6
10001	Z	"
11111	LTRS	LTRS
11011	FIGS	FIGS
00100	SPC	SPC
00010	CR	CR
01000	LF	LF
00000	NULL	NULL

each character code, as was described in Chapter 3 under asynchronous serial protocol, and is sometimes referred to as a *vertical redundancy check* (VRC).

Longitudinal redundancy check (LRC) codes and cyclic redundancy check (CRC) codes provide for an error check over an entire block of data. The LRC or CRC code is sent with the data block as the *block-check character* (BCC), as described in Chapter 6 under synchronous serial protocol.

7.2.1 LRC Codes

A common method employed to form a BCC for a block of data is to use longitudinal (sometimes called horizontal) parity across the character code bits in addition to vertical parity, as illustrated.

Character	A	B	C	D	E	F	G	BCC
	1	0	1	0	1	0	1	0
	0	1	1	0	0	1	1	0
ASCII	0	0	0	1	1	1	1	0
codes	0	0	0	0	0	0	0	0
	0	0	0	0	0	0	0	0
	0	0	0	0	0	0	0	0
	1	1	1	1	1	1	1	1
VRC bits	0	0	1	0	1	1	0	1
								LRC bits

Note: Even parity is shown.

TABLE 7.2 7-BIT ASCII CODES

Hex Low	Hex High	0	1	2	3	4	5	6	7
0		NUL	DLE	SP	0	@	P		p
1		SOH	DC1	!	1	A	Q	a	q
2		STX	DC2	=	2	B	R	b	r
3		ETX	DC3	#	3	C	S	c	s
4		EOT	DC4	$	4	D	T	d	t
5		ENQ	NAK	%	5	E	U	e	u
6		ACK	SYN	&	6	F	V	f	v
7		BEL	ETB	'	7	G	W	g	w
8		BS	CAN	<	8	H	X	h	x
9		HT	EM	>	9	I	Y	i	y
A		LF	SS	*	:	J	Z	j	z
B		VT	ESC	+	;	K	[	k	{
C		FF	FS	,	<	L	\	l	|
D		CR	GS	−	=	M	]	m	}
E		SO	RS	.	>	N	$\wedge$	n	~ `
F		SI	US	/	?	O		o	DEL

Note: The code is the least significant 7 bits of the two-digit hex number.

NUL	Null	DLE	Data link escape
SOH	Start of heading	DC1	Device control 1
STX	Start of text	DC2	Device control 2
ETX	End of text	DC3	Device control 3
EOT	End of transmission	DC4	Device control 4
ENQ	Enquiry	NAK	Negative acknowledge
ACK	Acknowledge	SYN	Synchronous idle
BEL	Audible signal (bell)	ETB	End of transmission block
BS	Backspace	CAN	Cancel
HT	Horizontal tab	EM	End of medium
LF	Line feed	SUB	Substitute
VT	Vertical tab	ESC	Escape
FF	Form feed	FS	File separator
CR	Carriage return	GS	Group separator
SO	Shift out	RS	Record separator
SI	Shift in	US	Unit separator
DEL	Delete	SP	Space

TABLE 7.3 EBCDIC CODES

HEX LOW \ HEX HIGH	0	1	2	3	4	5	6	7	8	9	A	B	C	D	E	F
0	NUL	DLE	DS		SP	&	-									0
1	SOH	DC1	SOS				/		a	j			A	J		1
2	STX	DC2	FS	SYN					b	k	s		B	K	S	2
3	ETX	DC3							c	l	t		C	L	T	3
4	PF	RES	BYP	PN					d	m	u		D	M	U	4
5	HT	NL	LF	RS					e	n	v		E	N	V	5
6	LC	BS	ETB	UC					f	o	w		F	O	W	6
7	DEL	IL	ESC	EOT					g	p	x		G	P	X	7
8		CAN							h	q	y		H	Q	Y	8
9	RLF	EM							i	r	z		I	R	Z	9
A	SMM	CC	SM		¢	!	¦	:								
B	VT				.	$	,	#								
C	FF	IFS		DC4	<	*	%	@								
D	CR	IGS	ENQ	NAK	(	)	_	'								
E	SO	IRS	ACK		+	;	>	=								
F	SI	IUS	BEL	SUB	|	¬	?	"								

EBCDIC control codes not found in the ASCII table are as follows:

PF	Punch off	CC	Cursor control
LC	Lowercase	IFS	Interchange file separator
UC	Uppercase	IGS	Interchange group separator
RLF	Reverse line feed	IRS	Interchange record separator
SMM	Start of manual message	IUS	Interchange unit separator
RES	Restore	DS	Digit select
NL	New line	SOS	Start of significance
IL	Idle	BYP	Bypass
SM	Set mode	PN	Punch on
RS	Reader stop		

When the BCC is formed this way, it is sometimes called a *checksum*. (Recall that the parity bits can be generated using exclusive-OR operations.)

7.2.2 CRC Codes

The LRC, or checksum, method of generating a block check character is simple to implement but is far from foolproof in enabling the receiver to catch errors. For example, double-bit errors can occur in the same positions in two characters of a frame and still result in the correct BCC. A much more powerful technique of generating an error-check code makes use of a CRC.

The CRC method involves shifting the message bits left and dividing by a predetermined binary number using modulo-2 arithmetic. The division results in a binary remainder, which is the CRC code, sent as the BCC with the message. The receiver performs an identical division of the received message and compares the resulting remainder with the received BCC. If the two remainders agree, the message is assumed to be error-free. CRC codes used in this way are usually 12 to 32 bits long.

If CRC codes are used in conjunction with automatic repeat request (ARQ) protocols, they are very effective in reducing the bit-error rate of a link. For example, it may be shown that a 16-bit CRC allows for only one undetected bit error in every 10^{14} bits transmitted!

To understand the procedure in more detail, it is important to know modulo-2 arithmetic and the concept of representing a bit stream as an algebraic polynomial.

Modulo-2 arithmetic.   MOD-2 arithmetic is performed by exclusive-OR gates. It is binary addition without carries:

$$0 + 0 = 0$$
$$0 + 1 = 1$$
$$1 + 0 = 1$$
$$1 + 1 = 0$$

Also, since the only allowed results are 0 and 1, there are no negatives in MOD-2 arithmetic—subtraction becomes the same as addition. It makes no difference which way we traverse the MOD-2 number line:

```
      0   1   0   1   0   1   0   1   0   1   0   1   0   1   0   1
    _____
    ----------------------------------------------------------> MOD-2 addition
    MOD-2 subtraction < ------------------------------------------------------
```

Polynomial representation.   The bits of a binary code, or sequence, can be interpreted as coefficients of a polynomial. For example, the sequence 110101 becomes:

$$(1)x^5 + (1)x^4 + (0)x^3 + (1)x^2 + (0)x^1 + (1)x^0$$

or simply,

$$x^5 + x^4 + x^2 + 1$$

Notice that for an n-bit code, the order (highest power of x) of the polynomial is $n - 1$.

Computing the CRC code.

1. We begin by assuming we have a message sequence to be transmitted and its corresponding polynomial $M(x)$. If the message is 110101, $M(x) = x^5 + x^4 + x^2 + 1$. We must also decide what length of error-check code to use for our protocol. Let the length of the desired CRC code be c bits.

   We then choose a *generating* polynomial $G(x)$ having order c. For the example, use $c = 3$, and define $G(x) = x^3 + 1$.

2. Next, we multiply $M(x)$ by x^c (x^3 here):

   $$x^3M(x)/G(x) = x^8 + x^7 + x^5 + x^3$$

   This is analagous to shifting the message bits left c places (giving 110101000 here).

3. We now divide $x^cM(x)$ by $G(x)$ using MOD-2 arithmetic, which results in a quotient polynomial $Q(x)$ and a remainder $R(x)$:

   $$x^cM(x) = Q(x) + R(x)/G(x)$$

   For the example, this division is

   or $Q(x) = x^5 + x^4 + x + 1$, and $R(x) = x + 1$

4. Next, we add the remainder $R(x)$ to the shifted message polynomial to obtain the transmitted sequence polynomial $T(x)$. That is,

   $$T(x) = x^cM(x) + R(x)$$

   or, in this case,

   $$T(x) = x^8 + x^7 + x^5 + x^3 + x + 1$$

We convert $T(x)$ to its corresponding binary sequence to obtain the final bit pattern to be transmitted, as follows:

$$(1)x^8 + (1)x^7 + (0)x^6 + (1)x^5 + (0)x^4 + (1)x^3 + (0)x^2 + (1)x^1 + (1)x^0 \text{ ----->}$$
$$110101011$$

The 3 rightmost bits form the CRC error-check code, and the first 6 bits are the original message.

The receiver CRC test.   To test for transmission errors, the receiver divides the received data block (polynomial) by the same generating polynomial $G(x)$ ($x^3 + 1$ in the example), using modulo-2 arithmetic. If the resulting remainder from this division is zero, the message is assumed to be error-free. Any remainder other than zero indicates an error has occurred.

For our example, the $T(x)/G(x)$ division becomes

$$0 \ R \text{ (no error)}$$

The remainder is zero, indicating no error. Notice also that the quotient, $x^5 + x^4 + x + 1$, is the same as $Q(x)$ defined earlier.

CRC proof.   It can readily be shown that the division performed in the receiver, $T(x)/G(x)$, will always result in quotient $Q(x)$ with remainder zero, providing MOD-2 arithmetic is used: We had

$$T(x) = x^c M(x) + R(x)$$

and

$$\frac{x^c M(x)}{G(x)} = Q(x) + \frac{R(x)}{G(x)}$$

Combining these gives us:

$$\frac{T(x)}{G(x)} = \frac{x^c M(x)}{G(x)} + \frac{R(x)}{G(x)} = Q(x) + \frac{R(x)}{G(x)} + \frac{R(x)}{G(x)}$$

or

$$\frac{T(x)}{G(x)} = Q(x) + (1 + 1)\left(\frac{R(x)}{G(x)}\right)$$

But $(1 + 1)_{MOD-2} = 0$, giving

$$\frac{T(x)}{G(x)} = Q(x) \qquad \text{(no remainder)}.$$

Implementation of CRC codes.   The operations required to generate a CRC code for a message can, of course, be done using arithmetic software routines. However, in the interest of speed and reduced microprocessor overhead, CRC code generation and checking is usually done using hardware.

The MOD-2 arithmetic and shift operations can be accomplished using a shift register having exclusive-OR feedback connections. The number of shift-register stages needed equals c, the order of the generating polynomial $G(x)$, or the number of bits in the CRC code. Figure 7.1 shows such a circuit to generate the 3-bit CRC for our previous

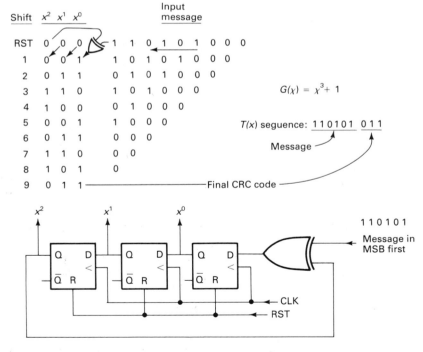

Figure 7.1 CRC generation for $G(x) = x^3 + 1$

example. The 6-bit message 110101 is shifted into the register, as shown, followed by three ("c") zeros. After nine shifts, the register contains the correct CRC bits (011 in this case).

Figure 7.2 shows a complete encoder circuit that generates the CRC and appends it to the message to form the final transmitted sequence.

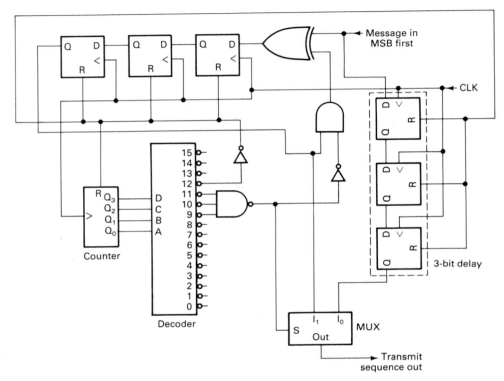

Figure 7.2   CRC encoder for $G(x) = x^3 + 1$

The preceding example used only a 3-bit CRC code and a 6-bit message. Much longer codes are needed to provide adequate error checking for correspondingly longer messages. Twelve-, 16- and 32-bit CRC codes are commonly used for the block-check or frame-check characters of practical data communication protocols. Sixteen-bit CRCs are most common, using generating polynomials $G(x) = x^{16} + x^{15} + x^2 + 1$ or $G(x) = x^{16} + x^{12} + x^5 + 1$. A 16-bit CRC circuit is shown in Figure 7.3.

The circuit for generating and checking the CRC sequence is usually included in the LSI communication controller chip. Motorola's MC6852 Advanced Data Link Controller and Intel's 8273 Programmable HDLC Protocol Controller perform 16-bit CRC functions automatically.

Frames of the Ethernet local area network (LAN) protocol contain up to 1500 bytes of information, followed by a 32-bit CRC frame check sequence. The generating polyno-

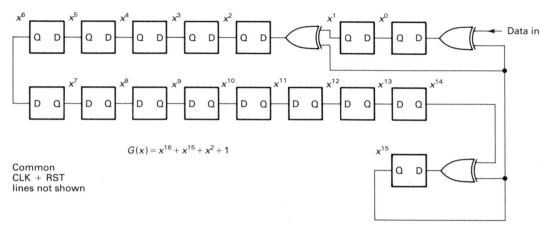

$$G(x) = x^{16} + x^{15} + x^2 + 1$$

Common
CLK + RST
lines not shown

Figure 7.3   16-bit CRC generation for $G(x) = x^{16} + x^{15} + x^2 + 1$

mial used is $G(x) = x^{32} + x^{26} + x^{23} + x^{22} + x^{16} + x^{12} + x^{11} + x^{10} + x^8 + x^7 + x^5 + x^4 + x^2 + x + 1$. The Intel 82586 LAN Coprocessor performs all Ethernet CRC functions on-chip!

7.3 ERROR CORRECTING CODES: HAMMING CODES

It is most efficient if we use only n bits per character to transmit data from a character set of 2^n characters, but this allows no possibility of error detection in the receiver. Any bit errors will result in another valid character code. If we add 1 redundant bit per character and use $n + 1$ bits, it becomes possible to detect single-bit errors in the receiver. This is analogous to using one parity check bit—sending 8 bits for each 7-bit ASCII code.

Richard Hamming of Bell Laboratories introduced the concept of *code distance*. The *Hamming distance* between two code words is equal to the number of bits that differ. For example, the distance between the ASCII code for B, 1000010, and the code for C, 1000011, is 1, since only 1 bit is different. If an even-parity check bit is added, the codes become 01000010 and 11000011, respectively. They now differ in 2 bit locations, and their Hamming distance is increased to 2.

By interspersing several check bits with the bits of each character code, it is possible to enable the receiver not only to detect but also to *correct* a limited number of bit errors per character. Hamming developed explicit procedures to do this; the resulting codes are known as *Hamming codes*. He published equations that allow calculation of the required number of check bits per character, their values, and their locations within the transmitted sequences.

To illustrate the application of Hamming error-correcting codes, suppose we want to encode the 16 hexadecimal numerals 0_{16}–F_{16}. By using 7-bit code words instead of the minimum 4 bits, we enable a receiver to detect double-bit errors and to correct single-bit errors. The seven bits of each code word consist of four message bits, $m_3m_2m_1m_0$, and three check bits, $c_2c_1c_0$. The bits of each code word are arranged as follows: $m_3m_2m_1c_2m_0c_1c_0$.

The three parity check bits are calculated by exclusive-ORing the message bits as follows:

$$c_0 = m_0 \oplus m_1 \oplus + m_3$$
$$c_1 = m_0 \oplus m_2 \oplus + m_3$$
$$c_2 = m_1 \oplus m_2 \oplus + m_3$$

For example, consider the code word for A_{16}:

$$m_3m_2m_1m_0 = 1010\ (A_{16})$$
$$c_0 = 0 \oplus 1 \oplus 1 = 0$$
$$c_1 = 0 \oplus 0 \oplus 1 = 1$$
$$c_2 = 1 \oplus 0 \oplus 1 = 0$$

Thus, the code word for A_{16} becomes 1010010 ($m_3m_2m_1c_2m_0c_1c_0$).

When the receiver receives a code word, it calculates three parity checks, as follows:

$$p_0 = c_0 \oplus m_0 \oplus m_1 \oplus m_3$$
$$p_1 = c_1 \oplus m_0 \oplus m_2 \oplus m_3$$
$$p_2 = c_2 \oplus m_1 \oplus m_2 \oplus m_3$$

If there is no error in the received code word, $p_0 = p_1 = p_2 = 0$. If an error has occurred, the binary number $p_2p_1p_0$ will "point" to the bit position of the error. Bit positions are numbered b_7–b_1.

To illustrate this error-correction power, assume the transmitted code for A_{16} (1010010) is received with an error in bit position 6—that is, the received code word is 1110010. The parity checks are calculated as follows:

$$p_0 = 0 \oplus 0 \oplus 1 \oplus 1 = 0$$
$$p_1 = 1 \oplus 0 \oplus 1 \oplus 1 = 1$$
$$p_2 = 0 \oplus 1 \oplus 1 \oplus 1 = 1$$

An error is indicated in bit position $p_2p_1p_0 = 110$: bit position 6.

Further information on Hamming codes may be found in his recent book, *Coding and Information Theory* (Englewood Cliffs, N.J.: Prentice-Hall, Inc., 1980).

7.4 DATA-COMPRESSION CODES

There are a variety of coding schemes that aim to reduce the total number of bits that must be transmitted to convey particular types of information. Four such examples are briefly described.

Run-length encoding.   Run-length encoding is used for data that are likely to contain long strings of repetitive bit patterns. Instead of the long repetitive strings, a control code is sent that tells the receiver to repeat the accompanying bit pattern a specified number of times, for example.

Differential Encoding.   With differential encoding only data changes are sent, instead of the data themselves. Again, this improves efficiency when many repetitive data are likely to occur.

(c) Huffman codes.   Huffman codes utilize the probability of occurrence of different characters and assign shorter codes to those characters that are transmitted most often. For example, instead of a 7-bit ASCII code for all letters of the alphabet, E may be assigned a 2-bit code and Z a 10-bit code, on the assumption that English-text data files contain many more E's than Z's. Huffman coding procedures provide a method of making such assignments so that the *average* number of bits per character may be reduced. Since the resulting character codes are of different lengths, they must be chosen such that no shorter code forms the first bits of one of the longer codes—so the receiver can recognize character boundaries. Such codes are referred to as *prefix* codes.

Figure 7.4 illustrates an example of Huffman encoding. A code table is developed in which the code words represent measured temperatures; 11 temperatures must be encoded, ranging from 20°C to 30°C, as shown. Without compression, a 4-bit binary code would be required. However, it is known that the probability of occurrence of the temperature values is quite varied; the probability distribution is shown in the figure. With Huffman encoding it is possible to assign code words of varying length such that the average transmitted code-word length will be less than 4.

Figure 7.4 shows a graphical method that is used to assign code words to the events (temperatures) such that the shortest codes are assigned to the events expected to occur most often (most probable), and the longest codes are assigned to the least probable events:

The events are listed in order of decreasing probability.

A 0-1 pair of bits is assigned to the two least probable events, as shown.

The two least probable events are then ''combined'' into one event, and their probabilities are added.

The new list of events is reordered, again to be in order of decreasing probability.

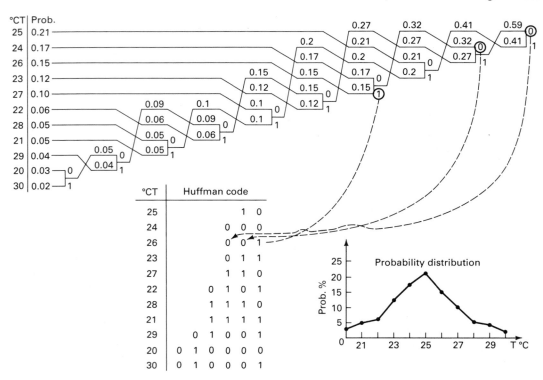

Figure 7.4 Huffman compression encoding example

The procedure is repeated, as shown, from left to right in Figure 7.4, until the last two events are combined.

The code word for each event is then written by traversing its line across the diagram.

Notice that if the codes are transmitted most significant bit (MSB) first, no code is the prefix of another.

For the example shown, the expected average code-word length may be calculated as follows:

Average code length $= (0.21 \times 2 + 0.17 \times 3 + 0.15 \times 3 + 0.12 \times 3 + 0.1 \times 3$
$+ 0.06 \times 4 + 0.05 \times 4 + 0.05 \times 4 + 0.04 \times 5$
$+ 0.03 \times 6 + 0.02 \times 6) = 3.18$ bits

This results in a reduction of data transmitted of approximately 20 percent (3.18-bit average word length compared with the uncompressed 4-bit code-word length).

It is interesting to develop a flowchart and program to implement Huffman encoding and decoding using software.

Graphics codes.   North American videotex systems use a table of *alphageo-metric* codes to transmit computer graphics, or video images. Each picture is conveyed as a list of its basic geometric shape components, with the location, color, and size of each (basic shapes include arc, circle, rectangle, and so forth). This is much more efficient than sending the coordinates and color of every point on the screen.

7.5 DATA ENCRYPTION

Pay-television signals are commonly *scrambled* to prevent their unauthorized use. Authorized (paid-up) users are issued a special *descrambler* unit by the pay-television company. This is an example of the *encryption* of an analog signal for commercial reasons.

Data signals are often used to carry confidential or secret information of individuals, governments, businesses, and the like. Data communication links used by the military and bank-to-bank transmissions involving monetary funds are prime examples where there is a need for data encryption.

In it simplest form, data encryption alters the transmitted data by rearranging the bit pattern according to a specified algorithm, or *key,* as it is called. Only authorized receivers know the secret key that enables them alone to decrypt the encrypted message.

Encryption or decryption often takes place at the link or network level, transparent to the users. Microprocessor-controlled data encryption units (DEUs) exist for this purpose. In 1977, the U.S. National Bureau of Standards published a data encryption standard (DES) algorithm as part of the Federal Information Processing Standards. It uses very complex bit-substitution and bit-transposition techniques. The algorithm provides for a 56-bit key word, which is periodically changed by the sender with the knowledge of the receiver.

Motorola's MC6859 Data Security Device (DSD), and Intel's 8294 Data Encryption Unit (DEU) are micro-bus-ready LSI chips designed to implement the DES algorithm automatically.

PROBLEMS

7.1.   Write the binary code for the string ''Prob. # 1'' using the following:
   (a)   Baudot code
   (b)   ASCII code
   (c)   EBCDIC code
   Which of the three codes is most efficient?

7.2.   Add an odd-parity bit to the codes of problem 7.1(b), and express them using two-digit hexadecimal numbers.

7.3.   Form a checksum byte for the character string of problem 7.2.

7.4.   **(a)**   Transmitting parity bits (VRC) with each ASCII code and a checksum (LRC) at the end of each block of characters enables the receiver not only to detect but also to correct an occurrence of one single-bit error per block. Explain.

(b)   Locate and correct the bit error in the following block; then decode the message. ASCII codes and even parity are used:

		MSB		LSB
First character			11101000	
			01101111	
			01110111	
			11100100	
Last character			11101001	
Received checksum			11101101	

7.5.   The EBCDIC code for the character A is to be transmitted, followed by a 2-bit CRC. The generating polynomial is $G(x) = x^2 + 1$.

(a)   Determine the correct transmitted bit sequence, with the CRC appended to the shifted message.

(b)   Confirm that the division $T(x)/G(x)$ results in 0 remainder.

7.6.   List and briefly describe the principle of three types of data-compression coding schemes.

7.7.   Develop a Huffman code for the set of four events A, B, C, D. The probability associated with each event is shown.
Calculate the average code-word length transmitted.

Event	Probability
A	0.5
B	0.26
C	0.14
D	0.1

7.8.   Continuing with the example of Hamming codes given in Section 7.3:

(a)   Write the transmitted code word for the hexadecimal numeric character C_{16}.

(b)   Introduce a bit error in bit position five and confirm that the receiver parity checks will locate the error.

7.9.   The following ASCII data block is encrypted using a simple key: The characters are numbered starting from 1 (first) to 6 (last), and the bits of each character code are numbered from 1 (LSB) to 7 (MSB). In each odd-numbered character, the even bits are complemented. In each even-numbered character, the odd bits are complemented.

$$1111001$$
$$0010000$$
$$1101001$$
$$0000111$$
$$1101111$$
$$0000001$$

Decipher (decrypt) the message.

8

Digital Techniques for Analog Signals

8.5 DELTA MODULATION AND DIFFERENTIAL PCM

8.5.1 Delta Modulation

Quantization Noise
Slope Overload
Bandwidth

8.5.2 Variable-Slope Delta Modulation

8.5.3 Differential PCM
Problems

Digital transmission of an analog signal requires sampling the signal and then encoding each sample voltage using a binary code. The binary code is sent over the communication link to the receiver in the form of a digital signal, as is done in data communication. The block diagram of a digital communication system was shown in Figure 1.10.

8.1 PAM (PULSE-AMPLITUDE MODULATION)

Except for the encoding and decoding by the transmitter and receiver, the operation of a digital communication system relies on the ability of the receiver to reconstruct the signal waveform from a series of sample pulses. This process of sending and receiving only periodic samples of a signal is known as pulse-amplitude modulation (PAM).

Figure 8.1 illustrates the main components of a PAM communication system. Such a system is analog, not digital, since the samples can take on any voltage amplitude; that is, their amplitude is not restricted to discrete values, as is the case for a digital signal. The samples are pulses. The amplitude of each represents the instantaneous voltage of the analog input signal, v_a. The pulses are transmitted at a continuous rate, determined by the sampling clock frequency, f_s.

Sampling theorem.   Provided that the transmitter samples the input signal often enough, the waveform can be reconstructed accurately in the receiver with a low-pass filter (LPF), as shown in Figure 8.1. It has been demonstrated mathematically that this reconstruction process is possible only if the sampling rate, f_s, is at least twice the highest input signal frequency, f_a. This fact is known as the *sampling theorem,* and can be stated as

$$f_s \geq 2f_a$$

where f_a is the upper boundary of the input signal spectrum or bandwidth, as shown, and f_s is the fundamental frequency or repetition rate of the sampling clock. This critical sampling rate is sometimes referred to as the *Nyquist rate,* after Nyquist, who conducted much original research in this field. The *sampling interval* or *sampling period* is $T_s = 1/f_s$.

PAM spectrum.   To understand the frequency spectrum of the PAM transmitted signal, it is helpful to consider the sampling clock as a carrier that is amplitude modulated

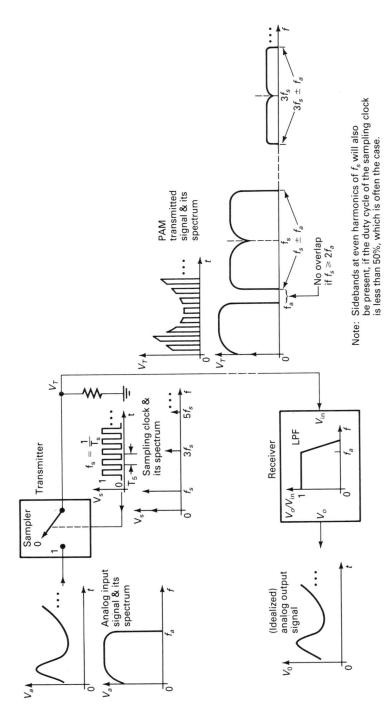

Figure 8.1 Pulse amplitude modulation

Note: Sidebands at even harmonics of f_s will also be present, if the duty cycle of the sampling clock is less than 50%, which is often the case.

by the input signal, producing upper and lower sidebands centered around the frequency components of the sampling clock. In Figure 8.1 the sampling clock is a square wave (50 percent duty cycle), which will contain fundamental and odd-harmonic components, as shown. Thus the spectrum of the PAM signal extends much higher in frequency than that of the input signal, which extends only to f_a.

The receiver low-pass filter allows only the baseband component (frequencies between 0 Hz and f_a) to pass, recovering the original signal. Notice that if f_s is less than twice f_a, portions of the PAM signal spectrum will overlap. This overlapping of the sidebands produces beat frequencies that interfere with the desired signal. This interference is referred to as *aliasing*. It results when the transmitter undersamples the input signal, and it makes accurate recovery of the signal by the receiver impossible.

8.2 PCM (PULSE-CODED MODULATION)

Figure 8.2 shows the block diagram of a PCM communication system. PCM transmission can be viewed as sending binary-encoded PAM samples digitally. Since an n-bit binary code can encode only 2^n different levels, the sample amplitudes must be rounded or *quantized* to the closest codable amplitude prior to encoding.

Usually transmission is serial, which means the sample codes must be shifted out serially, one bit at a time. Thus parallel-to-serial conversion is required in the transmitter and serial-to-parallel conversion is needed in the receiver, as shown in Figure 8.2. The serial bit stream is often sent synchronously. Figure 8.3 shows an example of transmitter and receiver waveforms; it assumes 5-bit PCM and that the analog input, v_a, varies over the range 0 to 7.75 V. The LSB represents 0.25 V in this case.

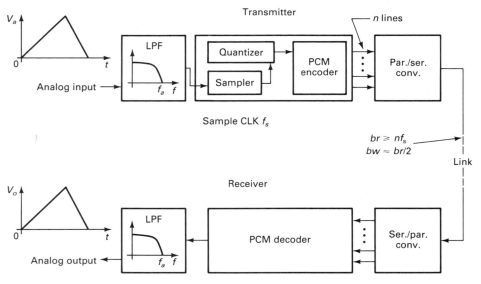

Figure 8.2   PCM communication system

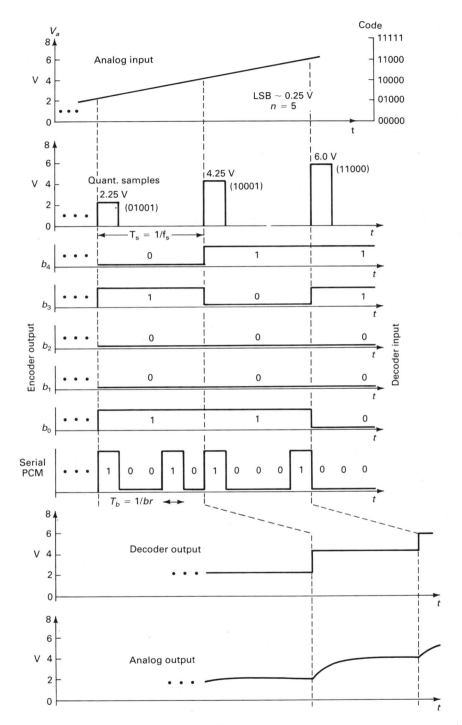

Figure 8.3 PCM waveforms ($n = 5$)

EXAMPLE

Write the PCM code for $v_a = 5$ V for the preceding PCM system.

Five-bit PCM allows for encoding $2^5 = 32$ sample voltages. There are 31 steps in the code range of 00000 to 11111, corresponding to a voltage range of 0 V to 7.75 V.

Thus each step equals $7.75/31 = 0.25$ V. The PCM code for 5 V may be calculated as

$$\frac{5}{0.25} = 20_{10} \quad \text{or} \quad 14_{16} \quad \text{or} \quad 1\ 0100_2$$

PCM bandwidth.   The major difficulty in converting analog communication systems to use PCM is the link bandwidth needed to carry the digital signal. Because a sequence of n bits must be sent during each sample interval, the bit rate on the link is quite high. (See the waveform Serial PCM in Figure 8.3, for example.)

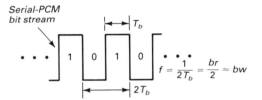

Figure 8.4   Serial-PCM bandwidth

The output br for the transmitter must be at least nf_s (f_s is the sample rate, as before) for n-bit serial PCM. Recall also that the sampling theorem requires $f_s \geqslant 2f_a$, where f_a is the highest frequency of the analog input signal. The length of one output bit time, T_b, is the inverse of br.

$$\text{br} \geqslant nf_s \geqslant 2nf_a \qquad \text{(br is in bits/second)}$$
$$T_b = 1/\text{br} \qquad (T_b \text{ in seconds})$$

EXAMPLE

What minimum sample clock frequency f_s and link bandwidth (BW) are required to transmit a 12-kHz tone, using 9-bit PCM (serial)?

To satisfy the sampling theorem, we have:

$$f_s = 2(12) \text{ kHz} = 24 \text{ kHz, minimum}$$

Each sample requires sending 9 bits serially. Consequently, the output PCM bit rate is 9×24 k $= 216$ bits/s, and the link bandwidth must be at least (216 K)/2 $= 108$ kHz.

The serial PCM signal requires maximum bandwidth when it is a 1-0-1-0-1-0-. . . square wave, in which case we get 2 bits per cycle, as shown in Figure 8.4. The (fundamental) frequency of the square wave is seen to be one-half the bit rate. Then br/2 hertz is an approximation for the minimum link bandwidth.

As an example of the preceding relationships, 8-bit PCM telephone systems usually restrict f_a to 4 kHz (voice) and use f_s = 8 kHz, giving a link bit rate of br = 64 bits/s. The approximate minimum bandwidth, BW, for such a system is 32 kHz.

Quantization error.   No matter how large we choose n, we can assign unique codes to only 2^n sample amplitudes. Thus, we must always quantize sample values prior to encoding. That is, we transmit the closest encodable voltage of the 2^n available, not the actual sample voltage. This introduces an error, called *quantization error* or quantization *noise*. We can make this error acceptably small in any PCM application by choosing n sufficiently large. Of course, choosing n unnecessarily large is undesirable, since it increases cost and transmission time and/or signal bandwidth.

Figure 8.5(a) shows the correlation between sample voltage, v_a, and the n-bit binary code value. v_a is assumed to fall within the range $+V_m$ to $-V_m$ volts. Figure 8.5(b) shows an example for n = 8 and V_m = 5.1 V. (Codes are shown in hexadecimal.) The voltage increment between successive codes, e, equals $2V_m/(2^n - 1)$; it corresponds to the voltage weight of the LSB. For the example in Figure 8.5(b), e = 10.2/255 = 0.04 V.

For any one sample, the maximum quantization error is $\pm e/2$. When we view this error as a fraction or percentage of v_a, we see that it is most significant when the magni-

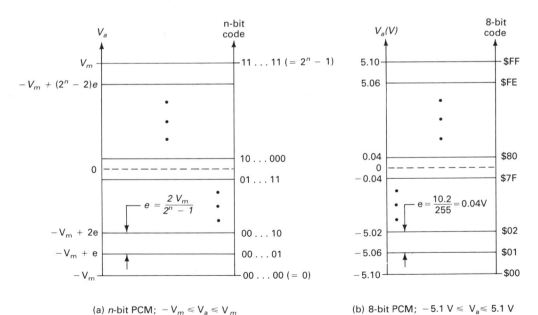

(a) n-bit PCM; $-V_m \leqslant V_a \leqslant V_m$ (b) 8-bit PCM; -5.1 V $\leqslant V_a \leqslant 5.1$ V

Figure 8.5 n-bit PCM coding of the analog signal, v_a

tude of v_a is small. This effect is illustrated in Figure 8.6. This fraction, q, can be expressed as

$$q = \frac{e}{(2\,|v_a|)}$$

and substitution for e gives

$$q = \frac{V_m}{(2^n - 1)\,|v_a|)}$$

Expressed as a percentage, $\%q$ becomes

$$\%q = \frac{100V_m}{(2^n - 1)\,|v_a|)}$$

The preceding equation can be rearranged to solve for n, giving

$$n = \frac{\log[(100/\%q)(V_m/|v_a|) + 1]}{\log 2}$$

$$n = 3.32\,\log\left[\left(\frac{100}{\%q}\right)\left(\frac{V_m}{|v_a|}\right) + 1\right]$$

In this form, the equation can be used to calculate the minimum n necessary to achieve a $\%q$ for a particular V_m/v_a ratio. For example, we might ask, What n is necessary for the percent quantization error not to exceed 10 percent when v_a is only 5 percent of its maximum?

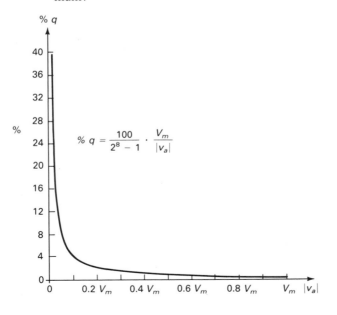

Figure 8.6   Percent quantization error

$$n \geq 3.32 \ \log \left[\left(\frac{100}{10} \right) \left(\frac{1}{.05} \right) + 1 \right] = 7.65$$

At least an 8-bit code is required to meet this objective.

Companding. The preceding description of PCM encoding relates to *linear PCM;* that is, the voltage increment between codes, *e,* is constant, and the relationship between the code values and the corresponding voltages is a straight line. This relationship is shown in Figure 8.7(a). As detailed in the previous section, linear PCM has the disadvantage that the quantization error is much more significant when the magnitude of v_a is small compared with v_a near its maximum. *Nonlinear PCM* overcomes this disadvantage by making *e,* the voltage increment, proportional to the amplitude of v_a. This system of encoding results in a logarithmic or exponential curve, as shown in Figure 8.7(b), and is referred to as *log PCM*. The quantization error for log PCM is constant for all values of v_a. This process of compressing the upper portion of the code-versus-v_a curve to provide more accuracy near the bottom is known as *companding.*

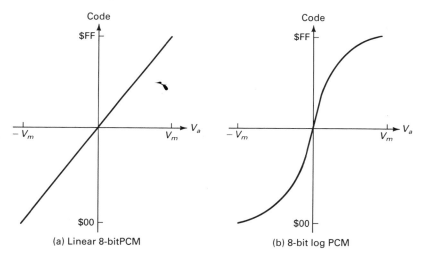

(a) Linear 8-bitPCM   (b) 8-bit log PCM

Figure 8.7 Linear and nonlinear PCM

The telephone industry in North America has adopted a specific code-voltage relationship, known as *μ-law* 255, which can be expressed mathematically as

$$y = \frac{V_m \ \log \ (1 \ + \ \mu \ v_a/V_m)}{\log \ (1 \ + \ \mu)}$$

where $\mu = 2^n - 1$ (255 for $n = 8$ bits), and v_a is confined to the range $\pm V_m$.

In practice, a piecewise-linear approximation to this equation is used, as shown in Figure 8.8. Note also the reversing of the codes used for positive v_a values and that two

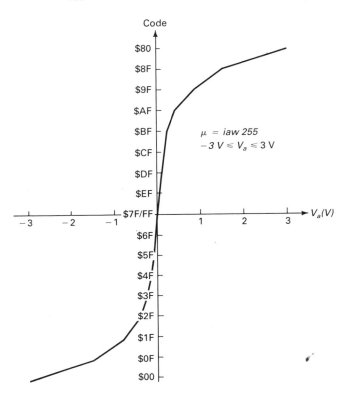

Figure 8.8 Mu-law 255 PCM

codes ($7F and $FF) are used for 0 V. A slightly different relationship, known as *A-law PCM* (the CCITT standard), is used in Europe.

8.3 PCM IN THE TELEPHONE NETWORK

Digital transmission is not used on the local loops, but PCM is used over interoffice four-wire links, where the encoded samples of 24 voice-frequency (VF) channels are multiplexed using TDM onto serial receive-and-transmit digital buses. The A/D conversion and multiplexing of the 24 channels is done in *channel-bank* circuits in the exchange office.

The common arrangement of channel-bank functions is shown in Figure 8.9(a), where the multiplexing and demultiplexing uses analog switches, with the A/D and D/A sections being shared by the 24 channels. More recently, the availability of coder-decoder (CODEC) ICs has made it practical for each channel to have its own conversion stages and for the multiplexing-demultiplexing to be done digitally, as shown in Figure 8.9(b). The channel bank includes low-pass filters, which limit the frequency spectrum of each analog input signal to 4 kHz maximum, and the sample rate used (f_s) is 8 kHz. Eight bits per sample is nominal for the encoders, although some of the 8 bits are diverted to signaling or timing periodically.

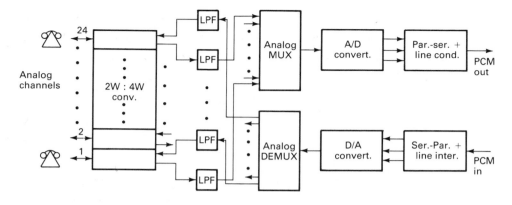

(a) Channel bank using shared A/D and D/A Conversion

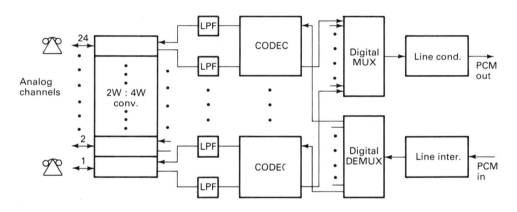

(b) Channel bank using CODEC ICs

Figure 8.9 PCM channel banks

TDM frame format for PCM.   Figure 8.10 shows the allocation of time slots within each 24-channel frame. Each frame contains 24 × 8 = 192 bits plus 1 additional bit (the s-bit) for synchronization, or 193 bits in total, per frame. As shown, a sequence of 12 such frames makes up a multiframe. Two lower-speed signaling channels are created by "stealing" bit 8 from each sample word in frames 6 and 12 in each multiframe. The 8-bits from the 6-frames form signaling channel A, and the 8-bits from the 12-frames make up signaling channel B for each voice channel. The signaling information includes ON HOOK/OFF HOOK status, dialing, and so forth. The data rate for each signaling channel is seen to be 1 bit/multiframe (1.5 ms) or 666 bits/s.

The s-bit is set or cleared for each frame to form a repetitive multiframe pattern, as shown in Figure 8.10. This pattern enables the receiver section of the channel bank to

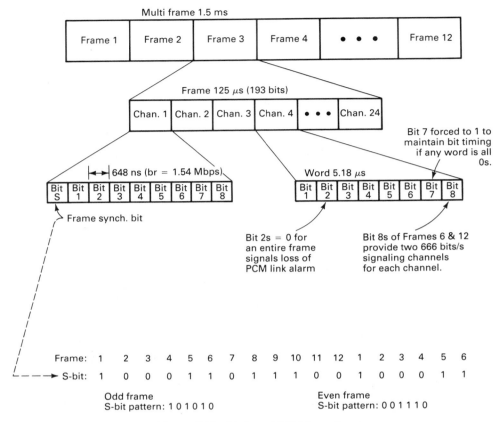

Figure 8.10 24-channel TDM frame format

frame the data and, in particular, to identify frames 6 and 12, which contain the signaling information.

In addition, the receiver monitors bit 2 of every channel. If a complete 24-channel frame is found in which all 2-bits are zero, it is assumed that the PCM link has failed, and an alarm condition is set. With the format of Figure 8.10, the bit rate on the PCM bus is 1.54 Mbits/s, and the required minimum bandwidth is 770 KHz.

Bit synch and pulse format. Bit synchronization of the receiver, as opposed to frame synchronization, is accomplished by PLL circuits, which lock to pulse transitions in the bit stream. Normally, we are accustomed to a nonreturn-to-zero (NRZ) logic signal format, as shown in Figure 8.11(a). Use of return-to-zero (RZ) format makes bit synchronization easier, since it ensures that a voltage transition occurs for every 1 state, as shown in Figure 8.11(b). To prevent the occurrence of long strings of 0s having no transitions, the transmitter sets bit 7 to 1 if all other bits of a channel word are 0s. Next to bit 8, a change in bit 7 causes minimal error in the data—recall that bit 8 doubles as a signaling bit.

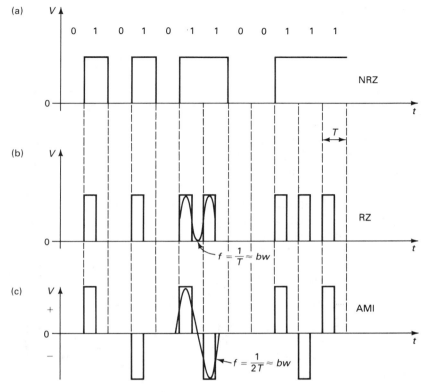

Figure 8.11 PCM line codes

NRZ and RZ pulse formats are both unipolar and therefore have a nonzero DC or average level, which is constantly varying depending upon the ratio of 1s to 0s transmitted. Coupling this varying DC component through network transformers and capacitors can distort the signal waveform and lead to errors. To eliminate this problem, the alternate mark inversion (AMI) format can be used, shown in Figure 8.11(c), where the pulse polarity of each successive 1 state is reversed. This essentially creates an AC signal having zero DC component. AMI format has the additional advantage of lower bandwidth (approximately half) compared with unipolar RZ. Also, it has some inherent error-checking capability for the receiver; detection of two successive pulses of the same polarity indicates an error due to noise, which is known as a *bipolar violation* error.

8.4 IC CODECS AND PCM FILTERS

Several IC manufacturers offer LSI codecs (PCM coder-decoders), PCM filters, and even *combos* or single-chip codec-filters. As an example, National Semiconductor's TP3020 codec and TP3040 filter can be combined to implement a complete PCM voice interface.

8.4.1 TP3020 Codec

A simplified block diagram of the TP3020 codec is shown in Figure 8.12. It is a CMOS LSI circuit, and it includes the following basic functions:

A/D and D/A conversion (PCM encoding or decoding), using μ-law companding.

Parallel/serial and serial/parallel conversion for the serial PCM data input and output.

Programmable receive-and-transmit time-slot assignment. Possible time slots number from 1 to 64 per frame.

Two-way signaling, using the LSBs of the PCM words during signaling frames.

Time-slot assignment. Assigning the receive-and-transmit time slots and selecting standby mode for the codec is done by loading the control register serially with the proper bit pattern, according to the chart given in Figure 8.12. The serial data applied to pin D_C is clocked into the register by the falling edge of the shift-clock signal on pin CLK_C. The frequency of CLK_C should be at least eight times the frame rate. The frame rate is usually 8 kHz. Referring to the chart in Figure 8.12, we see that B_1 is shifted in first and B_8 last. When a control word is not being loaded, CLK_C should normally be held LOW.

In the standby or power-down mode, IC dissipation is reduced from approximately 45 mW to 1 mW. Assigning a time slot automatically powers up the codec from the standby mode. Pin PDN is HIGH during power-down. It can be used to power-down other circuits (such as the PCM filter).

PCM receiver. PCM data bits are shifted in during the assigned time slot from pin D_R, timed by the falling edge of the clock signal on pin CLK_R. The receive clock should be 1.544 MHz for the format discussed in Section 8.3. Analog voice output from the decoder is from pin VF_R. The output voltage swing is typically $\pm$ 2 V peak. Data is shifted in MSB first.

Frame synchronization of the decoder is accomplished by the frame sync pulse applied to pin FS_R. The frame sync pulse is normally 1 bit-time wide; extending the frame sync pulse width to 2 or more bit-times "tells" the codec that the current frame is a signaling frame, in which case the least significant PCM bit is output to pin SIG_R instead of being applied to the decoder.

PCM transmitter. Analog voice-frequency input to the encoder is on pin VF_X. This signal is sampled once per frame at the end of the transmit time slot, and the resulting PCM word is shifted serially out pin D_X during the transmit time slot of the next frame. PCM words are shifted out MSB first, timed by the rising edge of the clock signal applied to pin CLK_X. The frequency of CLK_X is typically 1.544 MHz. The analog input swing should be approximately $\pm$ 2 V peak.

Frame synchronization of the encoder is accomplished by an 8-kHz frame sync pulse, applied to pin FS_X. The frame sync pulse is normally HIGH for one bit-time per

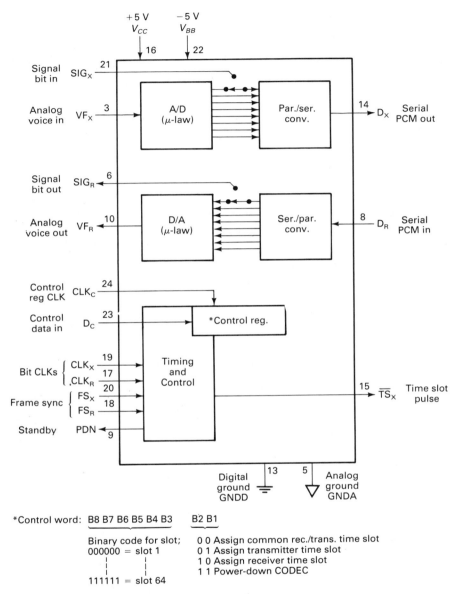

Figure 8.12 National's TP3020 CODEC

cycle; extending its width to 2 or more bit-times indicates a signaling frame, in which case the signal on pin SIG_X is substituted for the LSB of the PCM word shifted out pin D_X.

The output pin, D_X, is a three-state output, enabled only during the encoder time slot of each frame. This allows the sharing of a common digital bus among several codecs. Also, a time-slot pulse is available from pin TS_X, which is LOW during the encoder time slot and can be used to drive the ENABLE inputs of external three-state buffers if they are required.

Figure 8.13 illustrates the timing relationships among the CLK, FS, D, and TS_X signals. Figure 8.13 assumes that common bit clocks (CLK_X, CK_R) and frame sync pulses (FS_X, FS_R) are used for both the transmitter and receiver timing.

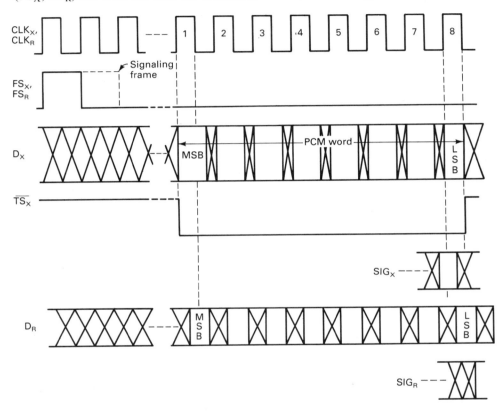

Figure 8.13   TP3020-CODEC timing waveforms

8.4.2 TP3040 PCM Filter

The PCM transmitter A/D operation must be preceded by a low-pass filter to limit the maximum input frequency to less than one-half the sampling rate. The sampling rate or frame rate used for PCM is normally 8 kHz. Also, a low-pass filter is required after the receiver D/A operation to smooth the stair-step output signal from the codec. The National Semiconductor TP3040 is a CMOS LSI device that includes both the transmit and the receive low-pass (switched-capacitor) filters. A simplified block diagram for the TP3040 is shown in Figure 8.14.

The transmit filter section actually provides a bandpass response: flat from 200 Hz

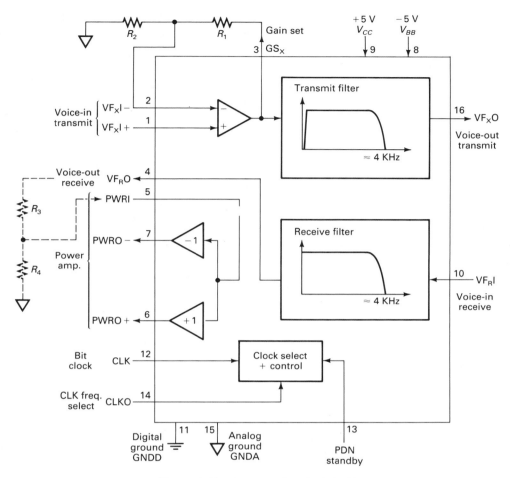

Figure 8.14   National's TP3040 PCM filter

to approximately 3 kHz, with greater than 30 dB attenuation above 4 kHz. The audio input is applied between the inverting and noninverting voice-frequency pins, $VF_X +$ and $VF_X -$. Transmit gain can be adjusted by selection of resistors R_1 and R_2. The output of the transmit filter is from pin VF_XO.

The receive filter provides a low-pass response: flat to approximately 3 kHz and 30 dB down at 4.5 kHz. Its input is applied (from the codec decoder) to pin VF_RI.

The receiver section of the TP3040 includes an output power amplifier, which is used when it is necessary to drive a 600-Ω load. The power amp is coupled to the receive filter output via R_3 and R_4, as shown in Figure 8.14. The amplifier can supply approximately 8 dB$_m$ of signal power to a 600-Ω load.

A power-down or standby mode is provided; it is selected by making input PDN HIGH (can be driven from codec PDN output).

The clock input for the TP3040 is applied to pin CLK. The clock frequency may be 1.536 MHz, 1.544 MHz, or 2.048 MHz and is selected by connecting pin CLKO to V_{BB}, GND, or V_{CC}, respectively. 1.544 MHz is the bit rate for the frame format discussed in Section 8.3.

The audio input and output levels for the filters (excluding the power amp) are nominally 1.54 V rms.

Figure 8.15 shows a typical application circuit using the TP3020 codec and TP3040 filter ICs.

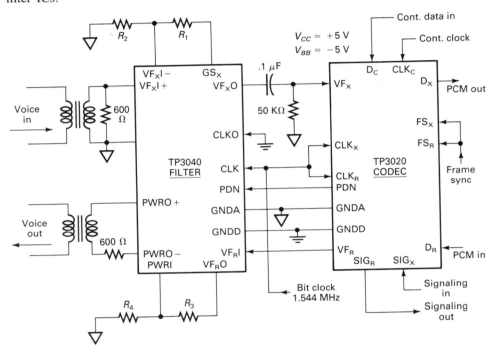

Figure 8.15   TP3020/3040 PCM voice channel (Adapted; courtesy National Semiconductor Corp.)

8.5 DELTA MODULATION AND DIFFERENTIAL PCM

In communication it is sometimes more efficient to transmit only signal changes instead of the absolute value of the signal. This is the basis of all delta or differential modulation systems. A delta modulation receiver constructs an approximation of the signal by summing (integrating) the received changes. Such an approach is most efficient when sending signals that infrequently undergo large changes in level. The author has had some success applying differential modulation to video communication. Video signals usually contain much repetitive information—picture backgrounds, for example. When delta modulation is applied to speech, the transmitted bit rate may be reduced by 50 percent, compared with standard PCM. There are fewer requirements for synchronizing the receiver with the transmitter for delta modulation than for PCM, but multiplexing sources may be more difficult.

8.5.1 Delta Modulation

A differential encoder could be implemented by simply comparing each new signal sample with the previous sample amplitude and transmitting the resulting difference signal to the receiver. The receiver decoder could then continuously add up all the previous difference signals to construct the absolute signal. Although this plan may appear workable at first, it suffers from a deadly flaw. Any system error or inaccuracy could be cumulative, and the receiver output signal would soon diverge from the transmitter input signal. The problem with such a system is that it is *open-loop:* The difference signal represents *change in the input signal* but not the actual *required change in the receiver output signal.* These two changes will not be the same unless the receiver output signal matches the transmitter input signal exactly.

To close the loop, the transmitter must be able to predict the actual receiver output signal at all times; then a true difference signal may be developed that indicates the actual change necessary in the receiver to match each new sample value. Figure 8.16 illustrates such a delta modulation system. The transmitter encoder includes an integrator identical with that of the receiver, and a comparator produces the difference signal, $e(t)$. The signal $e(t)$ has only two possible levels: A positive level indicates that the new signal value $s(t)$ is greater than the previous receiver output value $s'(t)$, and a negative $e(t)$ indicates that $s(t)$ is less than $s'(t)$. The D latch provides a one-sample-time delay, so that the input signal ($s(t)$) is always compared with the *previous* integrator output value ($s'(t)$). The output of each integrator increases at a constant rate when $e(t)$ is positive and decreases at a constant rate when $e(t)$ is negative.

Quantization noise.   In the waveforms of Figure 8.16, when the input signal $s(t)$ is not changing, the receiver output $s'(t)$ "hunts" above and below the correct level, and the difference signal $e(t)$ alternates between positive and negative. This incorrect variation in the receiver output is referred to as *quantization noise.* The severity of this quantization noise component in the output signal may be reduced by using a smaller step size (h) and/or a higher sampling frequency (f_s); however, this can lead to another problem, described shortly.

Slope overload.   If the transmitter input signal changes too rapidly, the receiver output is unable to keep up, and the output undergoes distortion due to *slope overload.* This effect is labeled on the waveforms of Figure 8.16. The maximum slope of the integrator output is h (step size) divided by one sample time, T_s. The highest frequency component of the input signal must be limited, such that its maximum slope does not exceed this value, to avoid slope overload.

If the input signal $s(t)$ is considered as a sine wave having amplitude V_m and frequency f_{in}, $s(t)$ may be written as

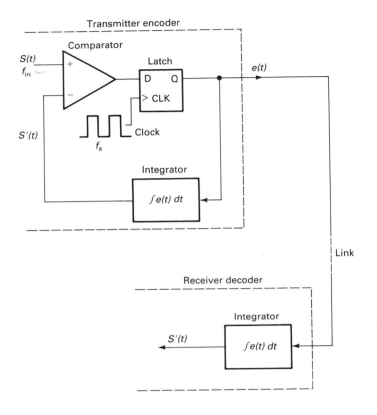

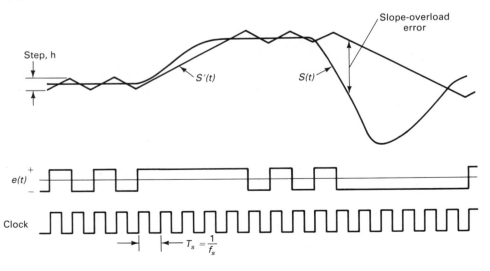

Figure 8.16 Delta modulation

$$s(t) = V_m sin(2\pi f_{in} t)$$

The slope of $s(t)$ is its derivative $ds(t)/dt$:

$$\frac{ds(t)}{dt} = 2\pi V_m f_{in} cos(2\pi f_{in} t)$$

This slope has a maximum when $t = 0$:

$$\left[\frac{ds(t)}{dt} \right]_{max} = 2\pi V_m f_{in}$$

The slope of the receiver integrator output is $h/T_s = hf_s$. Thus to avoid slope overload, we must have

$$2\pi V_m f_{in} \leq hf_s$$

or

$$f_{in} \leq \frac{(f_s h)}{(2\pi V_m)}$$

Bandwidth.   Notice from Figure 8.16 that the maximum fundamental frequency of the signal on the transmission link, $e(t)$, is $f_s/2$; then the approximate minimum link bandwidth required is

$$BW \approx \frac{f_s}{2} \geq \left(\frac{\pi V_m}{h} \right) f_{in}$$

This expression for the minimum bandwidth required to avoid slope overload may appear innocent, but it is not. Even if we can accept an h of, say, 5 percent of V_m, the bandwidth becomes nearly 63 times f_{in}! To illustrate this difficulty further, consider an example where delta modulation is compared with PCM.

EXAMPLE

A previous example dealt with transmitting a 12-kHz sine wave using 9-bit serial PCM. The required minimum sampling rate and bandwidth were calculated to be 216,000 samples/s and 108 kHz, respectively. Nine-bit PCM provides a voltage step size between adjacent codes of $2V_m/511$, where $\pm V_m$ is the peak-to-peak voltage range possible.

Using $2V_m/h = 511$, calculate the sampling rate, f_s, and minimum bandwidth necessary to avoid slope overload, using delta modulation to transmit the 12-kHz tone.

The bandwidth may be calculated as follows:

$$BW = \pi \left(\frac{V_m}{h} \right) f_{in} = \pi \times \frac{511}{2} \times 12 \text{ kHz} = 9.65 \text{ MHz}$$

f_s is twice BW, or 38.6 MHz.

In general, delta modulation is used only when significant quantization noise and/or the occasional occurrence of slope overload can be tolerated. Variable-slope delta modulation seeks to overcome this difficulty.

8.5.2 Variable-Slope Delta Modulation

In PCM systems, companding is used to decrease quantization noise without reducing the dynamic range of the input signals for a fixed number of bits per sample. A similar technique is employed in delta modulation systems, called variable-slope delta modulation (VSDM). In VSDM, the slope of the integrator output is increased or decreased, depending on the rate of change of the input signal. This is done to "help the integrator keep up" and to reduce the tendency for slope overload of the receiver without increasing quantization noise. Varying the slope of the integrator output may be thought of as varying the step size. The step size is made larger when the signal is changing most rapidly and is reduced when the signal is changing less.

Manufacturers have developed ICs that implement continuously variable slope delta (CVSD) modulation and demodulation economically. Figure 8.17 shows block diagrams for a CVSD modulator and demodulator. The algorithm combines the history of the previous two difference signal samples with the current one to modulate the integrator input signal amplitude. The two previous difference signal values $e(t)$ are temporarily stored in a shift register. A coincidence-detector circuit monitors these two previous values and the current value of $e(t)$ and produces a gain-control signal. The gain-control signal increases the integrator input signal whenever it detects three 1s or three 0s. Three 1s at the input to the coincidence detector indicates a steep increase in the magnitude of the analog signal. Three 0s indicates a steep decrease.

Illustrative waveforms for the input analog signal, the difference signal $e(t)$, and for the integrator output signal are shown in Figure 8.18. For the case shown, the analog input is an audio signal, and the waveforms are taken from the specification for Motorola's MC3417 CVSD Modulator/Demodulator IC. Figure 8.19 shows a complete modulator/demodulator circuit using the MC3417 for voice.

8.5.3 Differential PCM

Differential pulse code modulation (DPCM) combines the methods of delta modulation and pulse code modulation. A binary code is transmitted that represents the magnitude of the difference signal $e(t)$; thus, the encoded difference signal may have 2^m levels, assuming an m-bit code is transmitted for each sample of the difference signal. If one assumes that *only small changes occur between any two successive samples* of the input analog signal, then fewer bits are necessary to encode signal changes than to encode the absolute value of the signal itself.

Figure 8.20 illustrates a digital DPCM system. The encoder, shown in Figure 8.20(a), converts an 8-bit PCM signal into 4-bit DPCM. Integration is performed digitally using an adder, and the difference signal is generated using a subtracter. The decoder

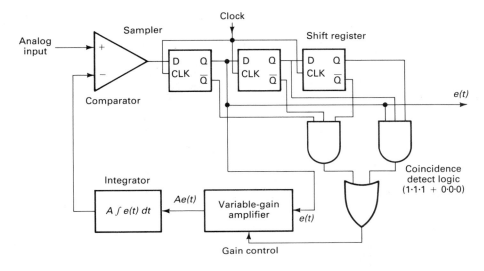

(a) CVSD modulator

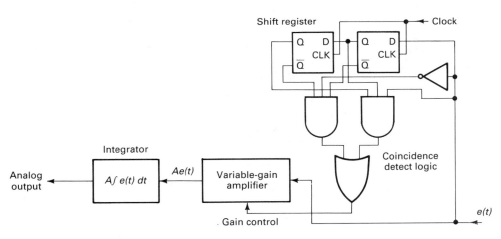

(b) CVSD demodulator

Figure 8.17 Variable slope delta modulation

integrates the received difference signal codes using an adder and thus reconstructs 8-bit PCM.

Although the system shown reduces the transmitted bit rate by 50 percent (4 bits/sample versus 8), slope overload can be a serious problem. In Figure 8.20, the range of PCM codes is ± 127. The range of the DPCM difference signal is ± 7; thus, slope over-

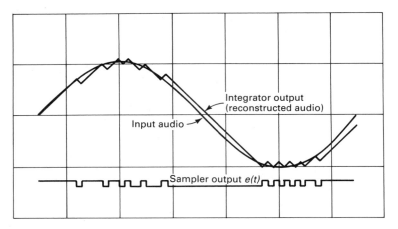

Figure 8.18 CVSD system waveforms (Reprinted courtesy Motorola, Inc.)

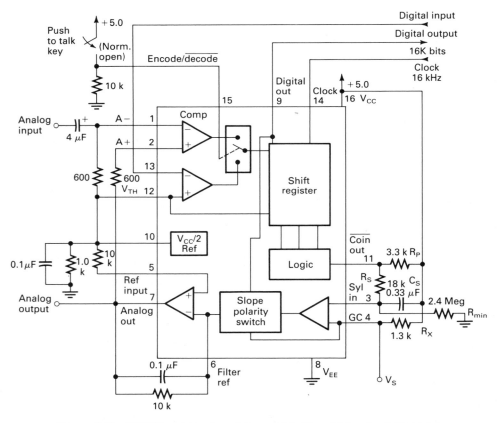

Figure 8.19 MC3417 variable slope delta modulator/demodulator circuit (Reprinted courtesy Motorola, Inc.)

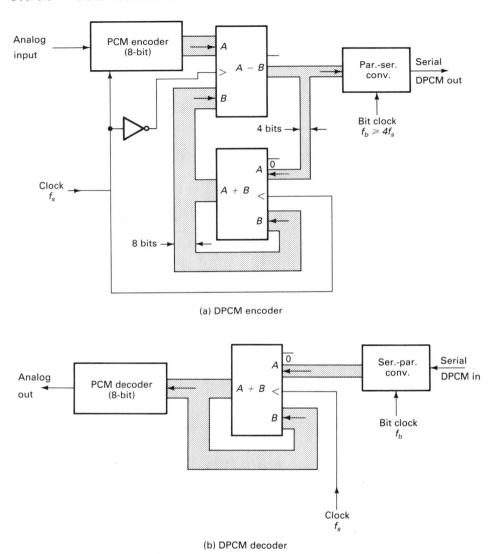

(a) DPCM encoder

(b) DPCM decoder

Figure 8.20   Differential PCM system

load will occur whenever the input signal changes by more than $\pm 7/254$ (about ± 3 percent) of its total dynamic range, from one sample to the next.

Nonlinearity (companding) and/or memory (history) may be added to a linear DPCM system to make it *adaptive* to the rate of change of the input signal. In adaptive differential PCM (ADPCM) systems, a third input is effectively applied to the adder, causing its output to increase more rapidly for larger signal changes.

PROBLEMS

8.1. A PAM communication system similar to that shown in Figure 8.1 uses a sampling clock having a period $T_s = 30$ μs.

Applying the sampling theorem, determine the maximum frequency to which the analog input signal should be limited.

8.2. What is meant by the following statement? Undersampling leads to aliasing distortion in the PAM receiver.

8.3. Describe the essential difference between a PAM system and a PCM communication system.

8.4. A PCM transmitter is designed for an analog input signal voltage range of approximately -5 V to $+5$ V. Each sample is encoded using a linear 4-bit binary code. Construct a possible table showing the voltage that corresponds to each of the 16 codes. Construct your code table such that the code for all negative voltages has its MSB = 1.

8.5. A music-recording format uses PCM and 16 bits/sample. The input audio signal may contain frequencies up to 17 kHz.

(a) What minimum bandwidth will such a system require if the resulting bit stream is to be processed serially?

(b) If the resulting data are stored using 2 bytes per 16-bit sample, how many seconds of music can be stored on a conventional 300-kbyte floppy disk?

8.6. How many bits/sample are required in a PCM system if the percent quantization error is not to exceed 1 percent when the analog signal has a level equal to 1 percent of its maximum?

8.7. Define companding, and describe its use in a PCM system.

8.8. **(a)** Sketch the line voltage waveform when AMI encoding is used for the bit stream

$$1\ 1\ 1\ 0\ 0\ 0\ 1\ 0\ 0\ 1\ 0$$

(b) What are the three advantages of AMI encoding, compared with NRZ?

(c) What is a bipolar violation error?

8.9. List the major functions included in the TP3020 CODEC IC.

8.10. Briefly describe how the telephone signaling channel is provided within the output bit stream of the CODEC.

8.11. A delta modulation transmitter is designed for an input analog signal voltage range of -5 V to $+5$ V. The maximum input frequency is 20 kHz. Compare the required bandwidth with that of an 8-bit PCM system for the same signal.

8.12. An 8-bit PCM signal is to be transmitted serially using 4-bit DPCM. The analog input signal amplitude range is ± 1 V; its maximum frequency component is 4 kHz. If slope overload is to be avoided for intersample changes of less than approximately 0.2 V, what must be the sampling rate (f_s) and the transmission-line bandwidth? Compare this bandwidth with that required for normal linear 8-bit PCM.

Hint: Assume the input is a sine wave having amplitude 1 V and frequency 4 kHz. Calculate its maximum slope in terms of T_s.

9

Videotex; A Case Study*

*Several of the figures included in this chapter have been reprinted or adapted from the standard for videotex presentation level protocol, North American PLPS, which was published jointly by ANSI and CSA:

This material is reproduced with permission from American National Standard X3.110, copyright 1983 by the American National Standards Institute. Copies of this standard may be purchased from the American National Standards Institute at 1430 Broadway, New York, N.Y. 10018.

Permission has been granted by Canadian Standards Association to make reference to CSA Standard T500-1983, Videotex/Teletext Presentation Level Protocol Syntax, which is copyrighted by CSA, and copies of which may be purchased from CSA Standards Sales, 178 Rexdale Blvd., Rexdale, Ontario, M9W 1R3.

173

9.1 INTRODUCTION

The term *Videotex* refers to a service whereby subscribers (users) may access a central data base (host computer) over the telephone network. The data base files contain encoded screens (pages) of video text and graphics information. The user places a call to the host computer and requests specific information, using a keypad or keyboard.

Videotext data bases can present a limitless variety of information. A data base is often tailored to meet the interests of a specific user group. Services for the general public may include such information as weather forecasts, investment help, shopping guides, and entertainment directories.

The host computer must have upstream links with information providers, who create and maintain the data base files. The pages are created and encoded using special computer-graphics workstations. Figure 9.1 shows the major network components.

The user's equipment must include three functional components:

A modem, to establish the data link over the telephone network,

A user terminal (or adapted microcomputer) to decode the received data and generate the video graphics,

A television set or monitor display.

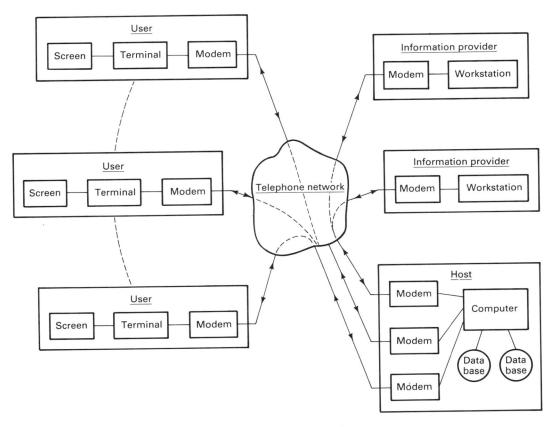

Figure 9.1 Videotex network components

Videotex is presented here as an excellent practical application of the fundamentals of data communication discussed earlier in the text.

9.2 VIDEOTEX STANDARDS

The challenges associated with developing a viable videotex service are in achieving good-quality color graphics while keeping the user terminal affordable for the average consumer and not requiring an excessive time for receiving a page over the telephone voice network. Practical, market-tested standards were first developed in Europe in the 1970s. Most notable were the British system (Prestel) and the French system (Teletel). They used a block-graphics or *mosaic* picture-encoding scheme. Objects were drawn using shapes from a limited set of graphics characters. The effect is similar to that of using a dot-matrix printer for graphics.

The British and French systems were later enhanced by a feature known as dynamically redefinable character sets (DRCS). In DRCS, different sets of graphics characters could be down-loaded to the user terminal and thus optimized for the picture to be constructed. Conceptually, this was a very powerful feature and added little cost to the user terminal; however, the algorithm required (in the page-creation workstations) to generate an optimum character set for a particular picture was very complex.

In 1979 Canada's Communication Research Center issued and began extensive field testing of the Telidon videotex standard. Telidon used geometric encoding of pictures. Picture description instructions (PDIs) were used to describe a picture in terms of its standard geometric component shapes (*primitives*). The primitives include point, circle, rectangle, line, and so forth. Telidon geometric graphics were superior to mosaic graphics, but the Telidon user terminal needed to decode the PDIs and generate the display video was expensive. Subsequently, the major strides made in custom LSI technology eliminated most of the cost penalty associated with the Telidon user terminal.

In May 1981 AT&T (the American Telephone and Telegraph Company) issued their standard, *Presentation Level Protocol,* for videotex in the United States. AT&T's document included provisions for both mosaic and geometric (PDI) picture-encoding options plus several other innovative features. Canada reissued its standard in February 1982, bringing it more in line with AT&T's.

A North American Standard (NAPLPS). Also in 1982, the Canadian Standards Association (CSA) and the American National Standards Institute (ANSI) began work toward a videotex standard for North America. The resulting standard for videotex, *North American Presentation Level Protocol Syntax* (NAPLPS), was issued jointly by CSA and ANSI in December 1983.

The term *presentation level* comes from the International Standards Organization (ISO) model of protocol levels. NAPLPS describes only the encoding of the material to be presented; it makes no attempt to specify the communication protocol or the user's application of the presented information.

The next section provides some detail regarding the NAPLPS picture-encoding procedures.

9.3 PICTURE-ENCODING BASICS

The encoding procedure uses the concept of an *in-use* code table. The NAPLPS document allows use of 8-bit or 7-bit code tables; the 7-bit approach is described here. The in-use table can be selected (at any time) to be either the standard 7-bit ASCII character set for text, a PDI code table for geometric graphics or a set of block-graphics characters for mosaic graphics.

The in-use code table is divided into two sections, as shown in Figure 9.2. The first two columns of the table are fixed (to be qualified later) and contain control characters— designated as control-character set C0. Most of the C0 characters are identical with the ASCII control set, and some are allocated to select the contents of the remainder of the in-use table (i.e., the rightmost six columns). SO (shift out), SI (shift in), SS2 (single shift

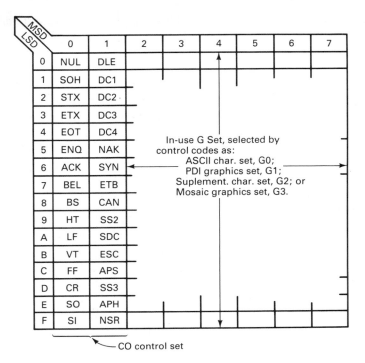

MSD / LSD	0	1	2	3	4	5	6	7
0	NUL	DLE						
1	SOH	DC1						
2	STX	DC2						
3	ETX	DC3						
4	EOT	DC4						
5	ENQ	NAK						
6	ACK	SYN						
7	BEL	ETB						
8	BS	CAN						
9	HT	SS2						
A	LF	SDC						
B	VT	ESC						
C	FF	APS						
D	CR	SS3						
E	SO	APH						
F	SI	NSR						

In-use G Set, selected by control codes as: ASCII char. set, G0; PDI graphics set, G1; Suplement. char. set, G2; or Mosaic graphics set, G3.

CO control set

Selection of in-use G Set:
SO Invoke the G1 set into in-use table.
SI Invoke the G0 set into in-use table.
SS2 Invoke the G2 set for next char. only.
SS3 Invoke the G3 set for next char. only.
G2 is invoked in a locking manner by the sequence ESC$6E.
G3 is invoked in a locking manner by the sequence ESC$6F.

Note: Default G set is G0, upon reset or power-up.

Figure 9.2 7-bit in-use code table

2), SS3 (single shift 3), and ESC (escape) are used to select the G set, as described in Figure 9.2. Other control codes that differ from ASCII include:

SDC (service delimiter character): Reserved for delimiting transmissions of *unprotected fields*—fields that may be edited by the user.

APS (active position set): Used to set the cursor position followed by the row and column addresses.

APH (active position home): Homes cursor to top left.

NSR (nonselective reset): Resets display parameters to default states.

The variable portion of the in-use table holds the current G set of characters. As listed in Figure 9.2, the G set can be selected as G0, the ASCII text characters; G1, the set of PDIs; G2, a supplementary character set for text; or G3, a set of mosaic-graphics characters. The default content of the in-use table, following power-up or reset, is the G0 ASCII character set.

Text.   In the strictly text mode, the ASCII set (G0) or the supplementary set (G2) is invoked into the in-use table. They are shown in Figures 9.3 and 9.4. User-terminal text displays are usually 40 characters wide by 20 lines; however, text size, color, orientation,

							10	11	12	13	14	15
					b_7		0	0	1	1	1	1
					b_6		1	1	0	0	1	1
					b_5		0	1	0	1	0	1
b_4	b_3	b_2	b_1	ROW	COL		2	3	4	5	6	7
0	0	0	0	0			SP	0	@	P		p
0	0	0	1	1			!	1	A	Q	a	q
0	0	1	0	2			"	2	B	R	b	r
0	0	1	1	3			#	3	C	S	c	s
0	1	0	0	4			$	4	D	T	d	t
0	1	0	1	5			%	5	E	U	e	u
0	1	1	0	6			&	6	F	V	f	v
0	1	1	1	7			'	7	G	W	g	w
1	0	0	0	8			(	8	H	X	h	x
1	0	0	1	9			)	9	I	Y	i	y
1	0	1	0	10			*	:	J	Z	j	z
1	0	1	1	11			+	;	K	[	k	{
1	1	0	0	12			,	<	L	\	l	|
1	1	0	1	13			-	=	M	]	m	}
1	1	1	0	14			.	>	N	^	n	~
1	1	1	1	15			/	?	O	_	o	DEL

Figure 9.3   The primary character set for text, G0 (Reprinted courtesy CSA/ANSI[1])

					10	11	12	13	14	15
			b7		0	0	1	1	1	1
			b6		1	1	0	0	1	1
			b5		0	1	0	1	0	1
b4	b3	b2	b1	COL / ROW	2	3	4	5	6	7
0	0	0	0	0		°	→	—	Ω	K
0	0	0	1	1	¡	±	`	¹	Æ	ae
0	0	1	0	2	¢	²	´	®	Đ	đ
0	0	1	1	3	£	³	ˆ	©	a	ð
0	1	0	0	4	$	×	~	™	Ħ	ħ
0	1	0	1	5	¥	μ	‾	♪	⊞	ı
0	1	1	0	6	#	¶	˘	⊟	IJ	ij
0	1	1	1	7	§	·	˙	⊟	Ŀ	ŀ
1	0	0	0	8	¤	÷	¨	◿	Ł	ł
1	0	0	1	9	'	′	/	◺	Ø	ø
1	0	1	0	10	''	″	°	◣	Œ	œ
1	0	1	1	11	«	»	˛	◤	º	β
1	1	0	0	12	←	¼	☐	⅛	Φ	φ
1	1	0	1	13	↑	½	˝	⅜	Ŧ	ŧ
1	1	1	0	14	→	¾	¸	⅝	η	η
1	1	1	1	15	↓	¿	˅	⅞	'n	

Figure 9.4 The supplementary character set for text, G2 (Reprinted courtesy ANSI/CSA[1])

and the like can be directly controlled (within the capabilities of the display), if necessary, by utilizing PDIs.

Graphics. The pages are "built up" on the user terminal display—element by element or layer upon layer—in any order, as codes are received. This overwriting of layers continues until a CLEAR SCREEN character (ASCII FORM FEED) is received.

Mosaic graphics use the character set shown in Figure 9.5. Notice that the 64 characters allow for the breaking up of a character field into six smaller rectangles. Mosaic pictures are constructed in a manner identical with that of text, approximating shapes using the characters available.

When PDI geometric graphics are used, elements are positioned on the display using a unit-coordinate system. The bottom left corner of the screen is taken as the origin (0, 0), and the top right corner is taken as location (1, 1).

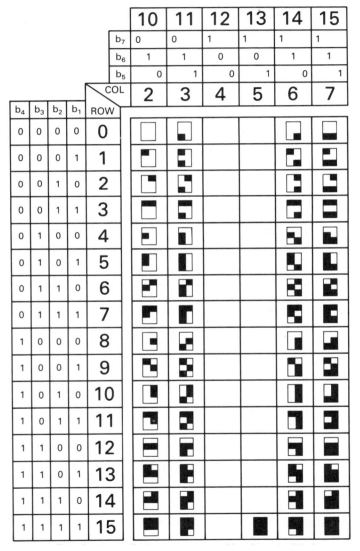

Figure 9.5 The mosaic-graphics character set, G3 (Reprinted courtesy CSA/ANSI[1])

The makeup of the PDI code table (G1) is shown in Figure 9.6. The two left columns (columns 2 and 3 of the in-use table) are used for *opcodes,* which identify the geometric shape to be constructed or issue a drawing control command. Columns 4, 5, 6, and 7 ($b_7 = 1$) are left open to allow coding of the numerical data that must follow many opcodes. The numerical data (operands) give necessary information such as size, position, and color.

				COL	10	11	12	13	14	15
				b_7	0	0	1	1	1	1
				b_6	1	1	0	0	1	1
				b_5	0	1	0	1	0	1
b_4	b_3	b_2	b_1	ROW	2	3	4	5	6	7
0	0	0	0	0	Control	Rectangle				
0	0	0	1	1	Control	Rectangle				
0	0	1	0	2	Control	Rectangle				
0	0	1	1	3	Control	Rectangle				
0	1	0	0	4	Point	Polygon				
0	1	0	1	5	Point	Polygon		Numeric data		
0	1	1	0	6	Point	Polygon				
0	1	1	1	7	Point	Polygon				
1	0	0	0	8	Line	Incremental				
1	0	0	1	9	Line	Incremental				
1	0	1	0	10	Line	Incremental				
1	0	1	1	11	Line	Incremental				
1	1	0	0	12	Arc	Control				
1	1	0	1	13	Arc	Control				
1	1	1	0	14	Arc	Control				
1	1	1	1	15	Arc	Control				

Figure 9.6 The PDI set for geometric graphics, G1 (Reprinted courtesy ANSI/CSA[1])

C1 control codes. As mentioned previously, the "permanent" resident of the first two columns of the in-use table is the ASCII control set, C0. However, provision is made temporarily (one character duration only) to substitute characters from a C1 control set, shown in Figure 9.7. The C1 controls allow extended (non-PDI) text control features, including size change, scrolling, underlining, and so forth. C1 codes DEF DRCS and END are used to down-load an optimized set of mosaic characters. This provides the dynamically redefinable character set (DRCS) feature mentioned earlier. Other codes from C1 are used to define MACROs, whereafter the predefined string is automatically generated by the user terminal upon receiving the single-character MACRO name.

				COL	0	1
			b_7		0	0
			b_6		0	0
			b_5		0	1
b_4	b_3	b_2	b_1	ROW		
0	0	0	0	0	NUL	DLE
0	0	0	1	1	SOH	DC1
0	0	1	0	2	STX	DC2
0	0	1	1	3	ETX	DC3
0	1	0	0	4	EOT	DC4
0	1	0	1	5	ENQ	NAK
0	1	1	0	6	ACK	SYN
0	1	1	1	7	BEL	ETB
1	0	0	0	8	APB (BS)	CAN
1	0	0	1	9	APF (HT)	SS2
1	0	1	0	10	APD (LF)	SDC
1	0	1	1	11	APU (VT)	ESC
1	1	0	0	12	CS (FF)	APS
1	1	0	1	13	APR (CR)	SS3
1	1	1	0	14	SO	APH
1	1	1	1	15	SI	NSR

Figure 9.7 The alternate control set, C1 (Reprinted courtesy CSA/ANSI[1])

9.4 GEOMETRIC GRAPHICS AND PDIS

A PDI consists of an opcode followed by its related bytes of numerical data. The numerical data specify the opcode's operand. As seen from Figure 9.6, all opcodes have $b_7 = 0$, and numerical data is coded such that $b_7 = 1$.

Some operands require only one byte of data—such as SELECT COLOR, where the byte following the opcode specifies the color to be used in subsequent drawing commands. Operands associated with a geometric shape PDI typically contain three bytes for each pair of coordinates and dimension given. For example, a line is drawn by issuing the LINE opcode byte, followed by six bytes of data—three used to specify the (x, y) coordinates of each end point.

PDIs are categorized as specifying either a geometric drawing primitive or a control attribute code. Figure 9.8 gives a detailed layout of the PDI set, with each form of the geometric primitives and control codes identified.

9.4.1 Attribute Control PDIs

The attribute control PDIs are listed next.

Domain.   Domain may be used to specify the number of bytes for each type of operand and the size of a logical picture element (e.g., the width of the ''brush stroke'').

Text.   Text may be used to specify text character size and orientation (rotation). It is also used to specify the cursor type (underscore, block, cross-hair, and so on).

Texture.   Texture selects line texture (solid, dashed, and the like) and the texture for filled areas (solid, cross-hatched, and so forth).

Select color.   Select color is used to select a color from a preloaded table of colors. A choice among eight gray scales and eight colors is typical.

Set color.   Set color may be used to down-load an alternative set of colors into the color table.

Blink.   Blink may be used to cause a portion of a picture to periodically alternate between two different colors.

Wait.   Wait causes a delay in the processing of PDIs by the user terminal for a specific time interval.

Reset.   Reset is used to reinitialize all attribute control parameters to their default values, clear the screen, and home the cursor.

As an example of an attribute control PDI, Figure 9.9 shows the two bytes that make up a SELECT COLOR instruction. The color—in this case blue-red—is selected by

b4	b3	b2	b1	ROW \ COL	2	3	4	5	6	7
				10 b7=0 b6=1 b5=0	**11** b7=0 b6=1 b5=1	**12** b7=1 b6=0 b5=0	**13** b7=1 b6=0 b5=1	**14** b7=1 b6=1 b5=0	**15** b7=1 b6=1 b5=1
0	0	0	0	0	RESET	RECT (OUTLINED)				
0	0	0	1	1	DOMAIN	RECT (FILLED)				
0	0	1	0	2	TEXT	SET & RECT (OUTLINED)				
0	0	1	1	3	TEXTURE	SET & RECT (FILLED)				
0	1	0	0	4	POINT SET (ABS)	POLY (OUTLINED)				
0	1	0	1	5	POINT SET (REL)	POLY (FILLED)				
0	1	1	0	6	POINT (ABS)	SET & POLY (OUTLINED)		Numeric data		
0	1	1	1	7	POINT (REL)	SET & POLY (FILLED)				
1	0	0	0	8	LINE (ABS)	FIELD				
1	0	0	1	9	LINE (REL)	INCR POINT				
1	0	1	0	10	SET & LINE (ABS)	INCR LINE				
1	0	1	1	11	SET & LINE (REL)	INCR POLY (FILLED)				
1	1	0	0	12	ARC (OUTLINED)	SET COLOR				
1	1	0	1	13	ARC (FILLED)	WAIT				
1	1	1	0	14	SET & ARC (OUTLINED)	SELECT COLOR				
1	1	1	1	15	SET & ARC (FILLED)	BLINK				

Figure 9.8 The PDI-graphics opcode set (Reprinted courtesy ANSI/CSA[1])

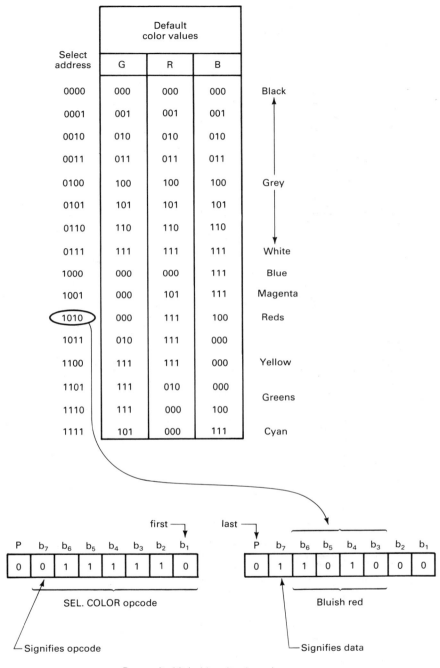

Figure 9.9 Color map and SEL. COLOR PDI

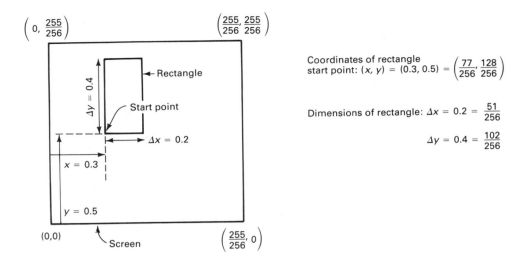

Coordinates of rectangle
start point: $(x, y) = (0.3, 0.5) = \left(\dfrac{77}{256}, \dfrac{128}{256} \right)$

Dimensions of rectangle: $\Delta x = 0.2 = \dfrac{51}{256}$

$\Delta y = 0.4 = \dfrac{102}{256}$

Rectangle opcode: $\_\, 0\ 1\ 1\ 0\ 0\ 1\ 0$ (from Fig. 9.8)
Coordinate codes: $x = 77 = 0\ 0\ 1\ 0\ 0\ 1\ 1\ 0\ 1$
$\qquad\qquad\qquad y = 128 = 0\ 1\ 0\ 0\ 0\ 0\ 0\ 0\ 0$
Dimension codes: $\Delta x = 51 = 0\ 0\ 0\ 1\ 1\ 0\ 0\ 1\ 1$
$\qquad\qquad\qquad \Delta y = 102 = 0\ 0\ 1\ 1\ 0\ 0\ 1\ 1\ 0$

Transmission Format:

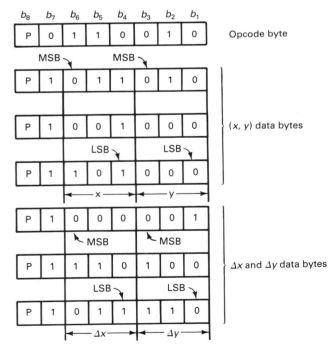

Figure 9.10 "SET and RECTANGLE" PDI example

specifying its address in the color map table, also shown. The opcode is taken from Figure 9.8. The 4-bit address (1010) is left-justified in the data byte. In this case, bits b_1 and b_2 of the data byte would be ignored by the user terminal.

9.4.2 Geometric Primitive PDIs

The PDIs that instruct the user terminal to create a geometric primitive shape are as follows.

Point.   Point sets the drawing point to any position in the unit screen and optionally displays a dot.

Line.   Line draws a line, based on its end points.

Arc.   Arc draws a circular arc, based on one end point, an intermediate point (on the arc), and a second end point.

A circle is defined as an arc having both end points the same, in which case the intermediate value is taken as its diameter.

Rectangle.   Rectangle draws a rectangle, based on a starting point, a length, and a height. The starting point is taken as the bottom left corner of the rectangle.

Polygon.   Polygon draws a polygon, based on a series of defined vertices.

Incremental.   Incremental draws a freehand shape or line in a point-by-point manner. It may also be used to create a "photographic" picture in a point-by-point manner within a specified area.

As an example, Figure 9.10 shows the makeup of the opcode and operand bytes for a SET and RECTANGLE PDI. SET refers to setting a new starting point instead of using the point where the previous command left off. Figure 9.10 shows the most common data format, where the drawing area is divided into 256×256 elements. Nine-bit twos-complement binary codes are used to specify dimensional and coordinate information.

In practice, most video screens are not square. A height-to-width ratio of 3:4 is used in television sets (*aspect ratio*). Consequently, pages are usually restricted to be no more than 200 picture elements high, although the coordinate system spans 256.

9.5 VIDEOTEX COMMUNICATION PROTOCOLS

Videotex is a data-communication service that must be provided using the switched telephone voice network. It is aimed at the general consumer market, and cost is a prime consideration.

The traffic pattern associated with videotex data is "bursty" by nature; it consists of short user commands sent upstream to the host computer and the requested page files sent downstream to the user terminal. Typically, the encoded page files contain in the order of 1000 bytes. For acceptable service, the system should require no more than a few seconds for a page to be transmitted, received, and displayed. Service should be full-duplex for satisfactory user-to-host interaction.

User terminals often include a Bell-202C—type originate modem. The Bell 202C is an asynchronous FSK modem, described briefly in Chapter 5. It provides a 1200-bits/s primary channel (host to user) and a 150-bits/s secondary channel (user to host). Figure 9.11 shows the modem frequency spectrum within the telephone network bandwidth. The mark-space frequencies are 1200 Hz and 2200 Hz for the primary channel and 390 Hz and 490 Hz for the secondary channel, as shown.

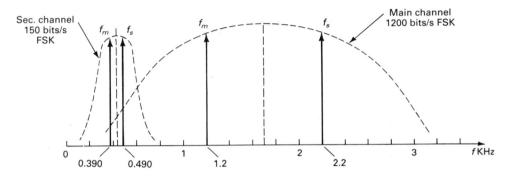

Figure 9.11   Bell 202C modem spectrum utilization

A bit rate of 1200 bits/s translates to approximately 120 bytes/s (assuming one start and one stop bit) which makes it possible to transmit a 1000-byte page file in 8.3 s.

If the user-terminal PDI decoder is occasionally unable to keep up with the rate at which codes are being received from the host, its receive buffer could overflow. To prevent this, flow control is provided by the ASCII control codes DC1 ("XON") and DC3 ("XOFF"), which may be transmitted to the host by the user terminal software as necessary.

In addition to having a Bell 202C modem built in, many terminals also provide an RS232 port for connecting an external modem. When an external modem is used, it is often a Bell 212A. The 212A provides 1200-bits/s channels in both directions (i.e., 1200 bits/s full-duplex).

9.6 THE VIDEOTEX USER TERMINAL

Figure 9.12 shows a representative block diagram of a user terminal. The major component groups and their functions are as follows:

CPU.   The CPU consists of the MPU (microprocessor), ROM, and static RAM. The software contained in the ROM consists of the overall operating system main pro-

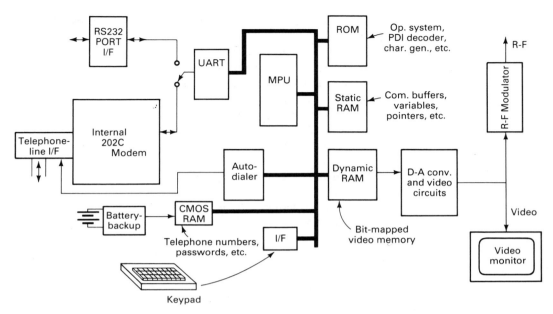

Figure 9.12 Videotex user terminal

gram, the communication/UART routines, the routines that decode the graphics codes, and the complex algorithms that generate the geometric shapes. The latter is often referred to as the PDI *decoder*.

Video memory. A geometric graphics display requires a *bit-mapped* video RAM memory. Each picture element (PEL) or *dot* is mapped to a specific memory location. Each memory location stores the color-map code for its respective picture element.

A 256-by-200 PEL display resolution dictates a bit-mapped memory size of 51,200 locations. Each location must store at least a 4-bit code corresponding to the select-address values given in Figure 9.9. Thus, the memory would contain $51,200 \times 4 = 2048$ bits, or approximately 26 kbytes. Dynamic RAM is used for the video memory.

Video circuits. The software PDI decoder "paints" the display in the bit-mapped memory by storing the proper 4-bit code in the proper location for each PEL. The D/A converter continually scans the memory, reading the codes and converting each to its proper video voltage level. Actually three voltages are generated in parallel, corresponding to red, green, and blue. The scanning of the video memory is synchronized with the scanning of the screen by the electron beam.

Remaining video circuits generate the synchronizing signals and mix (matrix) the signal components as required to drive the video display.

Some terminals include a radio-frequency (RF) modulator, which provides an output suitable for connecting to a television set. The modulation-demodulation process invariably degrades the signal somewhat, and the resolution of most television sets is inadequate for good graphics.

Communication circuits.   The terminal shown has a built-in Bell 202C modem. Page files are received at 1200 baud, and user-command codes are transmitted at 150 baud, using the 202C.

An RS232 port is provided as an alternative to the internal modem. The port may be used to connect an external modem (such as a Bell 212A) or to connect some other device—a videotex page-creation terminal, for example.

Keypad.   The keypad allows the user to input system commands, page numbers, telephone numbers, and the like. A typical keypad layout is shown in Figure 9.13. The layout shown is for an Electrohome terminal. Some of the user-command keys are listed along with their functions and transmitted codes.

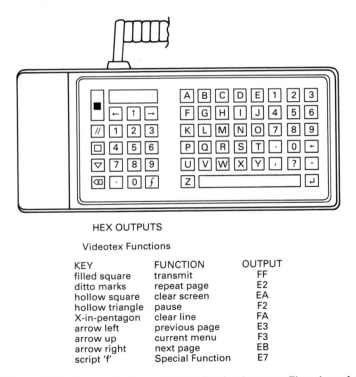

HEX OUTPUTS

Videotex Functions

KEY	FUNCTION	OUTPUT
filled square	transmit	FF
ditto marks	repeat page	E2
hollow square	clear screen	EA
hollow triangle	pause	F2
X-in-pentagon	clear line	FA
arrow left	previous page	E3
arrow up	current menu	F3
arrow right	next page	EB
script 'f'	Special Function	E7

Figure 9.13   User-terminal keypad layout (Reprinted courtesy Electrohome Ltd.)

10

Local Area Networks (LANs)

10.1 INTRODUCTION

The availability of low-cost powerful microcomputers has led to the decentralization of computer data processing within businesses and to a proliferation of computerized workstations or data bases used for design, budgeting, word processing, graphics preparation, scheduling, and so forth. To make possible the sharing of this information and resources within a company or department, networking is required. The network must provide reliable high-speed data communication links interconnecting the various pieces of computer equipment.

A LAN is a network that interconnects such computing workstations and peripherals located, at most, within a few kilometers of each other. The LAN is usually owned by a single private company. Small networks link equipment located within the same room or building floor. Medium-size LANs cover an entire building or plant, including links to corporate mainframes or minicomputers. Large LANs span several sites, such as over a university campus or government complex. Some LANs, notably digital PBXs, carry voice and data on the same network.

Figure 10.1 illustrates a small LAN that might be used in the engineering office of a small manufacturing firm. The communication medium for the network shown is a continuous data bus to which each station and resource is interfaced. The communication procedures and interfacing hardware used (i.e., the network protocol) must be carefully defined and implemented uniformly for the orderly sharing of the common bus. Only one station may transmit at a time, sending data to another station, or stations, in frames or packets that include source and destination addresses. All stations receive each packet and examine the contained destination address, copying in the data if the address is their own. Typical bit rates used on LANs fall in the 50-kbps to 15-Mbps range.

Baseband versus broadband. The most common type of LAN is that illustrated in Figure 10.1. It uses a bus or bus/tree architecture and provides baseband, usually serial synchronous half-duplex communications. As will be seen later, several other arrangements are possible. For example, the most powerful networks, in terms of bandwidth and distance, are *broadband* rather than baseband. Broadband networks transmit data by modulating RF analog carriers. Several carriers can be transmitted simultaneously using FDM to provide several communication channels at once on the same network. Dual cabling or assigning separate carriers for each direction is used to provide two-way communication over broadband networks. Broadband is an outgrowth of cable

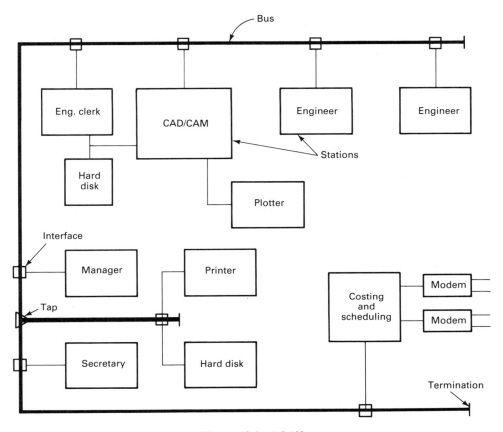

Figure 10.1 A LAN

television technology, and each network contains central *head-end* equipment for RF amplification and frequency translation of signals. This chapter is primarily concerned with baseband systems.

10.2 LAN TOPOLOGY

The term *topology* refers to the layout or interconnecting pattern used for a network. Figure 10.1 showed a bus or tree topology. The other basic arrangements used for local area networks are star and ring. All are illustrated in Figure 10.2.

Star.   The star arrangement uses a central switch or controller. A small telephone exchange is the classic example of a star topology. For a station to transmit data to another, it must first request the proper connection be made by the switch.

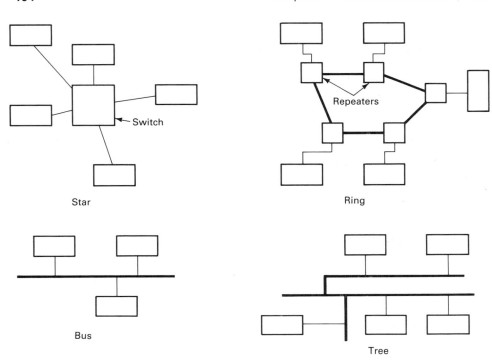

Figure 10.2 LAN topologies

Ring. The ring topology uses a ring of repeaters. Each repeater receives data, presents it to its station, and retransmits it to the next repeater. The repeaters are unidirectional, and data traverses the ring in one direction only (clockwise or counterclockwise). Each station examines the destination address field of each data packet and copies the data if the address is its own.

Bus and tree. The most popular LAN topology is the bus or bus/tree arrangement. No central switches or repeaters are involved. (Repeaters are used to interconnect separate buses on multibus networks.) The network bus is only the communication medium. Stations attach through interfacing units (sometimes called transceivers), which implement the required hardware and software procedures. All transmitted data packets travel the entire bus in either direction and are received by all stations. Each station examines the destination address of each packet, copying the data if the address matches its own.

10.3 LAN PROTOCOLS

In an assessment of the performance of a LAN, the transmission bit rate is only one consideration; the other important factor is how efficiently the network bus or ring is shared by the stations. This latter factor is primarily determined by the effectiveness of the medium-access protocol used (the medium being the bus or ring). The various access protocols used for LANs are based on one of four basic methods: contention, token passing, reservation, or slotted.

Contention protocols (CSMA/CD).   Using contention protocol, the stations compete for the right to transmit data over the network more or less at random or whenever the need to transmit data arises for each.

Each station monitors (listens to) the bus and begins transmission of a data packet only if the bus is clear (not busy). This protocol is referred to as *carrier sense,* or listen before talk, and is designated as carrier sense multiple access (CSMA).

With the CSMA method, it is inevitable that at times more than one station will begin data transmission at once, resulting in a ''collision'' that causes erroneous data to be received by all stations. Thus, for contention to work, each station must also be able to detect collisions. A transmitting station monitors the bus while it is transmitting to confirm that the actual bus signal is correct and is thus able to detect the occurrence of any collision. This collision detect (CD) feature leads to the acronym CSMA/CD to describe the complete protocol. When a collision is detected, the transmitting station immediately transmits a *jamming* pattern designed to inform all stations of the collision so that they will disregard the data packet. The transmitting station then defers or ''backs off'' for a random length of time before attempting retransmission.

The strength of CSMA/CD is its simplicity, flexibility, and its effectiveness when the network traffic is light and bursty in nature. Adding or removing stations on the bus does not affect the protocol procedures. The disadvantage of CSMA/CD is that the efficiency of bus utilization falls off sharply as the traffic loading becomes heavy. Some have described CSMA/CD as an ''uncoordinated free-for-all!'' Nonetheless, it remains the most popular LAN protocol.

CSMA/CD has its roots in a packet radio system developed by the University of Hawaii around 1970, known as ALOHANET. The modern benchmark LAN protocol based on CSMA/CD is the Ethernet, developed jointly between 1979 and 1982 by Xerox, Intel, and DEC corporations. Most microcomputer LANs use CSMA/CD, including PC Cluster (and the broadband PC Network) of IBM.

Token-passing protocols.   After CSMA/CD, the second most popular medium-access protocol for LANs is *token passing*. In this method, a network control block or token is passed in turn from station to station. When a station is in possession of the token, it may transmit one data packet. When it has transmitted the allowed data packet or if it has none to transmit, it sends the token on to the next station.

The token includes a destination address, and it circulates to the stations in a predetermined order. When a ring topology is used, the order of token circulation corresponds to the physical order of the station around the ring. When the network is arranged as a bus or tree, the order of circulation must be preset when the system is initialized and may bear no relationship to the physical location of the stations on the network—that is, a logical ring is superimposed on the physical network, as shown in Figure 10.3.

Token-passing protocol is more orderly but also more complex than CSMA/CD. Its strength is its superior performance under conditions of heavy data traffic. It enforces a

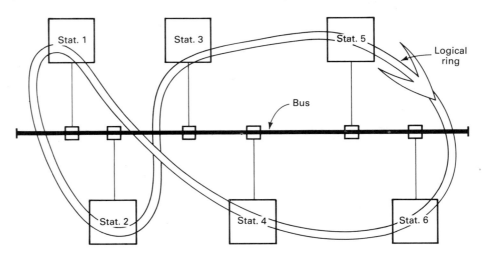

Token-passing order: 1, 2, 3, 5, 6, 4, 1, . . .

Figure 10.3 The token bus

fair sharing of the network medium, much like that of older computer networks that relied on polling of stations by a central controller to regulate bus access. Token passing replaces the need to have a central controller by distributing control throughout the network. Of course, token passing will not function if the ring is broken. The protocol must include token monitor procedures to allow recovery from a lost token or duplicate tokens situation and to provide means to modify the logical ring (add, subtract, or reorder stations).

In 1977, Datapoint introduced its LAN, ARCnet, using token passing. Recently, IBM announced a baseband token-passing ring protocol standard.

Reservation protocols.   When a reservation protocol is being used, a station wishing to transmit data on the network must make a request of a central controller or switch for a reservation to do so. A telephone PBX is most representative of this method of medium access. In general, the reservation may be in the form of allocating a switched circuit, a time slot, or a carrier frequency. The reservation method is not used extensively for LANs.

Slotted protocols.   *Slotted* refers to time slots, and this method is best illustrated by the slotted ring protocol. As shown in Figure 10.4, a limited number of fixed-length time slots circulate the ring continuously. Each slot includes a *leader,* or busy bit, that indicates if the slot is busy or available.

To transmit a data packet, a station must wait for an available slot to arrive, change its leader to busy, and insert its data packet as the slot goes by. All receivers monitor the destination addresses of busy slot packets, copying the data if the address is their own. The busy slot must traverse the entire ring before being restored to available status by the original transmitting station. A station is allowed to use just one slot for transmission per

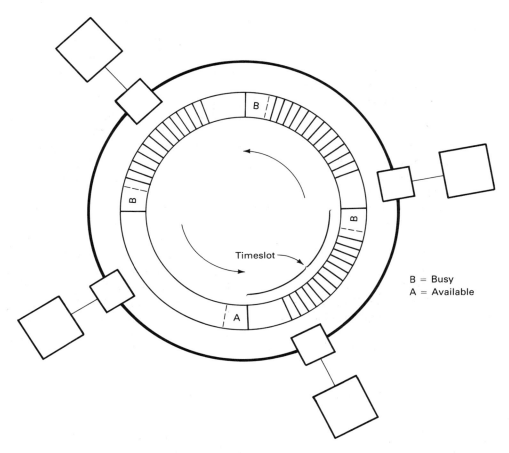

Figure 10.4   The slotted ring

ring cycle. The maximum number of slots that can circulate a ring is calculated by dividing the total ring delay (repeater delays plus propagation times) by the desired length of one time slot.

Commercial systems using the slotted ring are known as the *Pierce loop*, or Cambridge ring, after its developer and Cambridge University.

10.4 LAN STANDARDS

In the past, most LANs were installed using designs that were customized to interconnect a limited list of equipment. Often the LAN and the equipment were from the same vendor. For LANs to reach their full potential, standards must be adopted that allow the network to be open-ended so that it can service future applications unforeseen at the time of installation and that allow the networking of equipment from a variety of manufacturers.

The international standards body for LANs is the International Standards Organization (ISO) which is made up of representative groups from member countries. Work in North America has been under the direction of ANSI in the United States. ANSI, in turn, has commissioned the IEEE to develop and propose the technical standards for LANs.

As a structural guideline for member countries, ISO has proposed a seven-level hierarchy of protocols for networks known as the *Open Systems Interconnect*, or OSI model, which is shown in Figure 10.5. Current work on LAN standards relates to the first two levels of the OSI model: physical specifications and the data-link control procedures.

With the lack of any national standards in the past, Ethernet (Xerox, Intel, DEC), using CSMA/CD, and ARCnet (Datapoint), based on a token bus, evolved as common references or de facto standards due to their commercial success. Ethernet, in particular, is widely supported by products from several vendors.

However, there has been considerable activity on new commercial systems in the past few months—in particular, by General Motors, Boeing, and IBM:

> IBM token ring: IBM recently released specifications on a new LAN that uses token-passing ring protocol. It is baseband and uses twisted-pair cable. Texas Instruments has developed an LSI chip set for the LAN-to-station interface.
>
> MAP (manufacturing automation protocol): General Motors is well along in designing and implementing its MAP LAN, which is intended to link all computer-based manufacturing systems. MAP uses token-passing bus protocol. It is broadband and uses coaxial cable.

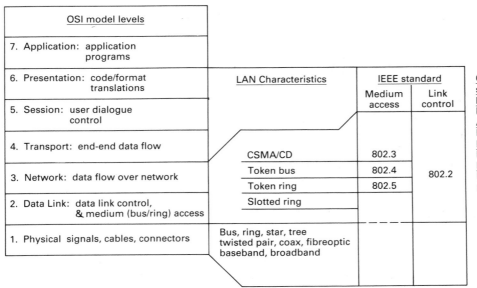

Figure 10.5 LAN protocol standards

TOP (technical and office protocols): TOP is being developed by Boeing and addresses the problem of engineering and other office communication. It uses much of the work done by GM on its MAP LAN.

Each of these newer systems is being developed in close cooperation with the IEEE to establish the required industry standards for each.

The IEEE LAN standards being developed are referred to by the IEEE committee number, 802. IEEE Standard 802.3 relates to CSMA/CD networks, including both baseband and broadband versions. The baseband 802.3 standard is very similar to Ethernet and is nearly finalized. IEEE Standard 802.4 relates to token-passing bus arrangements, and 802.5 involves token-passing rings. Figure 10.5 shows the relationship of these standards to the OSI model.

10.5 THE ETHERNET SPECIFICATION

Ethernet is a local area network developed jointly by Xerox, Intel, and Digital Equipment corporations. The published standard (available from Xerox) relates to level 1 (physical) and level 2 (data link) protocols of the OSI model, shown previously in Figure 10.5.

10.5.1 Overview of Ethernet

The Ethernet LAN carries data at 10 Mbits/s on a shielded coaxial cable bus. The maximum length of a bus cable segment is 500 m. Bus segments may be interconnected using repeaters; the maximum allowed station separation is stated as 2.8 km. Figure 10.6 illustrates a bus segment. Ethernet uses baseband signaling, and the bus-access, or medium-access, protocol is CSMA/CD. Data are sent in packets, and since Ethernet is a baseband system, only one station may drive the bus at one time. If more than one station inadvertently transmits simultaneously, a collision occurs, which causes an invalid packet to be received. Such invalid packets are discarded by all receiving stations, and the transmitting stations try again after waiting for a random period of time.

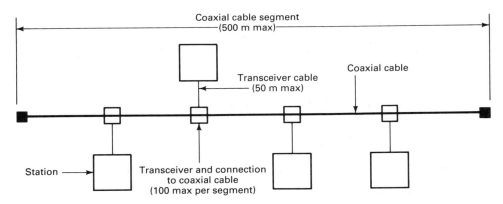

Figure 10.6 The Ethernet bus (Reprinted courtesy XEROX Corp.)

The Ethernet provides half-duplex, serial, synchronous communication over a single coaxial pair. Thus, receivers must recover the bit timing and synchronize their receive clock from the data stream—no separate clock signal is transmitted. To facilitate this, the data signal on the bus uses *Manchester encoding,* shown in Figure 10.7. The resultant Manchester waveform is said to be *self-clocking,* since each bit interval contains at least one voltage transition regardless of the data bit pattern. A positive-going transition at the center of a bit time signifies logic 1, and a negative-going transition at the center of a bit interval signifies logic 0.

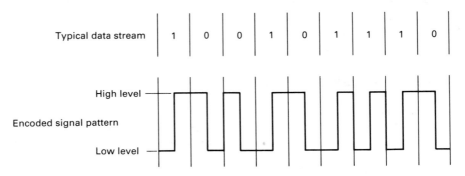

Figure 10.7   Manchester encoding (Reprinted courtesy XEROX Corp.)

Figure 10.8 illustrates the physical makeup of a station bus interface, and the relationship of each component to the protocol functions. The interface consists of the transceiver, which "sits" on the bus, and the controller board, which is usually located at the workstation. The transceiver cable interconnects the controller and transceiver. The transceiver cable uses four pairs of wires to carry power for the transceiver, the transmit data, receive data, and collision presence signals, as shown.

10.5.2 Ethernet Controller Functions

Figure 10.8 shows the functions of the controller as data encapsulation-decapsulation, link management, and encoding-decoding. It also provides the interface with the station microprocessor bus. These functions can be broken down further, as follows:

Data encapsulation-decapsulation
    Assembling and disassembling data packets
    Addressing
    Error detection
Link management
    Implementing the bus-access protocol, CSMA/CD
Encoding/decoding
    Translating NRZ to Manchester, and vice versa

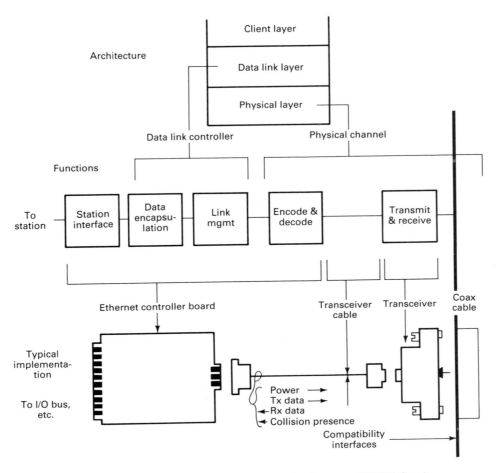

Figure 10.8 The Ethernet bus interface (Reprinted courtesy XEROX Corp.)

The format of the Ethernet data frame or packet is shown in Figure 10.9. Each frame is preceded by a 64-bit preamble, for receiver synchronization. The preamble consists of a sequence of alternate 1s and 0s, except for the last 2 bits, which are both 1s. The first bit of the preamble is a 1.

After the preamble, two 6-byte (6-"octet") address fields are transmitted for the destination and source addresses, respectively. The first bit of the destination address field is used to differentiate between addressing a single physical station (0) and addressing a group of stations (1). The latter mode is referred to as *multicast*. If the multicast is directed to *all* other stations on the network, it is termed *broadcast*, and the address $FF FF FF FF FF FF (all 1s) is used. Addresses are sent most significant byte first, and each byte is sent LSB first. For example, the address $F0 2E 15 6C 77 9B corresponds to the bit stream

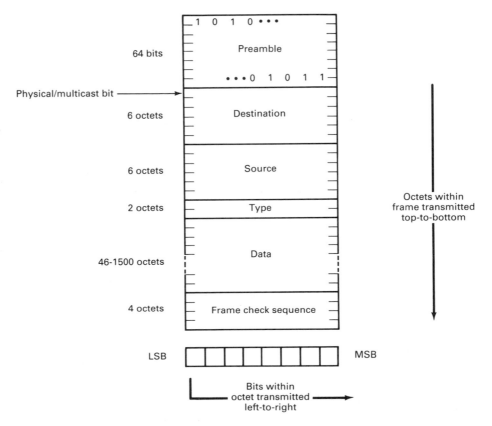

Figure 10.9 Ethernet packet or frame format (Adapted; courtesy XEROX Corp.)

0000 1111   0111 0100   1010 1000   0011 0110   1110 1110   1101 1001

with the left bit being transmitted first. The large address fields are provided to allow each
and every piece of Ethernet equipment manufactured to have a unique address. The service of assigning and recording addresses is currently offered by Xerox corporation. The
number of different addresses on any one network is limited to 1024.

Referring again to Figure 10.9, the address fields are followed by a 2-byte data type
field in order for the user to identify different types of data that may be carried over the
network, if necessary.

The allowed length of the data field is from 46 bytes minimum to 1500 bytes maximum. It must contain an integral number of bytes within this range. Each byte is
transmitted LSB first.

The 4-byte error check sequence is a CRC, which is calculated by combining all
previous bits of the frame (excluding the preamble), according to a prescribed mathemat-

ical procedure. This type of error-check code is more effective than a simple parity or checksum and is discussed more fully in Chapter 7. The CRC is transmitted MSB first.

Considering the allowed variation in the length of the data field, a complete frame or packet can range in length from 64 bytes minimum to 1518 bytes maximum.

The link management or bus-access protocol is CSMA/CD, which was described earlier in this chapter. The procedure for transmitting and receiving is best illustrated by the flowcharts shown in Figure 10.10. Transmission is deferred (delayed) until the bus is free. The controller ''listens'' via the receive data signal from the transceiver (see Figure 10.8). If two or more stations should inadvertently begin transmission more or less at the same time, the transceiver detects a collision condition on the bus and notifies the controller (of the collision) via the collision presence signal. The controller then issues a 32- to 48-bit jamming pattern (after completing the preamble, if necessary), which is to prolong the collision and ensure it is noticed by all transmitting stations. Following a collision, each transmitting station waits for a random length of time before attempting retransmission. Sixteen retries are allowed before an excessive-collisions error is flagged. Short packets (less than 64 bytes), which result from collisions or other irregularities, are discarded by receiving stations.

10.5.3 Ethernet Transceiver, Cables, and Signals

Figure 10.11 illustrates the transceiver input and output signals, showing typical voltage waveforms for each. All data lines use Manchester encoding, and the logic voltage levels are specified to match those of the high-speed emitter-coupled logic (ECL) family of devices. (For ECL, $V_H \geq -0.8$ V and $V_L \leq -1.7$ V.) The idle (no-signal) voltage on the coaxial cable and across the transceiver cable data pairs is 0 V. Notice, however, that when data are present, the DC levels (average voltages) on the coax and transceiver cable pairs are -1 V and 0 V, respectively.

The Ethernet document specifies 15-pin miniature D type connector assemblies for both ends of the transceiver cable. The pinout is as follows:

Signal	Pin No.	
Transmit data +	3	
-	10	
Receive data +	5	
-	12	(All other pins should
Collision presence +	2	have no connection)
-	9	
Power feed +	13	
Power return -	6	
Cable shield	1	

The Ethernet coaxial cable is a 50-Ω low-loss type, that uses foamed dielectric and multiple shielding. Its attenuation must not exceed 8.5 dB per 500 m at 10 MHz, and its velocity factor must be at least 0.77. (See Chapter 2 for a discussion of transmission-line parameters.)

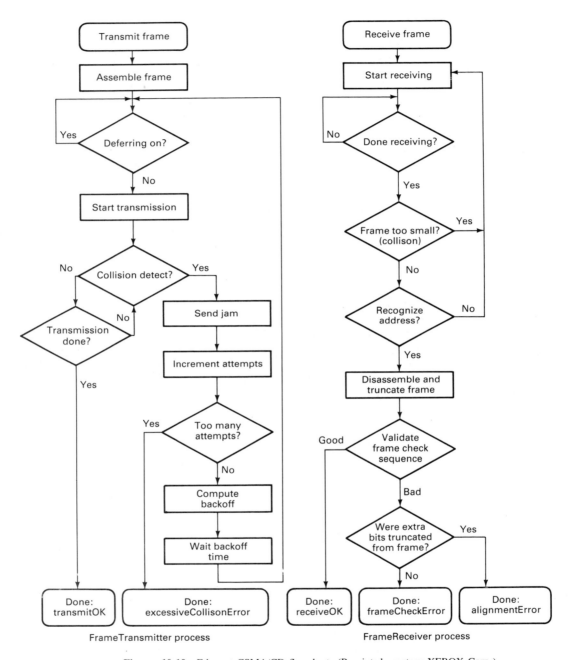

Figure 10.10 Ethernet CSMA/CD flowcharts (Reprinted courtesy XEROX Corp.)

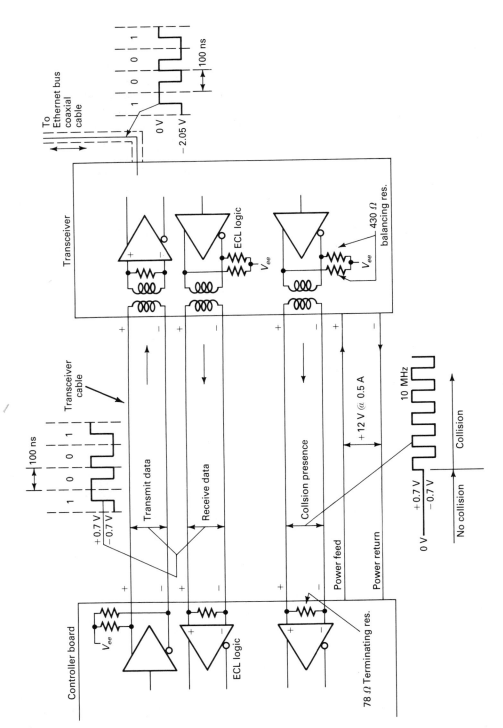

Figure 10.11 Ethernet transceiver signals

205

Figure 10.12 shows a simplified block diagram for a typical Ethernet transceiver. The LPF (low-pass filter) passes only the DC component of the signal from the coaxial cable to the inputs of the two voltage comparators shown. A DC level much less (negative) than -1 V indicates no signal is being received, and the output of the receive threshold comparator is such as to block (via the AND gate) any bus noise from being coupled to the transceiver cable receive data pair. If the DC level of the signal off the bus is excessive (much more negative than -1 V), the transceiver "assumes" this is due to the bus being driven by more than one transmitter, and the collision threshold comparator gates the 10-MHz oscillator signal onto the collision presence pair, informing the controller board of a collision condition on the bus.

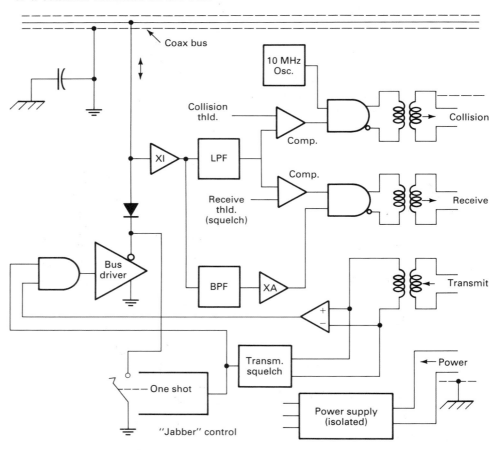

Figure 10.12   Ethernet transceiver

The transmit path includes provision to squelch (turn off) the transmit signal if the signal input from the controller is too low. This is to prevent noise and spurious signals from being transmitted when the transmitter is idle. Also, a "watchdog" timer circuit performs a function known as *jabber control* to prevent the station from inadvertently transmitting continuously for an extended period of time, should a fault occur. Recall from the previous section that the longest legal frame is 1518 bytes, plus preamble.

10.6 LSI ETHERNET INTERFACE

From the previous description of Ethernet, we see that the CSMA/CD bus-access procedures and the coax interface circuitry are fairly complex. Implementing the hardware interface using conventional MSI packages and discrete components is expensive and requires considerable PC board area. Also, implementing the bus-access procedures as part of the main station microprocessor software is undesirable because of the large overhead it places on the operating system—the CPU becomes *communication-bound* much of the time, unavailable for its main-user tasks. In any case, speed is likely to be a problem at 10 Mbps.

With Ethernet being accepted as, at least, an interim standard for LANs, IC manufacturers have developed LSI devices which make possible the implementation of an Ethernet station interface in a compact self-contained package. Intel corporation is probably the most advanced in this respect, being one of the developers of Ethernet. Intel has partitioned the interface into just two ICs, which take care of all the link control and hardware interface requirements between the station CPU bus and the Ethernet transceiver cable (see Figure 10.13). The "brains" of the interface is the controller chip, or LAN

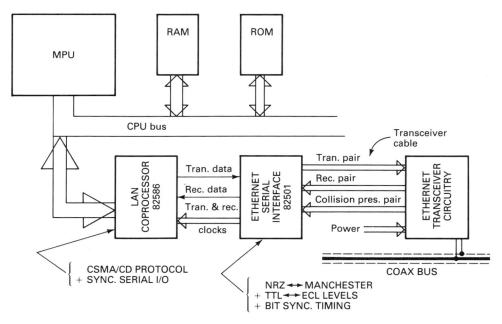

Figure 10.13   Ethernet interface architecture using LSI

coprocessor (82586). It includes the software (microcode) to implement automatically all the CSMA/CD procedures during transmission or reception of a frame. The Ethernet serial interface chip (82501) includes the circuitry to interface (drive-receive) with the transceiver differential pairs, to synchronize bit timing, and to perform the Manchester encoding-decoding function.

10.6.1 Intel's 82501 Ethernet Serial Interface

The block diagram and pinout for the 82501 are given in Figure 10.14. The 82501 is an NMOS device in a 20-pin dual in-line package. Its functions are as follows:

1. Receiving the ± 0.7 V Manchester-encoded data from the transceiver cable receive pair (RCV/$\overline{\text{RCV}}$), converting this data to TTL NRZ format, and outputting it to the RXD (receive data) pin 9.

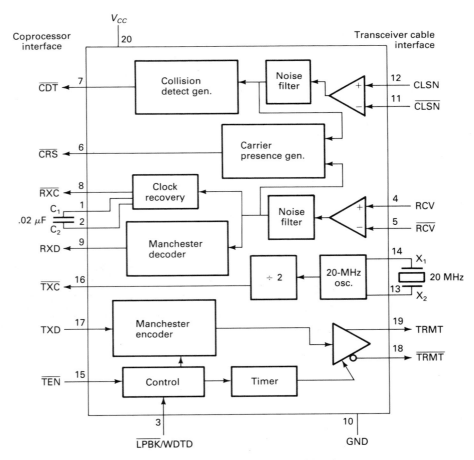

Figure 10.14 Intel's 82501 Ethernet serial interface

2. Extracting the bit timing from the received Manchester data signal and outputting the synchronized 10-MHz clock signal to the $\overline{\text{RXC}}$ (receive clock) pin 8.

3. Generating the carrier sense signal, making the $\overline{\text{CRS}}$ pin 6 LOW, only when a signal is being received from the transceiver cable receive or collision presence pairs.

4. Receiving TTL NRZ data from TXD (transmit data) pin 17, converting it to ± 0.7 Manchester format and outputting it to the transmit pair (TRMT/$\overline{\text{TRMT}}$).

5. Generating the transmit bit clock (derived from the 20-MHz crystal oscillator) and outputting it to the $\overline{\text{TXC}}$ (transmit clock) pin 16.

6. Generating the collision-detect signal, making the $\overline{\text{CDT}}$ pin 7 LOW only when a signal is detected on the transceiver cable collision presence pair (CLSN/$\overline{\text{CLSN}}$).

The $\overline{\text{TEN}}$ (transmit enable) pin 15 must be LOW for transmission to take place.

In addition, the 82501 contains a watchdog timer, which clamps the transmit output to 0-V differential should the transmitter input remain continuously active for longer than 25 ms. This function is referred to as *jabber control,* in the Ethernet specification and is to prevent the tying up of the bus for an extended period of time due to a local fault.

Recovery of the received bit timing and generation of the $\overline{\text{RXC}}$ signal uses a PLL circuit, which requires external connection of a capacitor, as shown. Approximately the first 12 bits of each received frame preamble are lost while the receiver achieves synchronization. Received data on RXD should be latched (into the LAN Coprocessor) coincident with the falling edge of the $\overline{\text{RXC}}$ signal.

Transmit data input on TXD is sampled on the falling edge of the $\overline{\text{transmit}}$ clock signal ($\overline{\text{TXC}}$).

Also, 78-Ω resistors should be connected across the RCV/$\overline{\text{RCV}}$ and CLSN/$\overline{\text{CLSN}}$ inputs to terminate the transceiver cable pairs properly. In addition, a 120-Ω resistor is required from both sides of the TRMT/$\overline{\text{TRMT}}$ output to ground for driver current sinking and line balancing.

Bringing $\overline{\text{LPBK}}$/WDTD (loopback/watchdog timer disable) pin LOW selects a loopback mode for testing, where serial data on pin TXD is routed back to RXD. Applying $+12$ V to this pin through a 4-Ω resistor selects normal operation, but with the timer disabled; $+5$ V selects normal operation with the timer enabled.

10.6.2 Intel's 82586 LAN Coprocessor

The 82586 is a specialized 16-bit microprocessor. It is designed to carry out all the Ethernet bus-access, frame-receiving and frame-transmitting procedures automatically. It functions as a dedicated I/O processor, sitting between the main station CPU bus and the Ethernet transceiver cable interface, as shown in Figure 10.13. It is an NMOS device, using a 48-pin dual in-line package.

A functional block diagram for the 82586 is shown in Figure 10.15. The receiving unit is prepared, at any time, to receive and store a frame of data. It automatically screens packets, storing only those having a correct destination address. Error (CRC) and correct frame length status are also reported. The command unit executes other commands (such as TRANSMIT) issued by the host (main station) CPU. The microinstruction ROM sec-

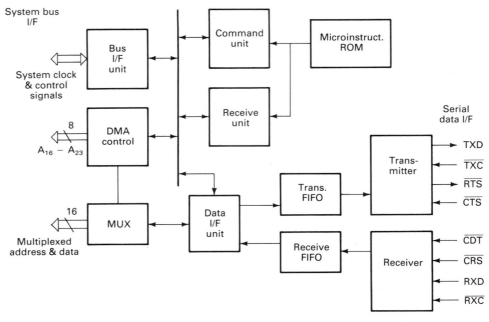

Figure 10.15   82586 functional block diagram (Adapted; courtesy Intel Corp.)

tion contains the microcode, which steps the receive and control units through the required sequence for each command. The 82586 also contains a complete serial synchronous receiver/transmitter, including the handshake lines (to mate with the Ethernet serial interface), and two 16-byte FIFO buffers.

Although the 82586 was specifically targeted toward Ethernet, it is highly flexible and may be programmed (configured) to implement other frame formats, including HDLC (high-level data-link control). Also, the receiver-transmitter will operate at data bit rates from 1 MHz to 10 MHz (the latter being that of Ethernet).

Of course, the coprocessor's bus interface lines match those of the Intel 16-bit microprocessor family (8088, 8086, 80186, and so on) most directly. The 82586 shares the CPU memory and includes DMA (direct memory access), which means its interface must include the CPU bus-access signals (HOLD and HOLDACK).

Direct interaction of the 82586 with the host takes place via two dedicated hardware lines and a shared RAM space, as shown in Figure 10.16. The CPU requests action of the 82586 using CA (channel attention), and the 82586 requests the attention of the CPU using an interrupt signal (INT). The shared memory space consists of four major sections:

Initialization root: This is an address pointer, to tell the coprocessor where the system control block begins in memory. This pointer must be stored a location $FFFF6. It serves somewhat like a reset vector for the 82586.

System control block (SCB): This serves as a "mailbox" for transferring control and status information between the CPU and coprocessor. It also includes pointers, giving the location in memory of the action command list and receive frame area.

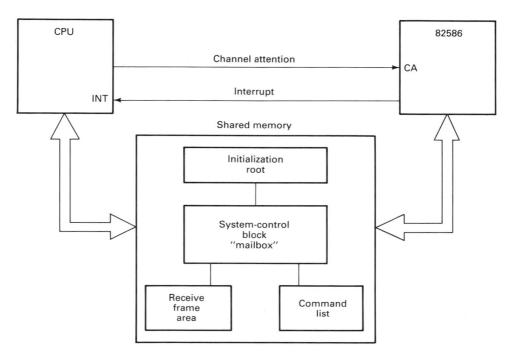

Figure 10.16   82586/CPU communication (Adapted; courtesy Intel Corp.)

Receive frame area: A section of memory set aside by the CPU for the storage of incoming frames by the 82586 as they are received. Provision is made for the automatic chaining together of receive buffers of varying sizes for more efficient use of RAM. Recall that Ethernet frames may vary in length from 64 bytes to 1518 bytes.

Action command list: This serves as the external program for the 82586. It is made up of a series of command blocks, one for each high-level action command, such as CONFIGURE, TRANSMIT, and so on. Each command block contains the necessary information for its execution and a pointer giving the location of the next command block.

Figure 10.17 shows the shared memory structure in somewhat more detail. The CPU accesses the system control block on its own or in response to an interrupt (INT) to read the status field and/or to issue a new control command. After issuing a new command, the CPU causes the 82586 to begin execution by pulsing the CA line HIGH.

The SCB status field is written only by the 82586, and typical information includes:

A frame has been received.

A command having its interrupt bit set has been executed.

Receiving unit is ready.

Command unit is busy.

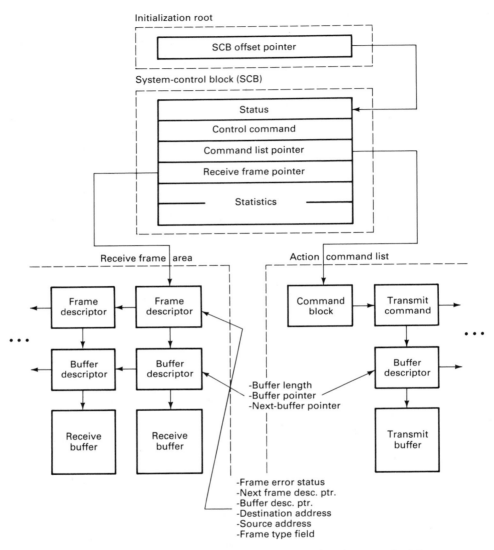

Figure 10.17 CPU/82586 shared memory structure (Adapted; courtesy Intel Corp.)

The list of control commands that may be issued by the CPU via the SCB includes:

Start executing the action command list.

Stop after current command.

Stop immediately.

Resume command execution.

Enable/disable receiving.

Software RESET.

There are four main action commands: IA-SETUP, CONFIGURE, MC-SETUP, and TRANSMIT. Each is described briefly as follows.

IA-SETUP: Used to load the 82586 with the individual address. The receive unit saves frames having a destination address that match this.

CONFIGURE: Used to program the operating protocol parameters, such as

Frame lengths

Address field length

Preamble length

Delay before retry, after collision

Number of retries allowed

CRC length

Note: The 82586 defaults to Ethernet configuration values upon RESET.

MC-SETUP: used to load the multicast addresses to which the 82586 should respond (in addition to its individual address).

TRANSMIT: Causes transmission of a frame. The TRANSMIT command block includes the frame destination address and type information, plus a pointer giving the location in memory of the data. The coprocessor automatically generates the preamble, assembles the frame, and appends the CRC character. In the event of a collision being detected ($\overline{CDT}$ going LOW), retries—up to the maximum number allowed—are also automatic.

Figure 10.18 shows the interconnection details for a complete station-to-Ethernet transceiver interface using the 82501 and 82586 ICs.

PROBLEMS

10.1. What type of data communication networks are classed as LANs?

10.2. Briefly describe and distinguish between the following LAN protocol families:
  (a) Contention or CSMA/CD
  (b) Token passing
  (c) Reservation
  (d) Slotted

10.3. Referring to the OSI model of network protocol levels, what level(s) does the Ethernet standard specify?

10.4. How can LANs be made full duplex?

10.5. Draw the voltage waveforms for the bit sequence 1 1 1 0 0 0 0 1 1 0:
  (a) Using NRZ coding
  (b) Using Manchester coding

10.6. Compare Manchester line coding with NRZI coding of the previous chapter.

10.7. List the functions of an Ethernet controller board assembly.

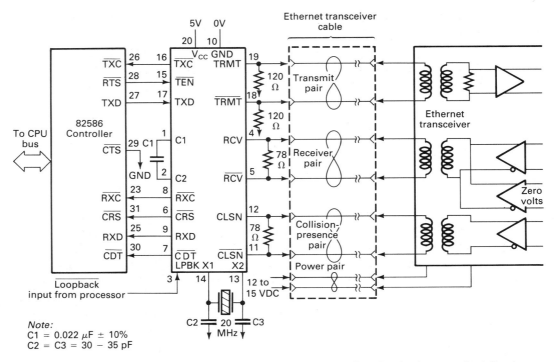

Figure 10.18   82586/82501/transceiver cable interface (Reprinted courtesy Intel Corp.)

10.8. How many unique Ethernet addresses could be assigned by Xerox, using the 6-octet address field allowed for in a packet?

10.9. The equivalent of approximately how many printed pages could be sent in one Ethernet data packet? Assume the data file uses EBCDIC coding.

10.10. How long does it take to transmit one Ethernet data packet, of maximum length? That is, how long is the bus occupied?

10.11. How are "defective" data packets, which may have been the result of a network collision, identified to be discarded by receiving stations?

10.12. How does an Ethernet transceiver circuit detect a network collision condition?

10.13. To what does the term *jabber control* refer?

10.14. Briefly describe the shared-memory concept of communication used between the Intel LAN Coprocessor and the main CPU.

Appendix

Network Standards:
The OSI Model
and X.21–X.27

A.1   THE OPEN SYSTEMS INTERCONNECTION MODEL

Physical Layer
Data-Link Layer
Network Layer
Transport Layer
Session Layer
Presentation Layer
Application Layer

A.2   PACKET-SWITCHING NETWORKS

Circuit Switching
Message Switching
Packet Switching

A.3   CCITT RECOMMENDATION X.25

Data Packet
Control Packet

A.1 THE OPEN SYSTEMS INTERCONNECTION MODEL

In 1977 a subcommittee of the ISO was directed to define a universal architecture that could be used as a reference model for the interconnection of distributed systems. CCITT is very active within this group. The subcommittee has proposed an OSI Model identifying seven specific data communication protocol layers, as shown in Figure A.1. The seven protocol layers exist at each station, and corresponding layers interact via the DTE-DCE interfaces and the network. Each layer is briefly described. Where possible, examples of specific protocols studied earlier in the text are given.

Physical layer. The physical-layer protocol specifies the various interconnecting circuits used, their functions, electrical characteristics, and the connector arrangement. EIA standards RS232 and RS449 (including electrical standards RS423/RS422) are examples of such physical-layer protocols.

CCITT's recommendation X.21 specifies its physical-layer protocols for the DTE-DCE link on public data networks. X.21 references functionality and electrical interface options comparable (but not identical) to those of RS449. X.24 defines the DTE/DCE interface circuits; see Figure A.2. Electrical characteristics are defined in X.26 (similar to RS423; unbalanced), and X.27 (similar to RS422; balanced).

Data-link layer. The data-link layer protocol describes the format used to "encapsulate" each basic unit of information for transmission between stations, over the data link. Examples include the following:

Asynchronous protocol: A start-stop protocol, where the basic unit of information is one character framed with start and stop bits.

BISYNC: A synchronous protocol, where the basic unit of information is the block. Each block of data contains a multicharacter message and the required control bytes (SOH, STX, ETX, and so on).

HDLC: Where the basic data unit is the frame bracketed by a unique bit pattern called a flag.

Asynchronous, BISYNC, and HDLC protocols were described earlier in the text.

CCITT's data-link protocol for public packet-switched networks is contained in its recommendation X.25. X.25 recommends HDLC.

Network layer. The network protocol layer relates to the procedures for the efficient routing of information packets across the network. CCITT's recommendation X.25 also describes this layer for packet-switched public networks. The network layer of X.25 is described in the next section.

Transport layer. The ISO intends for the transport layer to deal with the overall quality of service provided. It involves interfacing user service needs to the network. In particular, transport layer protocols deal with end-to-end data integrity and speed of delivery.

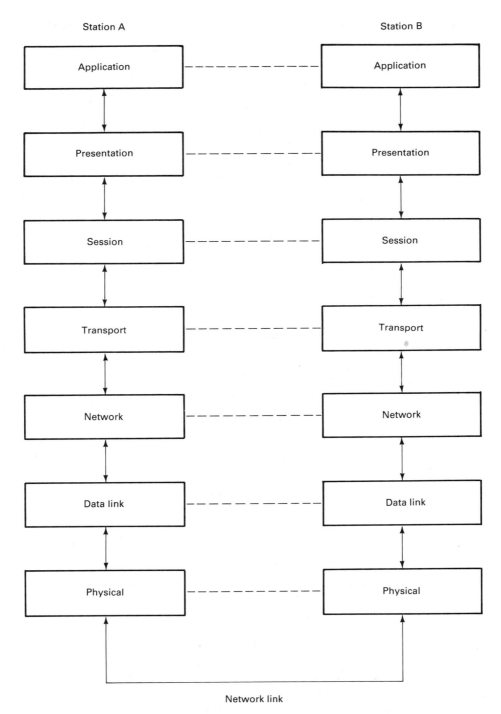

Figure A.1 OSI model protocol layers

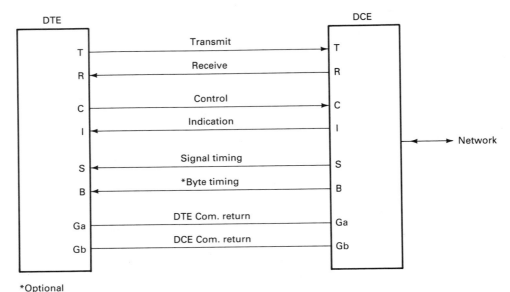

*Optional

Figure A.2   X.21/X.24 interface

The subcommittee is proposing that a gradation of different classes of service be defined, from the lowest (Class 0, an economy classification for less critical text messages) to Class 4, which would provide extensive error detection and correction facilities for critical data.

Session layer.   The session layer is required to control the initializing, conducting, and terminating a communication session.

Presentation layer.   The presentation protocol is responsible for any code, character, syntax, and other similar conversions necessary for the correct presentation of information. The videotex NAPLPS standard discussed earlier in the text is an example of a presentation protocol.

Application layer.   The application layer is the highest level protocol and, by necessity, includes elements that are very specific to each application. It describes the procedures associated with the end user's process.

A.2 PACKET-SWITCHING NETWORKS

Circuit switching.   Telephone voice traffic is carried over circuit-switching networks. Circuit switching implies establishing a physical connection between the users and maintaining the circuit for the duration of the call. Such a network provides full-duplex real-time (negligible delay) service.

Message switching.   For carrying computer data, the concept of message switching may be used. For message switching, it is not necessary for the network to establish a physical real-time connection between users. Instead, the network receives the message via the calling DTE-DCE link and stores the message temporarily in a queue for it to be delivered later. A queue is a waiting list or buffer containing prioritized messages for delivery. The network switch is a computer, which can offer service enhancements such as protocol conversion among users, establishing closed user groups, message broadcasting, and so forth. Electronic mail is a message-switched service. Each message must include its destination address when it is transmitted to the network.

Packet switching.   Packet-switching networks combine concepts of circuit and message switching. Messages are broken up and transmitted to the network in smaller packets. The network then circuit-switches each packet to its destination independently, using the most efficient route available at the time for each packet. Each packet includes

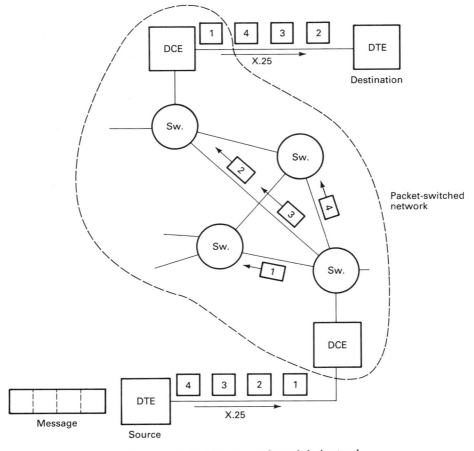

Figure A.3 Routing on a packet-switched network

identification and control data, such that each may take a different route to the destination node. At the destination DTE, the message is reassembled. Figure A.3 illustrates the concept of a packet-switched message.

Packet switching provides for real-time communication but allows network loading to be optimized dynamically, making best use of long-distance circuits.

A.3 CCITT RECOMMENDATION X.25

X.25 describes the protocols that a user must obey in attaching his or her DTE to the DCE of an X.25 packet network. It describes the three lower-level protocols: physical level, data-link level, and the network, or packet, level. The physical protocol section refers to recommendation X.21, and the data-link protocol uses HDLC, as described in Section A.1. The packet-level protocol is described briefly here.

X.25 packet level describes the sequence necessary for a DTE to place and clear (terminate) packet-switched calls as well as the procedure used to exchange data during a call. To place a call, the calling DTE sends a call request packet to the network DCE. The call request data packet includes the address of the called DTE. The network then attempts to establish a *virtual circuit* connection between the two DTEs. The term virtual circuit is used because there is no dedicated physical circuit maintained. Besides call request, the most commonly used control packets include incoming call, call accepted, call connected, clear requested, clear indication, and clear confirmation. Figure A.4 shows a simplified X.25 call sequence.

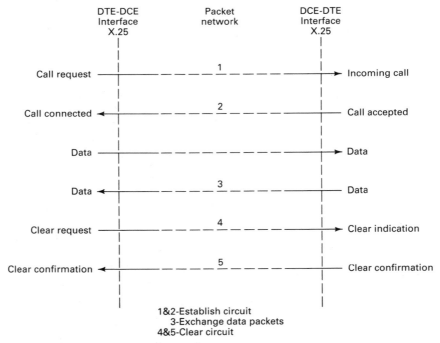

Figure A.4 X.25-call packet sequence

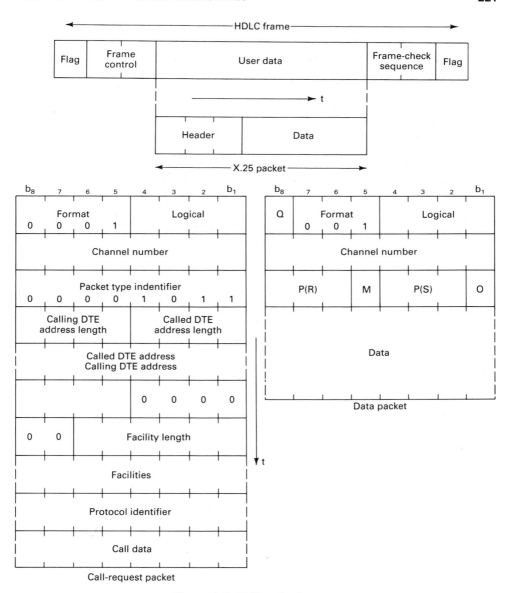

Figure A.5 X.25 packet formats

Each virtual circuit is allocated between two specific DTEs for the duration of a call. Each virtual connection is identified using a 12-bit logical channel number, and the channel number is included within the header of each packet. A DTE may have several calls (virtual circuits) active at one time, via one DCE.

Figure A.5 shows the relationship of a packet to its HDLC frame and the formats of the data packet and the call request control packet.

Data packet.   The data packet contains a 3-byte header, as shown. The logical channel number denotes a specific DTE-to-DTE virtual circuit for the duration of the call. The Q-bit is a data qualifier, which the users may employ to differentiate between two types of data. $P(R)$ and $P(S)$ are the packet receive and send counts, respectively, and are used for flow control between the DTE and DCE. Each increments $P(R)$ when a valid packet is received and increments $P(S)$ for each packet sent. These counts may be used to limit the number of outstanding (unacknowledged) packets on the network at any time and may also be used by the receiving DTE to reorder packets. The M bit is set to 1 when the transmitter wishes to indicate more data is to follow. Bits 5, 6, and 7 form the format identifier field. 001 identifies the data packet format shown. The length of the user data field is typically limited to 256 bytes maximum.

Control packet.   A call request packet is shown in Figure A.5, as an example of the control packet format. The third byte in a control packet identifies the packet type. The hexadecimal codes for the more common control packets are as follows:

Call Request	or Incoming Call	$0B
Call Accepted	or Call Connected	$0F
Clear Request	or Clear Indication	$13
	Clear Confirmation	$17

The facilities field allows for the selection among several special service features that may be offered by the network. Among such facilities is the fast select facility. Fast select allows the sending or receiving of 128 bytes of user data within the control packets. By using this facility, users may transfer short messages by exchanging call request and clear request control packets only.

IC Specifications (Excerpts)

 **MOTOROLA**

MC1488

QUAD LINE DRIVER

The MC1488 is a monolithic quad line driver designed to interface data terminal equipment with data communications equipment in conformance with the specifications of EIA Standard No. RS-232C.

Features:

- Current Limited Output
  ±10 mA typ
- Power-Off Source Impedance
  300 Ohms min
- Simple Slew Rate Control with External Capacitor
- Flexible Operating Supply Range
- Compatible with All Motorola MDTL and MTTL Logic Families

QUAD MDTL LINE DRIVER
RS-232C
SILICON MONOLITHIC
INTEGRATED CIRCUIT

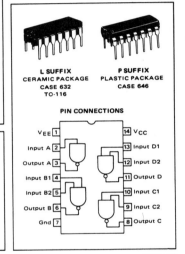

L SUFFIX
CERAMIC PACKAGE
CASE 632
TO-116

P SUFFIX
PLASTIC PACKAGE
CASE 646

PIN CONNECTIONS

V_{EE} 1	14 V_{CC}
Input A 2	13 Input D1
Output A 3	12 Input D2
Input B1 4	11 Output D
Input B2 5	10 Input C1
Output B 6	9 Input C2
Gnd 7	8 Output C

TYPICAL APPLICATION

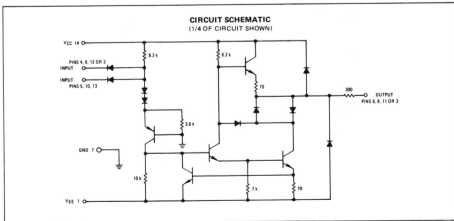

CIRCUIT SCHEMATIC
(1/4 OF CIRCUIT SHOWN)

Reprinted courtesy of Motorola, Inc.

MC1488

MAXIMUM RATINGS (T_A = +25°C unless otherwise noted.)

Rating	Symbol	Value	Unit
Power Supply Voltage	V_{CC} V_{EE}	+15 −15	Vdc
Input Voltage Range	V_{IR}	$-15 \leq V_{IR} \leq 7.0$	Vdc
Output Signal Voltage	V_O	±15	Vdc
Power Derating (Package Limitation, Ceramic and Plastic Dual-In-Line Package) Derate above T_A = +25°C	P_D $1/R_{\theta JA}$	1000 6.7	mW mW/°C
Operating Ambient Temperature Range	T_A	0 to +75	°C
Storage Temperature Range	T_{stg}	−65 to +175	°C

ELECTRICAL CHARACTERISTICS (V_{CC} = +9.0 ± 1% Vdc, V_{EE} = −9.0 ± 1% Vdc, T_A = 0 to +75°C unless otherwise noted.)

Characteristic	Figure	Symbol	Min	Typ	Max	Unit
Input Current — Low Logic State (V_{IL} = 0)	1	I_{IL}	−	1.0	1.6	mA
Input Current — High Logic State (V_{IH} = 5.0 V)	1	I_{IH}	−	−	10	µA
Output Voltage — High Logic State	2	V_{OH}				Vdc
(V_{IL} = 0.8 Vdc, R_L = 3.0 kΩ, V_{CC} = +9.0 Vdc, V_{EE} = −9.0 Vdc)			+6.0	+7.0	−	
(V_{IL} = 0.8 Vdc, R_L = 3.0 kΩ, V_{CC} = +13.2 Vdc, V_{EE} = −13.2 Vdc)			+9.0	+10.5	−	
Output Voltage — Low Logic State (V_{IH} = 1.9 Vdc, R_L = 3.0 kΩ, V_{CC} = +9.0 Vdc, V_{EE} = −9.0 Vdc)	2	V_{OL}	−6.0	−7.0	−	Vdc
(V_{IH} = 1.9 Vdc, R_L = 3.0 kΩ, V_{CC} = +13.2 Vdc, V_{EE} = −13.2 Vdc)			−9.0	−10.5	−	
Positive Output Short-Circuit Current (1)	3	I_{OS+}	+6.0	+10	+12	mA
Negative Output Short-Circuit Current (1)	3	I_{OS-}	−6.0	−10	−12	mA
Output Resistance (V_{CC} = V_{EE} = 0, $|V_O|$ = ±2.0 V)	4	r_o	300	−	−	Ohms
Positive Supply Current (R_L = ∞)	5	I_{CC}				mA
(V_{IH} = 1.9 Vdc, V_{CC} = +9.0 Vdc)			−	+15	+20	
(V_{IL} = 0.8 Vdc, V_{CC} = +9.0 Vdc)			−	+4.5	+6.0	
(V_{IH} = 1.9 Vdc, V_{CC} = +12 Vdc)			−	+19	+25	
(V_{IL} = 0.8 Vdc, V_{CC} = +12 Vdc)			−	+5.5	+7.0	
(V_{IH} = 1.9 Vdc, V_{CC} = +15 Vdc)			−	−	+34	
(V_{IL} = 0.8 Vdc, V_{CC} = +15 Vdc)			−	−	+12	
Negative Supply Current (R_L = ∞)	5	I_{EE}				
(V_{IH} = 1.9 Vdc, V_{EE} = −9.0 Vdc)			−	−13	−17	mA
(V_{IL} = 0.8 Vdc, V_{EE} = −9.0 Vdc)			−	−	−15	µA
(V_{IH} = 1.9 Vdc, V_{EE} = −12 Vdc)			−	−18	−23	mA
(V_{IL} = 0.8 Vdc, V_{EE} = −12 Vdc)			−	−	−15	µA
(V_{IH} = 1.9 Vdc, V_{EE} = −15 Vdc)			−	−	−34	mA
(V_{IL} = 0.8 Vdc, V_{EE} = −15 Vdc)			−	−	−2.5	mA
Power Consumption		P_C				mW
(V_{CC} = 9.0 Vdc, V_{EE} = −9.0 Vdc)			−	−	333	
(V_{CC} = 12 Vdc, V_{EE} = −12 Vdc)			−	−	576	

SWITCHING CHARACTERISTICS (V_{CC} = +9.0 ± 1% Vdc, V_{EE} = −9.0 ± 1% Vdc, T_A = +25°C.)

Propagation Delay Time (z_I = 3.0 k and 15 pF)	6	t_{PLH}	−	275	350	ns
Fall Time (z_I = 3.0 k and 15 pF)	6	t_{THL}	−	45	75	ns
Propagation Delay Time (z_I = 3.0 k and 15 pF)	6	t_{PHL}	−	110	175	ns
Rise Time (z_I = 3.0 k and 15 pF)	6	t_{TLH}	−	55	100	ns

(1) Maximum Package Power Dissipation may be exceeded if all outputs are shorted simultaneously.

Reprinted courtesy of Motorola. Inc.

B.2 RS232 RECEIVER: MC1489

 **MOTOROLA**

MC1489L
MC1489AL

QUAD LINE RECEIVERS

The MC1489 monolithic quad line receivers are designed to interface data terminal equipment with data communications equipment
in conformance with the specifications of EIA Standard No. RS-232C.

- Input Resistance — 3.0 k to 7.0 kilohms
- Input Signal Range — ± 30 Volts
- Input Threshold Hysteresis Built In
- Response Control
  a) Logic Threshold Shifting
  b) Input Noise Filtering

QUAD MDTL
LINE RECEIVERS
RS-232C

SILICON MONOLITHIC
INTEGRATED CIRCUIT

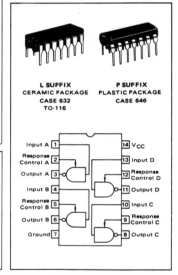

L SUFFIX
CERAMIC PACKAGE
CASE 632
TO-116

P SUFFIX
PLASTIC PACKAGE
CASE 646

Input A	1	14	V_CC
Response Control A	2	13	Input D
Output A	3	12	Response Control D
Input B	4	11	Output D
Response Control B	5	10	Input C
Output B	6	9	Response Control C
Ground	7	8	Output C

TYPICAL APPLICATION

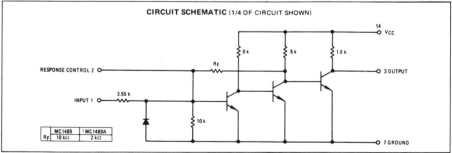

CIRCUIT SCHEMATIC (1/4 OF CIRCUIT SHOWN)

R_F	MC1489	MC1489A
	10 kΩ	2 kΩ

Reprinted courtesy of Motorola, Inc.

MC1489L, MC1489AL

MAXIMUM RATINGS (T_A = +25°C unless otherwise noted)

Rating	Symbol	Value	Unit
Power Supply Voltage	V_{CC}	10	Vdc
Input Voltage Range	V_{IR}	±30	Vdc
Output Load Current	I_L	20	mA
Power Dissipation (Package Limitation, Ceramic and Plastic Dual In-Line Package)	P_D	1000	mW
Derate above T_A = +25°C	$1/\theta_{JA}$	6.7	mW/°C
Operating Ambient Temperature Range	T_A	0 to +75	°C
Storage Temperature Range	T_{stg}	–65 to +175	°C

ELECTRICAL CHARACTERISTICS (Response control pin is open.) (V_{CC} = +5.0 Vdc ±1%, T_A = 0 to +75°C unless otherwise noted)

Characteristics		Figure	Symbol	Min	Typ	Max	Unit
Positive Input Current	(V_{IH} = +25 Vdc)	1	I_{IH}	3.6	–	8.3	mA
	(V_{IH} = +3.0 Vdc)			0.43	–	–	
Negative Input Current	(V_{IL} = –25 Vdc)	1	I_{IL}	–3.6	–	–8.3	mA
	(V_{IL} = –3.0 Vdc)			–0.43	–	–	
Input Turn-On Threshold Voltage		2	V_{IHL}				Vdc
(T_A = +25°C, $V_{OL} \leq 0.45$ V) MC1489				1.0	–	1.5	
MC1489A				1.75	1.95	2.25	
Input Turn-Off Threshold Voltage		2	V_{ILH}				Vdc
(T_A = +25°C, $V_{OH} \geq 2.5$ V, I_L = –0.5 mA) MC1489				0.75	–	1.25	
MC1489A				0.75	0.8	1.25	
Output Voltage High	(V_{IH} = 0.75 V, I_L = –0.5 mA)	2	V_{OH}	2.6	4.0	5.0	Vdc
	(Input Open Circuit, I_L = –0.5 mA)			2.6	4.0	5.0	
Output Voltage Low	(V_{IL} = 3.0 V, I_L = 10 mA)	2	V_{OL}	–	0.2	0.45	Vdc
Output Short-Circuit Current		3	I_{OS}	–	3.0	–	mA
Power Supply Current	(V_{IH}= +5.0 Vdc)	4	I_{CC}	–	20	26	mA
Power Consumption	(V_{IH} = +5.0 Vdc)	4	P_C	–	100	130	mW

SWITCHING CHARACTERISTICS (V_{CC} = 5.0 Vdc ± 1%, T_A = +25°C)

Propagation Delay Time	(R_L = 3.9 kΩ)	5	t_{PLH}	–	25	85	ns
Rise Time	(R_L = 3.9 kΩ)	5	t_{TLH}	–	120	175	ns
Propagation Delay Time	(R_L = 390 Ω)	5	t_{PHL}	–	25	50	ns
Fall Time	(R_L = 390 Ω)	5	t_{THL}	–	10	20	ns

TYPICAL CHARACTERISTICS
(V_{CC} = 5.0 Vdc, T_A = +25°C unless otherwise noted)

FIGURE 7 – INPUT CURRENT

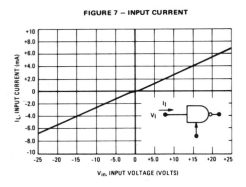

FIGURE 8 – MC1489 INPUT THRESHOLD
VOLTAGE ADJUSTMENT

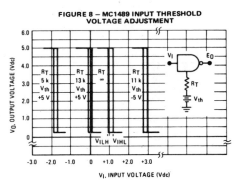

FIGURE 9 – MC1489A INPUT THRESHOLD
VOLTAGE ADJUSTMENT

FIGURE 10 – INPUT THRESHOLD VOLTAGE
versus TEMPERATURE

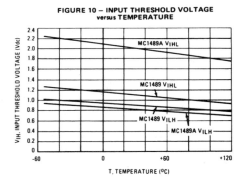

FIGURE 11 – INPUT THRESHOLD versus
POWER-SUPPLY VOLTAGE

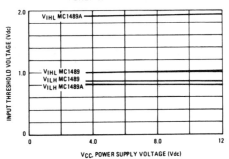

Reprinted courtesy of Motorola, Inc.

 **MOTOROLA**

MC3486

QUAD RS-422/423 LINE RECEIVER

Motorola's Quad RS-422/3 Receiver features four independent receiver chains which comply with EIA Standards for the Electrical Characteristics of Balanced/Unbalanced Voltage Digital Interface Circuits. Receiver outputs are 74LS compatible, three-state structures which are forced to a high impedance state when the appropriate output control pin reaches a logic zero condition. A PNP device buffers each output control pin to assure minimum loading for either logic one or logic zero inputs. In addition, each receiver chain has internal hysteresis circuitry to improve noise margin and discourage output instability for slowly changing input waveforms. A summary of MC3486 features include:

- Four Independent Receiver Chains
- Three-State Outputs
- High Impedance Output Control Inputs (PIA Compatible)
- Internal Hysteresis — 30 mV (Typ) @ Zero Volts Common Mode
- TTL Compatible
- Single 5 V Supply Voltage
- DS 3486 Second Source

QUAD RS-422/3 LINE RECEIVER WITH THREE-STATE OUTPUTS

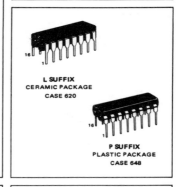

L SUFFIX
CERAMIC PACKAGE
CASE 620

P SUFFIX
PLASTIC PACKAGE
CASE 648

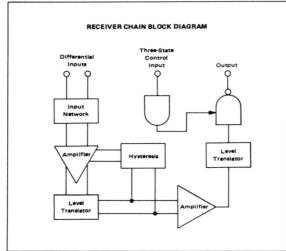

RECEIVER CHAIN BLOCK DIAGRAM

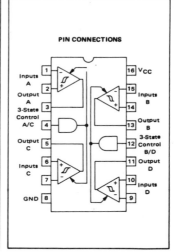

PIN CONNECTIONS

Reprinted courtesy of Motorola, Inc.

MC3486

ABSOLUTE MAXIMUM RATINGS (Note 1)

Rating	Symbol	Value	Unit
Power Supply Voltage	V_{CC}	8.0	Vdc
Input Common Mode Voltage	V_{ICM}	±15	Vdc
Input Differential Voltage	V_{ID}	±25	Vdc
Three-State Control Input Voltage	V_I	8.0	Vdc
Output Sink Current	I_O	50	mA
Storage Temperature	T_{stg}	-65 to +150	°C
Operating Junction Temperature	T_J		°C
Ceramic Package		+175	
Plastic Package		+150	

Note 1: "Absolute Maximum Ratings" are those values beyond which the safety of the device cannot be guaranteed. They are not meant to imply that the devices should be operated at these limits. The "Table of Electrical Characteristics" provides conditions for actual device operation.

RECOMMENDED OPERATING CONDITIONS

Rating	Symbol	Value	Unit
Power Supply Voltage	V_{CC}	4.75 to 5.25	Vdc
Operating Ambient Temperature	T_A	0 to +70	°C
Input Common Mode Voltage Range	V_{ICR}	-7.0 to +7.0	Vdc
Input Differential Voltage Range	V_{IDR}	6.0	Vdc

ELECTRICAL CHARACTERISTICS (Unless otherwise noted minimum and maximum limits apply over recommended temperature and power supply voltage ranges. Typical values are for T_A = 25°C, V_{CC} = 5.0 V and V_{IK} = 0 V. See Note 1.)

Characteristic	Symbol	Min	Typ	Max	Unit
Input Voltage — High Logic State (Three-State Control)	V_{IH}	2.0	—	—	V
Input Voltage — Low Logic State (Three-State Control)	V_{IL}	—	—	0.8	V
Differential Input Threshold Voltage (Note 4) (-7.0 V < V_{IC} < 7.0 V, V_{IH} = 2.0 V)	$V_{TH(D)}$				V
(I_O = 0.4 mA, $V_{OH} \geqslant$ 2.7 V)		—	—	0.2	
(I_O = 8.0 mA, $V_{OL} \geqslant$ 0.5 V)		—	—	-0.2	
Input Bias Current (V_{CC} = 0 V or 5.25) (Other Inputs at 0 V)	$I_{IB(D)}$				mA
(V_I = -10 V)		—	—	-3.25	
(V_I = -3.0 V)		—	—	-1.50	
(V_I = +3.0 V)		—	—	+1.50	
(V_I = +10 V)		—	—	+3.25	
Input Balance and Output Level (-7.0 V < V_{IC} < 7.0 V, V_{IH} = 2.0 V, See Note 3)					V
(I_O = 0.4 mA, V_{ID} = 0.4 V)	V_{OH}	2.7	—	—	
(I_O = 8.0 mA, V_{ID} = 0.4 V)	V_{OL}	—	—	0.5	
Output Third State Leakage Current ($V_{I(D)}$ = +3.0 V, V_{IL} = 0.8 V, V_{OL} = 0.5 V)	I_{OZ}	—	—	-40	μA
($V_{I(D)}$ = -3.0 V, V_{IL} = 0.8 V, V_{OL} = 2.7 V)		—	—	40	
Output Short-Circuit Current ($V_{I(D)}$ = 3.0 V, V_{IH} = 2.0 V, V_O = 0 V) See Note 2)	I_{OS}	-15	—	-100	mA
Input Current — Low Logic State (Three-State Control) (V_{IH} = 0.5 V)	I_{IL}	—	—	-100	μA
Input Current — High Logic State (Three-State Control)	I_{IH}				μA
(V_{IH} = 2.7 V)		—	—	20	
(V_{IH} = 5.25 V)		—	—	100	
Input Clamp Diode Voltage (Three-State Control) (I_{IK} = -10 mA)	V_{IK}	—	—	-1.5	V
Power Supply Current (V_{IL} = 0 V)	I_{CC}	—	—	85	mA

Reprinted courtesy of Motorola, Inc.

B.4 RS422 DRIVER: MC3487

 **MOTOROLA**

QUAD LINE DRIVER WITH THREE-STATE OUTPUTS

Motorola's Quad RS-422 Driver features four independent driver chains which comply with EIA Standards for the Electrical Characteristics of Balanced Voltage Digital Interface Circuits. The outputs are three-state structures which are forced to a high impedance state when the appropriate output control pin reaches a logic zero condition. All input pins are PNP buffered to minimize input loading for either logic one or logic zero inputs. In addition, internal circuitry assures a high impedance output state during the transition between power up and power down. A summary of MC3487 features include:

- Four Independent Driver Chains
- Three-State Outputs
- PNP High Impedance Inputs (PIA Compatible)
- Fast Propagation Times (Typ 15 ns)
- TTL Compatible
- Single 5 V Supply Voltage
- Output Rise and Fall Times Less Than 20 ns
- DS 3487 Second Source

QUAD RS-422 LINE DRIVER WITH THREE-STATE OUTPUTS

SILICON MONOLITHIC INTEGRATED CIRCUIT

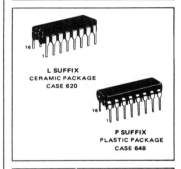

L SUFFIX
CERAMIC PACKAGE
CASE 620

P SUFFIX
PLASTIC PACKAGE
CASE 648

PIN CONNECTIONS

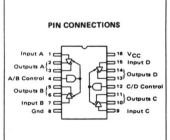

	Pin		Pin	
Input A	1		16	V_CC
Outputs A	2, 3		15	Input D
A/B Control	4		14, 13	Outputs D
Outputs B	5, 6		12	C/D Control
Input B	7		11, 10	Outputs C
Gnd	8		9	Input C

DRIVER BLOCK DIAGRAM

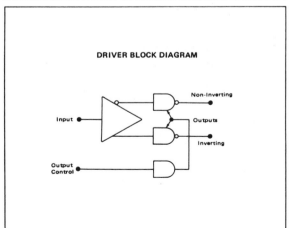

TRUTH TABLE

Input	Control Input	Non-Inverting Output	Inverting Output
H	H	H	L
L	H	L	H
X	L	Z	Z

L = Low Logic State
H = High Logic State
X = Irrelevant
Z = Third-State (High Impedance)

Reprinted courtesy of Motorola, Inc.

*ABSOLUTE MAXIMUM RATINGS

Rating	Symbol	Value	Unit
Power Supply Voltage	V_{CC}	8.0	Vdc
Input Voltage	V_I	5.5	Vdc
Operating Ambient Temperature Range	T_A	0 to +70	°C
Operating Junction Temperature Range Ceramic Package Plastic Package	T_J	 175 150	°C
Storage Temperature Range	T_{stg}	–65 to +150	°C

*"Absolute Maximum Ratings" are those values beyond which the safety of the device cannot
be guaranteed. They are not meant to imply that the devices should be operated at these limits.
The "Table of Electrical Characteristics" provides conditions for actual device operation.

ELECTRICAL CHARACTERISTICS (Unless otherwise noted specifications apply 4.75 V < V_{CC} < 5.25 V and 0°C < T_A < 70°C.
Typical values measured at V_{CC} = 5.0 V, and T_A = 25°C.)

Characteristic	Symbol	Min	Typ	Max	Unit
Input Voltage — Low Logic State	V_{IL}	—	—	0.8	Vdc
Input Voltage — High Logic State	V_{IH}	2.0	—	—	Vdc
Input Current — Low Logic State (V_{IL} = 0.5 V)	I_{IL}	—	—	–400	µA
Input Current — High Logic State (V_{IH} = 2.7 V) (V_{IH} = 5.5 V)	I_{IH}	 — —	 — —	 +50 +100	µA
Input Clamp Voltage (I_{IK} = -18 mA)	V_{IK}	—	—	–1.5	V
Output Voltage — Low Logic State (I_{OL} = 48 mA)	V_{OL}	—	—	0.5	V
Output Voltage — High Logic State (I_{OH} = –20 mA)	V_{OH}	2.5	—	—	V
Output Short-Circuit Current (V_{IH} = 2.0 V) [2]	I_{OS}	–40	—	–140	mA
Output Leakage Current — Hi-Z State (V_{IL} = 0.5 V, $V_{IL(Z)}$ = 0.8 V) (V_{IH} = 2.7 V, $V_{IL(Z)}$ = 0.8 V)	$I_{OL(Z)}$	 — —	 — —	 ±100 ±100	µA
Output Leakage Current — Power OFF (V_{OH} = 6.0 V, V_{CC} = 0 V) (V_{OL} = -0.25 V, V_{CC} = 0 V)	$I_{OL(off)}$	 — —	 — —	 +100 -100	µA
Output Offset Voltage Difference[1]	$V_{OS} - \bar{V}_{OS}$	—	—	±0.4	V
Output Differential Voltage 1	V_T	2.0	—	—	V
Output Differential Voltage Difference 1	$V_T - \bar{V}_T$	—	—	±0.4	V
Power Supply Current (Control Pins = Gnd)[3] (Control Pins = 2.0 V)	 I_{CCX} I_{CC}	 — —	 — —	 105 85	mA

1. See EIA Specification RS-422 for exact test conditions.
2. Only one output may be shorted at a time.
3. Circuit in three-state condition.

SWITCHING CHARACTERISTICS (V_{CC} = 5.0 V, T_A = 25°C unless otherwise noted.)

Characteristic	Symbol	Min	Typ	Max	Unit
Propagation Delay Times High to Low Output Low to High Output	 t_{PHL} t_{PLH}	 — —	 — —	 20 20	ns
Output Transition Times — Differential High to Low Output Low to High Output	 t_{THL} t_{TLH}	 — —	 — —	 20 20	ns
Propagation Delay — Control to Output (R_L = 200 Ω, C_L = 50 pF) (R_L = 200 Ω, C_L = 50 pF) (R_L = ∞, C_L = 50 pF) (R_L = 200 Ω, C_L = 50 pF)	 $t_{PHZ(E)}$ $t_{PLZ(E)}$ $t_{PZH(E)}$ $t_{PZL(E)}$	 — — — —	 — — — —	 25 25 30 30	ns

Reprinted courtesy of Motorola, Inc.

 **MOTOROLA**

AM26LS31

QUAD LINE DRIVER WITH NAND ENABLED THREE-STATE OUTPUTS

The Motorola AM26LS31 is a quad differential line driver intended for digital data transmission over balanced lines. It meets all the requirements of EIA Standard RS-422 and Federal Standard 1020.

The AM26LS31 provides an enable/disable function common to all four drivers as opposed to the split enables on the MC3487 RS-422 driver.

The high impedance output state is assured during power down.

- Full RS-422 Standard Compliance
- Single +5 V Supply
- Meets Full V_O = 6.0 V, V_{CC} = 0 V, I_O < 100 μA Requirement
- Output Short Circuit Protection
- Complementary Outputs for Balanced Line Operation
- High Output Drive Capability
- Advanced LS Processing
- PNP Inputs for MOS Compatibility

QUAD RS-422 LINE DRIVER WITH THREE-STATE OUTPUTS

SILICON MONOLITHIC INTEGRATED CIRCUIT

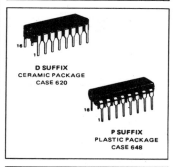

D SUFFIX
CERAMIC PACKAGE
CASE 620

P SUFFIX
PLASTIC PACKAGE
CASE 648

PIN CONNECTIONS

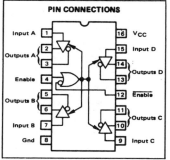

Input A	1		16	V_{CC}
Outputs A	2		15	Input D
	3		14	Outputs D
Enable	4		13	
Outputs B	5		12	Enable
	6		11	Outputs C
Input B	7		10	
Gnd	8		9	Input C

DRIVER BLOCK DIAGRAM

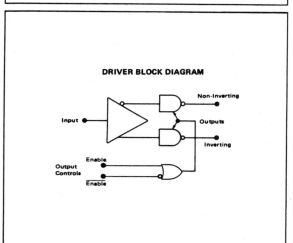

TRUTH TABLE

Input	Control Inputs (E/Ē)	Non-Inverting Output	Inverting Output
H	H/L	H	L
L	H/L	L	H
X	L/H	Z	Z

L = Low Logic State
H = High Logic State
X = Irrelevant
Z = Third-State (High Impedance)

Reprinted courtesy of Motorola, Inc.

AM26LS31

Reprinted courtesy of Motorola, Inc.

•ABSOLUTE MAXIMUM RATINGS

Rating	Symbol	Value	Unit
Power Supply Voltage	V_{CC}	8.0	Vdc
Input Voltage	V_I	5.5	Vdc
Operating Ambient Temperature Range	T_A	0 to +70	°C
Operating Junction Temperature Range Ceramic Package Plastic Package	T_J	 175 150	°C
Storage Temperature Range	T_{stg}	-65 to +150	°C

•"Absolute Maximum Ratings" are those values beyond which the safety of the device cannot
be guaranteed. They are not meant to imply that the devices should be operated at these limits.
The "Table of Electrical Characteristics" provides conditions for actual device operation.

ELECTRICAL CHARACTERISTICS (Unless otherwise noted specifications apply 4.75 V ≤ V_{CC} ≤ 5.25 V and 0°C ≤ T_A ≤ 70°C.
Typical values measured at V_{CC} = 5.0 V, and T_A = 25°C.)

Characteristic	Symbol	Min	Typ	Max	Unit
Input Voltage — Low Logic State	V_{IL}	–	–	0.8	Vdc
Input Voltage — High Logic State	V_{IH}	2.0	–	–	Vdc
Input Current — Low Logic State (V_{IL} = 0.4 V)	I_{IL}	–	–	–360	μA
Input Current — High Logic State (V_{IH} = 2.7 V) (V_{IH} = 7.0 V)	I_{IH}	 – –	 – –	 +20 +100	μA
Input Clamp Voltage (I_{IK} = –18 mA)	V_{IK}	–	–	–1.5	V
Output Voltage — Low Logic State (I_{OL} = 20 mA)	V_{OL}	–	–	0.5	V
Output Voltage — High Logic State (I_{OH} = –20 mA)	V_{OH}	2.5	–	–	V
Output Short-Circuit Current (V_{IH} = 2.0 V) [2]	I_{OS}	–30	–	–150	mA
Output Leakage Current — Hi-Z State (V_{OL} = 0.5 V, $V_{IL(E)}$ = 0.8 V, $V_{IH(\overline{E})}$ = 2.0 V) (V_{OH} = 2.5 V, $V_{IL(E)}$ = 0.8 V, $V_{IH(\overline{E})}$ = 2.0 V)	$I_{O(Z)}$	 – –	 – –	 –20 +20	μA
Output Leakage Current — Power OFF (V_{OH} = 6.0 V, V_{CC} = 0 V) (V_{OL} = –0.25 V, V_{CC} = 0 V)	$I_{O(off)}$	 – –	 – –	 +100 –100	μA
Output Offset Voltage Difference [1]	$V_{OS} - \overline{V}_{OS}$	–	–	±0.4	V
Output Differential Voltage [1]	V_T	2.0	–	–	V
Output Differential Voltage Difference [1]	$V_T - \overline{V}_T$	–	–	±0.4	V
Power Supply Current (Output Disabled) [3]	I_{CCX}	–	60	80	mA

1. See EIA Specification RS-422 for exact test conditions.
2. Only one output may be shorted at a time.
3. Circuit in three-state condition.

SWITCHING CHARACTERISTICS (V_{CC} = 5.0 V, T_A = 25°C unless otherwise noted.)

Characteristic	Symbol	Min	Typ	Max	Unit
Propagation Delay Times High to Low Output Low to High Output	 t_{PHL} t_{PLH}	 – –	 – –	 20 20	ns
Output Skew		–	–	6.0	ns
Propagation Delay — Control to Output (C_L = 10 pF, R_L = 75 Ω to Gnd) (C_L = 10 pF, R_L = 180 Ω to V_{CC}) (C_L = 30 pF, R_L = 75 Ω to Gnd) (C_L = 30 pF, R_L = 180 Ω to V_{CC})	 $t_{PHZ(E)}$ $t_{PLZ(E)}$ $t_{PZH(E)}$ $t_{PZL(E)}$	 – – – –	 – – – –	 30 35 40 45	ns

MC8T13
MC8T23

DUAL LINE DRIVERS

The MC8T13 and MC8T23 are designed to drive transmission lines with impedances of 50 Ω to 500 Ω. The MC8T23 specifically meets all of the input/output requirements of the IBM System 360/System 370 specifications (IBM Specification GA 22-6974-0).

- High Output Drive Capability —
  I_O = -75 mA (Min) @ V_O = 2.4 V — MC8T13
  I_O = -59.3 mA (Min) @ V_O = 3.11 V — MC8T23
- High Speed Operation —
  t_{PLH} = t_{PHL} = 20 ns (Max) with 50 Ω Load
- MTTL and MDTL Compatible Inputs
- Uncommitted Emitter Output Structures Permit Party-Line Operation
- Designed to Operate with MC8T14 or MC8T24 Line Receivers
- Outputs are Short-Circuit Protected
- Equivalent to SN75121 and SN75123 Respectively.

DUAL LINE DRIVERS
SILICON MONOLITHIC INTEGRATED CIRCUIT

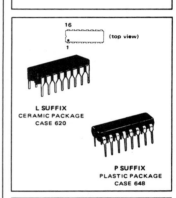

L SUFFIX
CERAMIC PACKAGE
CASE 620

P SUFFIX
PLASTIC PACKAGE
CASE 648

TYPICAL APPLICATION

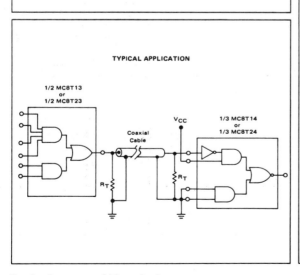

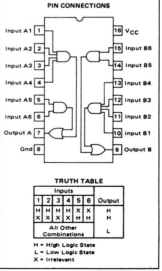

PIN CONNECTIONS

Input A1 [1]	[16] V_{CC}
Input A2 [2]	[15] Input B6
Input A3 [3]	[14] Input B5
Input A4 [4]	[13] Input B4
Input A5 [5]	[12] Input B3
Input A6 [6]	[11] Input B2
Output A [7]	[10] Input B1
Gnd [8]	[9] Output B

TRUTH TABLE

Inputs						Output
1	2	3	4	5	6	
H	H	H	H	X	X	H
X	X	X	X	H	H	H
All Other Combinations						L

H = High Logic State
L = Low Logic State
X = Irrelevant

Reprinted courtesy of Motorola, Inc.

MC8T13, MC8T23

MAXIMUM RATINGS (T_A = +25°C unless otherwise noted.)

Rating	Symbol	Value	Unit
Power Supply Voltage	V_{CC}	7.0	Vdc
Input Voltage	V_I	5.5	Vdc
Output Voltage	V_O	7.0	Vdc
Power Dissipation @ T_A = +25°C Derate above 25°C	P_D	1000 6.7	mW mW/°C
Operating Ambient Temperature Range	T_A	0 to +75	°C
Storage Temperature Range	T_{stg}	-65 to +150	°C

ELECTRICAL CHARACTERISTICS (Unless otherwise noted, 4.75 V $\leqslant V_{CC} \leqslant$ 5.25 V and 0°C $\leqslant T_A \leqslant$ 75°C)

Characteristics	Symbol	MC8T13 Min	MC8T13 Typ	MC8T13 Max	MC8T23 Min	MC8T23 Typ	MC8T23 Max	Unit
Input Voltage — Low Logic State	V_{IL}	–	–	0.8	–	–	0.8	V
Input Voltage — High Logic State	V_{IH}	2.0	–	–	2.0	–	–	V
Input Current — Low Logic State (V_{IL} = 0.4 V)	I_{IL}	-0.1	–	-1.6	-0.1	–	-1.6	mA
Input Current — High Logic State (V_{IH} = 4.5 V) (V_{IH} = 5.5 V, V_{CC} = 5.0 V)	I_{IH1} I_{IH2}	– –	– –	40 10	– –	– –	40 10	μA mA
Input Clamp Voltage (I_I = -12 mA, V_{CC} = 5.0 V)	$V_{I(clamp)}$	–	–	-1.5	–	–	-1.5	V
Output Voltage — High Logic State (V_{IH} = 2.0 V, I_{OH} = -75 mA) (V_{CC} = 5.0 V, V_{IH} = 2.0 V, I_{OH} = -59.3 mA) (T_A = 25°C)	V_{OH1} V_{OH2}	2.4 – –	– – –	– – –	– 2.9 3.11	– – –	– – –	V V
Output Current — High Logic State (V_{IH} = 4.5 V, V_{CC} = 5.0 V, V_O = 2.0 V, T_A = 25°C)	I_{OH}	-100	–	-250	-100	–	-250	mA
Output Current — Low Logic State (V_{IL} = 0.8 V, V_O = 0.4 V) (V_{IL} = 0.8 V, V_O = 0.15 V)	I_{OL1} I_{OL2}	– –	– –	-800 –	– –	– –	– -240	μA μA
Output Reverse Leakage Current — Low Logic State (V_{IL} = 0 V, V_O = 3.0 V) (V_{IL} = 0 V, V_O = 3.0 V, V_{CC} = 0 V)	I_{OR1} I_{OR2}	– –	– –	80 500	– –	– –	– 40	μA μA
Output Short-Circuit Current (V_{IH} = 4.5 V, V_{CC} = 5.0 V, V_O = 0 V, T_A = 25°C)	I_{OS}	–	–	-30	–	–	-30	mA
Power Supply Currents (I_O = 0 mA) Outputs — Low Logic State, V_{IL} = 0.8 V Outputs — High Logic State, V_{IH} = 2.0 V	I_{CCL} I_{CCH}	– –	– –	60 28	– –	– –	60 28	mA mA

SWITCHING CHARACTERISTICS (V_{CC} = 5.0 V, T_A = 25°C unless otherwise noted.) Figure 1

Characteristic	Symbol	MC8T13 Min	MC8T13 Typ	MC8T13 Max	MC8T23 Min	MC8T23 Typ	MC8T23 Max	Unit
Propagation Delay Time — Low to High Level Output (R_L = 37 Ω, C_L = 15 pF) (R_L = 37 Ω, C_L = 1000 pF) (R_L = 50 Ω, C_L = 15 pF) (R_L = 50 Ω, C_L = 100 pF)	t_{PLH}	– – – –	11 22 – –	20 50 – –	– – – –	– – 12 20	– – 20 35	ns
Propagation Delay Time — High to Low Level Output (R_L = 37 Ω, C_L = 15 pF) (R_L = 37 Ω, C_L = 1000 pF) (R_L = 50 Ω, C_L = 15 pF) (R_L = 50 Ω, C_L = 100 pF)	t_{PHL}	– – – –	8.0 20 – –	20 50 – –	– – – –	– – 12 15	– – 20 25	ns

Reprinted courtesy of Motorola, Inc.

 **MOTOROLA**

MC8T14
MC8T24

TRIPLE LINE RECEIVERS WITH HYSTERESIS

SILICON MONOLITHIC
INTEGRATED CIRCUIT

TRIPLE LINE RECEIVERS WITH HYSTERESIS

. . . specifically designed to meet the input/output specifications for IBM 360/370 Systems (IBM specification GA 22-6974-0). Each receiver incorporates hysteresis to provide high noise immunity and also high input impedance to minimize loading on the related driver.

- Each Channel Can Be Independently Strobed
- High Speed — $t_{PLH} = t_{PHL} = 20$ ns
- Input Gating Provided on Each Line
- Operates on a Single +5.0 V Power Supply
- Fully Compatible with MTTL or MDTL Logic Systems
- Input Hysteresis Results in High Noise Immunity

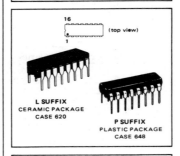

L SUFFIX
CERAMIC PACKAGE
CASE 620

P SUFFIX
PLASTIC PACKAGE
CASE 648

16   (top view)
1

TYPICAL APPLICATION

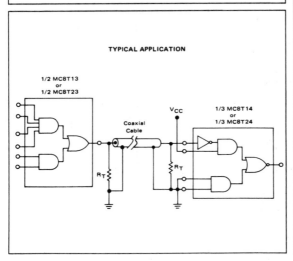

1/2 MC8T13
or
1/2 MC8T23

Coaxial
Cable

V_{CC}

1/3 MC8T14
or
1/3 MC8T24

R_T

R_T

PIN CONNECTIONS

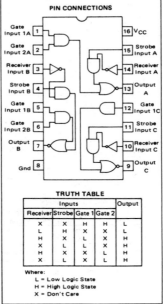

Gate Input 1A	1		16	V_{CC}
Gate Input 2A	2		15	Strobe Input A
Receiver Input B	3		14	Receiver Input A
Strobe Input B	4		13	Output A
Gate Input 1B	5		12	Gate Input 1C
Gate Input 2B	6		11	Strobe Input C
Output B	7		10	Receiver Input C
Gnd	8		9	Output C

TRUTH TABLE

Inputs				Output
Receiver	Strobe	Gate 1	Gate 2	
X	X	H	H	L
L	H	X	X	L
H	X	L	X	H
X	L	L	X	H
H	X	X	L	H
X	L	X	L	H

Where:
L = Low Logic State
H = High Logic State
X = Don't Care

Reprinted courtesy of Motorola, Inc.

MC8T14, MC8T24

MAXIMUM RATINGS (T$_A$ = 25°C unless otherwise noted.)

Rating	Symbol	Value	Unit
Power Supply Voltage	V$_{CC}$	7.0	Vdc
Receiver Input Voltage (V$_{CC}$ = 0)	V$_{I(R)}$	7.0 6.0	Vdc
Strobe or Gate Input Voltage	V$_{I(S)}$ or (G)	5.5	Vdc
Output Voltage	V$_O$	7.0	Vdc
Output Current	I$_O$	±100	mA
Power Dissipation (Package Limitation) Ceramic Package Derate above 25°C	P$_D$	1000 6.7	mW mW/°C
Plastic Package Derate above 25°C		830 6.7	mW mW/°C
Junction Temperature Ceramic Package Plastic Package	T$_J$	 175 150	°C
Operating Ambient Temperature Range	T$_A$	0 to +75	°C
Storage Temperature Range	T$_{stg}$	–65 to +150	°C

ELECTRICAL CHARACTERISTICS (Unless otherwise noted, 4.75 ≤ V$_{CC}$ ≤ 5.25 V and 0°C ≤ T$_A$ ≤ 75°C)

Characteristic	Symbol	MC8T14 Min	Typ	Max	MC8T24 Min	Typ	Max	Unit
Gate or Strobe Input Voltage — High Logic State	V$_{IH(G)}$ or (S)	2.0	–	–	2.0	–	–	V
Gate or Strobe Input Voltage — Low Logic State	V$_{IL(G)}$ or (S)	–	–	0.8	–	–	0.8	V
Receiver Input Voltage — High Logic State	V$_{IH(R)}$	2.0	–	–	1.7	–	–	Vdc
Receiver Input Voltage — Low Logic State	V$_{IL(R)}$	–	–	0.8	–	–	0.7	Vdc
Receiver Input Hysteresis (1) (V$_{CC}$ = 5.0 V, T$_A$ = 25°C, V$_{IL(G)}$ = 0, V$_{IH(S)}$ = 4.5 V)	V$_{H(R)}$	0.3	0.5	–	0.2	0.4	–	V
Input Clamp Voltage (V$_{CC}$ = 5.0 V, T$_A$ = 25°C, I$_I$ = –12 mA) (Strobe or Gate Inputs)	V$_{IC(G)}$ or (S)	–	–	1.5	–	–	1.5	V
Input Breakdown Voltage (V$_{CC}$ = 5.0 V, I$_I$ = 10 mA) (Strobe or Gate Inputs)	V$_{I(G)}$ or (S)	5.5	–	–	5.5	–	–	V
Receiver Input Current — High Logic State (V$_{IH(R)}$ = 3.8 V) (V$_{IH(R)}$ = 3.11 V) (V$_{IH(R)}$ = 7.0 V) (V$_{IH(R)}$ = 6.0 V, V$_{CC}$ = 0 V)	I$_{IH(R)}$	 – – – –	 – – – –	 0.17 – – –	 – – – –	 – – – –	 – 0.17 5.0 5.0	mA
Gate or Strobe Input Current — High Logic State (V$_{IH(S)}$ = 4.5 V, V$_{IH(R)}$ = 3.11 V) (V$_{IH(G)}$ = 4.5 V)	I$_{IH(G)}$ or (S)	 – –	 – –	 40 40	 – –	 – –	 40 40	µA
Gate or Strobe Input Current — Low Logic State (V$_{IL(G)}$ or (S) = 0.4 V, V$_{IL(R)}$ = 0 V)	I$_{IL(G)}$ or (S)	–0.1	–	–1.6	–0.1	–	–1.6	mA
Output Voltage — High Logic State (V$_{IH(R)}$ = 2.0 V, V$_{IH(S)}$ = 2.0 V, V$_{IL(G)}$ = 0.8 V, I$_{OH}$ = –800 µA) (V$_{IH(R)}$ = 0.8 V, V$_{IL(S)}$ = 0.8 V, V$_{IL(G)}$ = 0.8 V, I$_{OH}$ = –800 µA) (V$_{IH(R)}$ = 1.7 V, V$_{IH(S)}$ = 2.0 V, V$_{IL(G)}$ = 0.8 V, I$_{OH}$ = –800 µA) (V$_{IH(R)}$ = 0.7 V, V$_{IL(S)}$ = 0.8 V, V$_{IL(G)}$ = 0.8 V, I$_{OH}$ = –800 µA)	V$_{OH}$	 2.6 2.6 – –	 3.5 3.5 – –	 – – – –	 – – 2.6 2.6	 – – 3.4 3.4	 – – – –	V
Output Voltage — Low Logic State (V$_{IL(R)}$ = 0.8 V, V$_{IH(S)}$ = 2.0 V, V$_{IL(G)}$ = 0.8 V, I$_{OL}$ = 16 mA) (V$_{IL(R)}$ = 0.8 V, V$_{IL(S)}$ = 0.8 V, V$_{IH(G)}$ = 2.0 V, I$_{OL}$ = 16 mA) (V$_{IL(R)}$ = 0.7 V, V$_{IH(S)}$ = 2.0 V, V$_{IL(G)}$ = 0.8 V, I$_{OL}$ = 16 mA) (V$_{IL(R)}$ = 0.7 V, V$_{IL(S)}$ = 0.8 V, V$_{IH(G)}$ = 2.0 V, I$_{OL}$ = 16 mA)	V$_{OL}$	 – – – –	 – – – –	 0.4 0.4 – –	 – – – –	 – – – –	 – – 0.4 0.4	V
Output Short-Circuit Current (2) (V$_{IH(R)}$ = 3.8 V, V$_{IL(G)}$ = 0 V, V$_{IL(S)}$ = 0, V$_{CC}$ = 5.0 V, T$_A$ = 25°C) (V$_{IH(R)}$ = 3.11 V, V$_{IL(G)}$ = 0 V, V$_{IL(S)}$ = 0 V, V$_{CC}$ = 5.0 V, T$_A$ = 25°C)	I$_{OS}$	 –50 –	 – –	 –100 –	 – –50	 – –	 – –100	mA
Power Supply Current (V$_{CC}$ = 5.25 V, T$_A$ = 25°C)	I$_{CC}$	–	60	72	–	60	72	mA

(1) The Input Hysteresis is defined as the difference the input voltage at which the output begins to go from the high logic state to the low logic state and the input voltage which causes the output to begin to go from the low logic state to the high logic state.

(2) Only one output may be shorted at a time.

Reprinted courtesy of Motorola, Inc.

238

B.8 IBM-SYSTEM DRIVER/RECEIVER: SN75123/SN75124

LINE CIRCUITS

- Meet IBM System 360 Input/Output Interface Specifications
- Operate from Single 5-V Supply
- TTL Compatible

additional features of SN75123 line driver

- Plug-In Replacement for Signetics 8T23
- 3.11-V Output at I_{OH} = −59.3 mA
- Uncommitted Emitter-Follower Output Structure for Party-Line Operation
- Short-Circuit Protection
- AND-OR Logic Configuration

additional features of SN75124 line receiver

- Plug-In Replacement for Signetics 8T24
- Built-In Input Threshold Hysteresis
- High Speed . . . Typical Propagation Delay Time = 20 ns
- Independent Channel Strobes
- Input Gating Increases Application Flexibility

SN75123
J OR N
DUAL-IN-LINE PACKAGE (TOP VIEW)

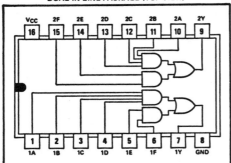

SN75124
J OR N
DUAL-IN-LINE PACKAGE (TOP VIEW)

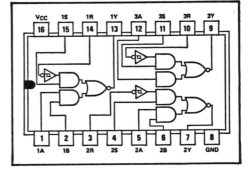

description

The SN75123 dual line driver and the SN75124 triple line receiver are both specifically designed to meet the input/output interface specifications for IBM System 360. They are also compatible with standard TTL logic and supply voltage levels.

The low-impedance emitter-follower outputs of the SN75123 will drive terminated lines such as coaxial cable or twisted pair. Having the outputs uncommitted allows wired-OR logic to be performed in party-line applications. Output short-circuit protection is provided by an internal clamping network which turns on when the output voltage drops below approximately 1.5 volts. All of the inputs are in conventional TTL configuration and the gating can be used during power-up and power-down sequences to ensure that no noise is introduced to the line.

The SN75124 has receiver inputs with built-in hysteresis to provide increased noise margin for single-ended systems. An open line will affect the receiver input as would a low-level input voltage and the receiver input can withstand a level of −0.15 volt with power on or off. The other inputs are in TTL configuration. The S input must be high to enable the receiver input. Two of the line receivers have A and B inputs which, if both are high, will hold the output low. The third receiver has only an A input which, if high, will hold the output low.

TEXAS INSTRUMENTS
INCORPORATED

SN75123 absolute maximum ratings over operating free-air temperature range (unless otherwise noted)

Supply voltage, V_{CC} (see Note 1)	7 V
Input voltage	5.5 V
Output voltage	7 V
Continuous total dissipation at (or below) 25°C free-air temperature (see Note 2)	1 W
Operating free-air temperature range	0°C to 75°C
Storage temperature range	−65°C to 150°C
Lead temperature 1/16 inch from case for 60 seconds: J package	300°C
Lead temperature 1/16 inch from case for 10 seconds: N package	260°C

SN75123 recommended operating conditions

	MIN	NOM	MAX	UNIT
Supply voltage, V_{CC}	4.75	5	5.25	V
High-level output current, I_{OH}			−100	mA
Operating free-air temperature, T_A	0		75	°C

SN75123 electrical characteristics, V_{CC} = 4.75 V to 5.25 V, T_A = 0°C to 75°C (unless otherwise noted)

PARAMETER		TEST CONDITIONS			MIN	TYP	MAX	UNIT
V_{IH}	High-level input voltage				2			V
V_{IL}	Low-level input voltage						0.8	V
V_{IK}	Input clamp voltage	V_{CC} = 5 V,	I_I = −12 mA				−1.5	V
$V_{(BR)I}$	Input breakdown voltage	V_{CC} = 5 V,	I_I = 10 mA		5.5			V
V_{OH}	High-level output voltage	V_{CC} = 5 V, I_{OH} = −59.3 mA,	V_{IH} = 2 V, See Note 3	T_A = 25°C	3.11			V
				T_A = 0°C to 75°C	2.9			
I_{OH}	High-level output current	V_{CC} = 5 V, T_A = 25°C,	V_{IH} = 4.5 V, See Note 3	V_{OH} = 2 V,	−100		−250	mA
V_{OL}	Low-level output voltage	V_{IL} = 0.8 V,	I_{OL} = −240 μA,	See Note 3			0.15	V
$I_{O(off)}$	Off-state output current	V_{CC} = 0,	V_O = 3 V				40	μA
I_{IH}	High-level input current	V_I = 4.5 V					40	μA
I_{IL}	Low-level input current	V_I = 0.4 V			−0.1		−1.6	mA
I_{OS}	Short-circuit output current ‡	V_{CC} = 5 V,	T_A = 25°C				−30	mA
I_{CCH}	Supply current, outputs high	V_{CC} = 5.25 V, Outputs open	All inputs at 2 V,				28	mA
I_{CCL}	Supply current, outputs low	V_{CC} = 5.25 V, Outputs open	All inputs at 0.8 V,				60	mA

‡ Not more than one output should be shorted at a time.

SN75123 switching characteristics, V_{CC} = 5 V, T_A = 25°C

PARAMETER		TEST CONDITIONS	MIN	TYP	MAX	UNIT
t_{PLH}	Propagation delay time, low-to-high-level output	R_L = 50 Ω, C_L = 15 pF, See Figure 1		12	20	ns
t_{PHL}	Propagation delay time, high-to-low-level output			12	20	
t_{PLH}	Propagation delay time, low-to-high-level output	R_L = 50 Ω, C_L = 100 pF, See Figure 1		20	35	ns
t_{PHL}	Propagation delay time, high-to-low-level output			15	25	

NOTES: 1. Voltage values are with respect to network ground terminal.
2. For operation above 25°C free-air temperature, refer to the Dissipation Derating Curves in the Thermal Information section, which starts on page 21. In the J package, SN75123 chips are glass-mounted.
3. The output voltage and current limits are guaranteed for any appropriate combination of high and low inputs specified by the function table for the desired output.

TYPE SN75124
TRIPLE LINE RECEIVER

SN75124 absolute maximum ratings over operating free-air temperature range (unless otherwise noted)

Supply voltage, V_{CC} (see Note 1)	7 V
Input voltage: R input with V_{CC} applied	7 V
R input with V_{CC} not applied	6 V
A, B, or S input	5.5 V
Output voltage	7 V
Output current	±100 mA
Continuous total dissipation at (or below) 25°C free-air temperature (see Note 4)	1 W
Operating free-air temperature range	0°C to 75°C
Storage temperature range	−65°C to 150°C
Lead temperature 1/16 inch from case for 60 seconds: J package	300°C
Lead temperature 1/16 inch from case for 10 seconds: N package	260°C

SN75124 recommended operating conditions

	MIN	NOM	MAX	UNIT
Supply voltage, V_{CC}	4.75	5	5.25	V
High-level output current, I_{OH}			−800	µA
Low-level output current, I_{OL}			16	mA
Operating free-air temperature, T_A	0		75	°C

SN75124 electrical characteristics, V_{CC} = 4.75 V to 5.25 V, T_A = 0°C to 75°C (unless otherwise noted)

PARAMETER			TEST CONDITIONS		MIN	TYP	MAX	UNIT
V_{IH}	High-level input voltage	A,B, or S			2			V
		R			1.7			
V_{IL}	Low-level input voltage	A,B, or S					0.8	V
		R					0.7	
$V_{T+}-V_{T-}$	Hysteresis†	R	V_{CC} = 5 V,	T_A = 25°C	0.2	0.4		V
V_{IK}	Input clamp voltage	A,B, or S	V_{CC} = 5 V,	I_I = −12 mA			−1.5	V
$V_{(BR)I}$	Input breakdown voltage	A,B, or S	V_{CC} = 5 V,	I_I = 10 mA	5.5			V
V_{OH}	High-level output voltage		V_{IH} = V_{IH} min, $\quad$ V_{IL} = V_{IL}max, $\quad$ I_{OH} = −800 µA, See Note 3		2.6			V
V_{OL}	Low-level output voltage		V_{IH} = V_{IH} min, $\quad$ V_{IL} = V_{IL}max, $\quad$ I_{OL} = 16 mA, See Note 3				0.4	V
I_I	Input current at maximum input voltage	R	V_I = 7 V				5	mA
			V_I = 6 V,	V_{CC} = 0			5	
I_{IH}	High-level input current	A,B, or S	V_I = 4.5 V				40	µA
		R	V_I = 3.11 V				170	
I_{IL}	Low-level input current	A,B, or S	V_I = 0.4 V		−0.1		−1.6	mA
I_{OS}	Short-circuit output current‡		V_{CC} = 5 V,	T_A = 25°C	−50		−100	mA
I_{CC}	Supply current		V_{CC} = 5.25 V				72	mA

†Hysteresis is the difference between the positive-going input threshold voltage, V_{T+}, and the negative-going input threshold voltage, V_{T-}. See Figure 4.

‡Not more than one output should be shorted at a time, and duration of the short-circuit should not exceed one second.

SN75124 switching characteristics, V_{CC} = 5 V, T_A = 25°C

PARAMETER	TEST CONDITIONS	MIN	TYP	MAX	UNIT
t_{PLH} Propagation delay time, low-to-high-level output from R input	See Figure 2		20	30	ns
t_{PHL} Propagation delay time, high-to-low-level output from R input			20	30	

NOTES: 1. Voltage values are with respect to network ground terminal.
        3. The output voltage and current limits are guaranteed for any appropriate combination of high and low inputs specified by the function table for the desired output.
        4. For operation above 25°C free-air temperature, refer to the Dissipation Derating Curves in the Thermal Information section, which starts on page 21. In the J package, SN75124 chips are glass-mounted

Reprinted courtesy of Texas Instruments, Inc.

 **National Semiconductor**

PRELIMINARY

microCMOS

MM54HC4016/MM74HC4016
Quad Analog Switch

General Description

These devices are digitally controlled analog switches implemented in microCMOS Technology, 3.5 micron silicon gate P-well CMOS. These switches have low 'on' resistance and low 'off' leakages. They are bidirectional switches, thus any analog input may be used as an output and vice-versa. The '4016 devices allow control of up to 12V (peak) analog signals with digital control signals of the same range. Each switch has its own control input which disables each switch when low. All analog inputs and outputs and digital inputs are protected from electrostatic damage by diodes to V_{CC} and ground.

Features

- Typical switch enable time: 15 ns
- Wide analog input voltage range: 0–12V
- Low 'on' resistance: 50Ω typical
- Low quiescent current: 80 μA maximum (74HC)
- Matched switch characteristics
- Individual switch controls

Connection Diagram

Dual-In-Line Package

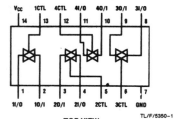

TL/F/5350–1

TOP VIEW
MM54HC4016/MM74HC4016

54HC4016 (J)   74HC4016 (J,N)

Truth Table

Input	Switch
CTL	I/O-O/I
L	"OFF"
H	"ON"

Schematic Diagram

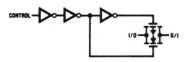

TL/F/5350–2

Absolute Maximum Ratings (Notes 1 & 2)

Supply Voltage (V_{CC})	-0.5 to $+15$V
DC Control Input Voltage (V_{IN})	-1.5 to $V_{CC}+1.5$V
DC Switch I/O Voltage (V_{IO})	-0.5 to $V_{CC}+0.5$V
Clamp Diode Current (I_{IK}, I_{OK})	± 20 mA
DC Output Current, per pin (I_{OUT})	± 25 mA
DC V_{CC} or GND Current, per pin (I_{CC})	± 50 mA
Storage Temperature Range (T_{STG})	$-65°$C to $+150°$C
Power Dissipation (P_D) (Note 3)	500 mW
Lead Temperature (T_L) (Soldering 10 seconds)	260°C

Operating Conditions

	Min	Max	Units
Supply Voltage(V_{CC})	2	12	V
DC Input or Output Voltage (V_{IN}, V_{OUT})	0	V_{CC}	V
Operating Temperature Range(T_A)			
MM74HC	-40	$+85$	°C
MM54HC	-55	$+125$	°C
Input Rise or Fall Times			
(t_r, t_f) $V_{CC}=2.0$V		1000	ns
$V_{CC}=4.5$V		500	ns
$V_{CC}=6.0$V		400	ns

DC Electrical Characteristics (Note 4)

Symbol	Parameter	Conditions	V_{CC}	$T_A=25°$C Typ	74HC $T_A=-40$ to 85°C	54HC $T_A=-55$ to 125°C	Units
					Guaranteed Limits		
V_{IH}	Minimum High Level Input Voltage		2.0V	1.5	1.5	1.5	V
			4.5V	3.15	3.15	3.15	V
			9.0V	6.3	6.3	6.3	V
			12.0V	8.4	8.4	8.4	V
V_{IL}	Maximum Low Level Input Voltage		2.0V	0.3	0.3	0.3	V
			4.5V	0.9	0.9	0.9	V
			9.0V	1.8	1.8	1.8	V
			12.0V	2.4	2.4	2.4	V
R_{ON}	Maximum 'ON' Resistance (See Note 5)	$V_{CTL}=V_{IH}$, $I_S=1.0$ mA $V_{IS}=V_{CC}$ to GND (Figure 1)	4.5V	100			Ω
			9.0V	50			Ω
			12.0V	30			Ω
		$V_{CTL}=V_{IH}$, $I_S=1.0$ mA $V_{IS}=V_{CC}$ or GND (Figure 1)	2.0V	120			Ω
			4.5V	50			Ω
			9.0V	35			Ω
			12.0V	20			Ω
R_{ON}	Maximum 'ON' Resistance Matching	$V_{CTL}=V_{IH}$ $V_{IS}=V_{CC}$ to GND	4.5V	10			Ω
			9.0V	5			Ω
			12.V	5			Ω
I_{IN}	Maximum Control Input Current	$V_{IN}=V_{CC}$ or GND $V_{CC}=2-6$V		± 0.1	± 1.0	± 1.0	μA
I_{IZ}	Maximum Switch 'OFF' Leakage Current	$V_{OS}=V_{CC}$ or GND $V_{IS}=$ GND or V_{CC} $V_{CTL}=V_{IL}$ (Figure 2)	5.5V	10			nA
			9.0V	15			nA
			12.0V	20			nA
I_{IZ}	Maximum Switch 'ON' Leakage Current	$V_{OS}=V_{CC}$ or GND $V_{CTL}=V_{IH}$ (Figure 3)	5.5V	10			nA
			9.0V	15			nA
			12.0V	20			nA
I_{CC}	Maximum Quiescent Supply Current	$V_{IN}=V_{CC}$ or GND $I_{OUT}=0$ μA	5.5V	2.0	20	40	μA
			9.0V	8.0	80	160	μA
			12.0V	16.0	160	320	μA

Note 1: Absolute Maximum Ratings are those values beyond which damage to the device may occur.

Note 2: Unless otherwise specified all voltages are referenced to ground.

Note 3: Power Dissipation temperature derating — plastic "N" package: -12 mW/°C from 65°C to 85°C; ceramic "J" package: -12 mW/°C from 100°C to 125°C.

Note 4: For a power supply of 5V ± 10% the worst case on resistances (R_{ON}) occurs for HC at 4.5V. Thus the 4.5V values should be used when designing with this supply. Worst case V_{IH} and V_{IL} occur at $V_{CC}=5.5$V and 4.5V respectively. (The V_{IH} value at 5.5V is 3.85V.) The worst case leakage current occur for CMOS at the higher voltage and so these values should be used.

Note 5: At supply voltages ($V_{CC}-V_{EE}$) approaching 2V the analog switch on resistance becomes extremely non-linear. Therefore it is recommended that these devices be used to transmit digital only when using these supply voltages.

Reprinted courtesy of National Semiconductor Corp.

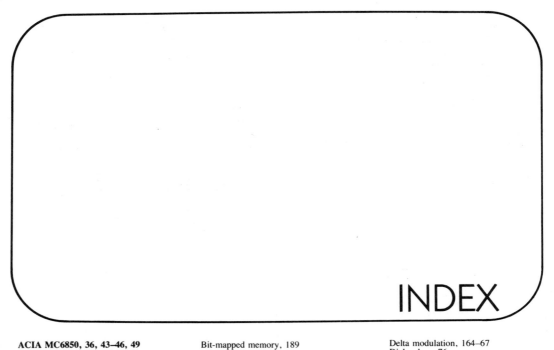

INDEX